Growing Business Innovation

Creating, Marketing and Monetising IP

Edited by
Jonathan Reuvid

Legend Business Ltd,
107-111 Fleet Street, London, EC4A 2AB
info@legend-paperbooks.co.uk | www.legendpress.co.uk

Print ISBN 978-1-78719-893-7
Ebook ISBN 978-1-78719-892-0
Set in Times. Printed by Opolgraf SA.
Cover design by Simon Levy www.simonlevyassociates.co.uk

Publishers Note

GROWING BUSINESS INNOVATION

CREATING, MARKETING AND MONETISING IP

Editor: Jonathan Reuvid, Legend Business Books

Foreword	*Tim Moss, CBE, UK Intellectual Property Office*	**7**
Preface	*Professor Graham Richards CBE*	**9**
List of Contributors		**11**
Introduction	*The Editor*	**21**
Part One	**Preparing for Innovation**	**23**
1.1	**Business Structures**	**25**
	Gary McGonagle, Howman Solicitors	
1.2	**Mastering Business Plans**	**33**
	Allison McSparron-Edwards, Consultrix Ltd	
1.3	**The Pros and Cons of University Innovation and Exploitation**	**44**
	Paul O'Brien, The School of Chemistry and The School of Materials, Manchester University	
1.4	**Developing an Innovative Mindset in Leaders and Teams**	**50**
	Sarah McCloughry, STEMM Commercial Ltd and Charlie Wilson, Bosideon Consulting Ltd	
1.5	**New Innovation Programmes for UK Industry: Urgent Imperatives**	**56**
	Jeremy Tear, GovGrant Ltd and Karren Brooks	

1.6	**Cracking Open The World's Finest Academic Minds to Drive Innovation in Business**	**63**
	Dirk Mersch, Cambridge Innovation Consulting Ltd	
1.7	**The Lean Start-up Policy – a Framework and Philosophy for Innovation**	**69**
	Andy Hill, Fieldridge Ltd	
Part Two	**Focus on Intellectual Property**	**79**
2.1	**The Importance of Patents – UK Ingredients for a successful patent regime**	**81**
	Will Steele, Intellectual Property Office	
2.2	**Strategic IP Management**	**86**
	Dr. Nicholas Acham, Stratagem IPM Limited	
2.3	**Cost-effective Handling of Intellectual Property**	**91**
	Ilya Kazi, Mathys & Squire LLP	
2.4	**Keep Informed about IP Rights**	**98**
	Margit Hoehne, Patentgate GmbH	
2.5	**Business and Making the Most of Your IP**	**106**
	Guy Robinson, Intellectual Property Office	
2.6	**Using Trademarks, Design Rights and Copyright to Protect Innovation**	**110**
	Gregor Kleinknecht, Hunters	
2.7	**Protecting against IP Disputes**	**118**
	Keeley Patten, Miller Insurance Services LLP	
Part Three	**Aids to Innovation**	**123**
3.1	**Information Services Supporting Innovation and IP Protection**	**127**
	Steven Johnson and Vedran Biondic, J & B Partners Ltd	
3.2	**Business Growth through Industry-Academia Interactions**	**131**
	Dr. Brian More, Coventry University	
3.3	**Online Presence: Ignite the Digital Spark**	**140**
	Yasmin El-Saie, UK2 Group	
3.4	**The Use of Patent Information for Innovation and Competitive Intelligence**	**148**
	Rahman Hyatt and James Cooper, Minesoft Ltd	
3.5	**Protecting Innovation without Patents**	**164**
	Aaron Wood, Wood IP Ltd	

3.6   **Reserving Patent Rights for Your Secret Processes**   169
John Moetteli, Da Vinci Partners

3.7   **Grants and Incentives within the UK**   175
Olaf Swanzy, PNO Group

Part Four   **Extended Thinking**   185

4.1   **Developing a Patent Portfolio Strategy for Technology Start-ups: optimised for venture capital investment**   187
Dr. Mark Graves and Julia May, May Figures Ltd

4.2   **Innovation in HR Practice**   193
Claire Vane, Integrated Resources Ltd

4.3   **Adapting Defence Technology to Business Enterprise**   199
Paddy Bradley, Swindon & Wiltshire LEP

4.4   **Embracing Tech Transforms a Business Practice**   206
Sumit Agarwal, DNS Accountants

4.5   **Scotland's Innovation Journey**   210
Jim Watson, Scottish Enterprise

4.6   **Innovation, Creativity and Consciousness**   217
Karren Brooks, Whitespace

4.7   **The End Game: Monetizing Innovation**   222
Jonathan Reuvid, Legend Business

FOREWORD

The innovative spirit is a fundamental essence which contributes to economies and societies moving forward. However you choose to define it, it is the drive to improve through new approaches, methods or ideas; it is this element which captures the core of a new business idea. But from this beginning turning ideas into a reality, whether it be from a back room to a local market or a laboratory to a global marketplace, is a challenging process.

This book provides an invaluable starting point, a framework for aspiring or established entrepreneurs, those looking for the ideas to flourish and their businesses to grow. A framework is the right place to start. There is no one perfect solution to the challenge, no one size fits all. This guide is an invaluable piece of the jigsaw in this framework – providing information, support and advice from a range of people who have been there and are doing it.

This guide also delves into some depth about an essential part of this framework that provides support to the process of innovation: intellectual property. From practical advice to strategic thinking it unveils the value of investing in IP protection and how to get the most out of it by sharing and maximising its use. The relevance and value of IP should not be underestimated: research commissioned by the UK Intellectual Property Office shows that UK firms have been investing more in the knowledge-based economy than in tangible assets such as buildings and machinery for nearly two decades. Intangible investment has grown at a more consistent rate and seems unaffected by wider economic difficulties. Around half of this investment is protected by formal IP rights.

Despite these impressive figures much more needs to be done to engage, support and educate businesses, from start-ups to well established firms, about the benefits of making the most of your IP. Wherever you are on your innovation journey, just setting out or preparing for the end game, this guide should help you along that path.

Tim Moss CBE
Chief Executive and Comptroller General, UK Intellectual Property Office.

PREFACE

Innovation is not just important: it is vital. This is particularly true in the United Kingdom, where we need new industries to replace those whose time is over or where they have been transferred overseas.

Our history in this respect has been less than encouraging. Many times we have developed novel technologies but failed to convert them into major industries. The science behind dyestuffs, television and even computers was conducted in Britain, but not developed into world ranking companies.

The record of protecting and exploiting intellectual property has been dismal. Penicillin, radar and the jet engine, all British inventions, were given away as part of the Lend Lease Agreement between Churchill and Roosevelt. In that case there were strategic reasons as part of the war effort and encouraging the USA to enter the conflict. However, after the war there was little improvement. The Attlee government set up the National Research for Development Corporation (later the British Technology Group) which owned the intellectual property of all Government funded research. Despite the notable successes of the cephalosporin drugs from Oxford and the pyrethroids from Rothamsted, the overall success was poor. Monoclonal antibodies were not patented and yet that technology is now the basis of multi billion pound companies.

A significant step forward came under Margaret Thatcher when she gave the intellectual property of work funded by the state in universities to the universities providing they created a mechanism for exploitation. This followed some ten years after the similar highly influential Bayh-Dole Act in the USA which has had a massive impact. As a result, universities have become a major source of spin-out companies, although many remain too small.

The present volume provides the information and background to ameliorate the current situation. It starts at the beginning prior to company foundation. Firstly we have to generate the novel ideas. Universities are one obvious source, but there are potential conflicts and academics are rarely suitable as chief executive officers of companies. Industry itself is a major provider of novel technologies, while the combination of academia plus commerce is perhaps a more fruitful starting point. The preparation for innovation constitutes Part One of this guide.

The second part focuses on the absolutely fundamental aspect of intellectual property. It cannot be overstated as to just how vital the possession of patents and their management is to innovative businesses. IP is at the heart of the value of high tech companies. In addition, trademarks, copyright and know-how play a crucial underlying role. Handling IP in a cost effective way is at the core of new businesses.

Having set up a company, the next step is to grow it. This will involve generating new IP and creating a web presence. Help in both these vital aspects is provided as is information on grants and incentives for innovation.

The final section embraces extended thinking, getting set for venture capital involvement and maintaining the culture for innovation. Having been personally involved in the setting up of a number of high tech companies, including a couple of notable successes and a couple of dismal failures, I wish that I had had access to the information contained in this volume some years ago. It would have made life easier and mistakes could have been avoided. The volume ends up as does the life of the innovative business with the word 'exit'. The people who back new companies do so in the hope and expectation that at some time in the not too distant future they will be able to multiply their investment by means of an IPO, floating on the stock exchange or a trade sale. As the final chapter emphasises, the end game is monetisation.

If done wisely the rewards can be not inconsiderable. My own single Department of Chemistry at Oxford has earned for the University in excess of £100 million, without, it must be emphasised, compromising its essential raison d'être of teaching and research. Perhaps most noteworthy in this respect has been the fact that the major successes have been derived from what is clearly 'blue skies' research and not by consciously directing efforts towards application.

Prof Graham Richards CBE
Oxford Drug Design Ltd

LIST OF CONTRIBUTORS

Dr. Nicholas Acham entered the patent profession in 2000 after several years of R&D in the surface coatings industry in France and the UK. A short period in private practice was followed by 12 years at a multinational fast-moving consumer goods company supporting numerous different businesses during which time he acquired extensive experience in invention harvesting, drafting and examination of applications, opposing and defending patents before the EPO both at first and second instances, managing extensive patent portfolios and providing advice on technical agreements. A Chartered and European Patent Attorney, Nicholas joined Stratagem IPM Limited in 2017 as a senior attorney.

Sumit Agarwal founded DNS Accountants as a young chartered accountant in 2005, having come to the UK in 2003, and qualified in CIMA the following year. Through its acumen and experience DNS has provided a strong foothold for hundreds of companies, both big and small, to run their own businesses successfully and grow exponentially. After 12 years, DNS Accountants has a large clientele of over 3,000 with eight branches nationally (in Central and Greater London, Regent Street, Harrow, and Hounslow; Surrey; the North, in Hull and Wigan; and Southeast in Cornwall). The success and approach of the firm have put it among the Top 200 Accountants in the UK (VouchedFor.co.uk, 2016). Specialising in tax advice, tax investigation, tax planning and accounting services, DNS provides a proactive service geared toward the needs of its clientele. In 2017 Sumit won the British Indian Award; DNS was shortlisted for the Practice Excellence Awards Practice Growth of the Year; and a finalist in the British Accountancy Awards (BAA) Independent Firm of the Year. In 2015 DNS was a finalist for the BAA Practitioner of the Year; and Nominated Best Contractor by Contractor UK. In 2013 DNS won the BAA Best Online Accounting Firm Award.

Paddy Bradley is Director of the Swindon and Wiltshire Local Enterprise Partnership and has overall responsibility for the day-to-day running of the partnership and its operations. A highly experienced local government director, Paddy was previously Head of Economy, Skills and Property Development at Swindon Borough Council. In that role, he regularly provided strategic and operational support to SWLEP. Paddy has a wide range of experience in the public and private sectors, working as a business analyst and system designer. He also spent 20 years in education as a teacher, headteacher and education inspector.

Karren Brooks founded Whitespace at the request of her successful client base from the London Leadership Centre. She is passionate about global consciousness and the neurosciences, which help explain the emotional and mental performance required for the attainment of success and happiness. Karren is an innovative media entrepreneur and brings that valuable experience to her advisory services for business, legacy families and elite sports organisations and athletes. She is known for her provocative interviews and remarkable breakthrough results with her clients. Karren is writing her latest book *Spiritual Currency – Life's Capital* which will be published early in 2018.

James Cooper is currently a support executive at Minesoft Ltd. Having completed his degree in Biomedical Science in 2012, James started his career in the healthcare sector to support an application to study Medicine. He worked a centre for the treatment of traumatic brain injury for 2 years, monitoring patient response to treatment and assessing efficacy of treatment based on patient meta-data in addition to assisting the healthcare team and nursing staff. In mid-2015, James joined Minesoft to provide support for the new chemical explorer module and now assists with the company's marketing, customer relationship management and support services for all products.

Yasmin El-Saie is Content Manager at UK2 Group, where her passion for websites and writing about online technology fuses into strategic content creation and planning. Originally a Physics graduate, her creative passions led her into the world of programming and website building, as a means for growing and promoting her ideas into a blog and business to reach a whole new audience. The science of search engine optimisation became her next challenge, as well as tapping into the power of social media. She is a convert to the online world.

Dr. Mark Graves gained a first-class MEng degree in Electronic and Structural Materials Engineering from Oxford University, where he won the Maurice Lubbock prize in the final year examinations, and a PhD in Computer Science from the University of Wales, Cardiff, winning a Royal Commission 1851 Industrial Fellowship. Mark spent 20 years running engineering and software development projects with teams in Europe, the USA and India in fields ranging from food manufacturing control to wireless sensor networks. He is the named inventor of 4 granted patents, has published 10 academic papers and book chapters in the field of machine vision and is co-editor of the book 'Machine Vision for Inspection of Natural Products.' Mark moved into the R&D Tax Credit and Patent Advisory field in 2010 and has since prepared over 700 technical claim reports in technologies ranging from software/IT, electronics and mechanical engineering through to food production and beauty products. He is a part-qualified patent attorney, having completed a post-graduate certificate in Intellectual Property Law from Bournemouth University and qualified as a Certified Patent Valuation Analyst, and has advised on and written patents for many companies including leading x-ray engineering and medical device patents. Mark is an active investor himself in early stage technology companies having shareholdings in more than 25.

Andy Hill is a strategy consultant and MBA with a background in early-stage businesses in the medical technology industry. He also has a background in sales and marketing and general management and for seven years ran a small UK-based medical device plc. Andy co-funded and spun-out a medical software imaging business from the University of Oxford and has an ongoing interest in making the technology transfer process more effective - for the benefit of inventors, entrepreneurs and society as a whole.

Margit Hoehne is CEO of patentGate GmbH since 2008. She has 20 years' experience with patent information, starting as a research assistant at PATON, the patent information centre In Ilmenau, Germany. Since then she has specialised in developing solutions for in-house patent monitoring workflows. Margit has a degree in business and computer science from the Technical University Ilmenau.

Rahman Hyatt is a Director of Minesoft with over 20 years' experience in the information industry. He grew up in France, Switzerland and the UK, and as a tri-lingual Business Studies graduate he gained experience in the Intellectual Property field at Questel, Orbit, Dialog and Minesoft, working with companies on site in Europe, North America, Australia and Asia. Rahman is an experienced senior member of the management team, as well as a Minesoft director and shareholder. He plays an active role in business and product development and leads specific development projects for corporate clients in addition to overseeing the sales and client service teams, combining his expertise in technology and patents.

Steven Johnson and Vedran Biondic are the founding directors of J&B Partners Ltd. and have over 20 years of searching experience between them. With degrees from Oxford University, Queen Mary, University of London and Zagreb University, they hold a wealth of technical knowledge in the areas of Chemistry, Life Sciences and Mechanical, Electrical and Aerospace Engineering. After working for larger independent search companies, J&B Partners was set up 7 years ago to provide high quality client-focused searching and IP consulting services. Working with clients large and small, they are familiar with all types of searching, with patent systems from across the globe, and using the most up-to-date databases.

Ilya Kazi is a partner at Mathys & Squire with over 20 years' experience in IP, working with companies from start-ups to multinationals. He has an exceptionally successful track record in EPO Opposition and Appeal practice, both as Opponent and Patentee and is a Higher Court Litigator who represented the successful defendant British Gas in the UK High Court in Meter-Tech v British Gas. He has been named by Intellectual Asset Management 3 years running as "One of the world's leading IP strategists" and uses his contentious experience to assist advising companies on cost-effectively obtaining and managing an IP portfolio and adopting an integrated IP strategy that will really work commercially.

Gregor Kleinknecht LLM MCIArb is a dual qualified German Rechtsanwalt and English solicitor. Following a career at large international law firms in the City of London, Gregor founded the award-winning boutique firm Klein Solicitors. He joined Hunters upon the merger of the two firms in February 2014. Gregor has a strong and broadly based contentious and non-contentious IP practice, focusing on brand protection and the exploitation, protection and enforcement of trademarks, domain names, design rights and copyright. Gregor has been recognised as the Corporate Live Wire 2014 Lawyer of the Year in the category Intellectual Property - UK .

Julia May is a prize winning Chartered Accountant and Chartered Tax Advisor, formerly an Arthur Andersen corporation tax specialist. She has a BEng Honours Degree in Engineering Science from the University of Liverpool, specializing in electrical, nuclear and mechanical engineering, and broad based industry experience working for a number of software and IT consultancy firms before moving into the R&D Tax Credit field. One of the UK's leading R&D Tax Credit tax advisors, a delegate of the HMRC's Research & Development Consultative Committee and a member of the HMTC i-File Working Party, Julia has personally prepared and reviewed hundreds of R&D tax credit and, more recently, Patent Box claims. Specialising in handling HMRC inquiries on issues ranging from complications over offshore shareholder structures and taxation of capitalisation of intangible assets to basics such as inadequate record-keeping, Julia offers financial, tax modellng, fundraising and EIS or SEIS investment advice to a number of early stage technology companies where she is able to provide clients and their accountants with pragmatic commercial advice when faced with multiple interactive issues, always prioritising the overall needs of the business holistically.

Dr. Brian More works as Director for Intellectual Property Commercialisation at Coventry University with responsibility for policy, protection, valuation and commercialisation of all forms of IP. He manages a portfolio of 20 patent families, 22 trademarks, designs and copyright. He has had 40 years' experience working with Intellectual Property, as inventor on 6 patents and jointly owned 4 trademarks. Brian has been active in starting 18 companies, using IP and attracting investment in them. Brian studied for a PhD in Grenoble as an employee of the CEA and subsequently worked at the NPL and BNFL's Company Research Laboratory. Prior to joining Coventry University, he worked as Business Development Manager for the School of Physics and Astronomy at the University of Birmingham. He is a Director of 4 companies and sits on 3 national advisory panels. Brian has worked for private contractors on assessment of development proposals in the field of nanotechnology and on EU Framework projects as commercialisation consultant. He has an MBA in Technology Transfer and Innovation from Coventry University and was awarded the 2009 Lord Stafford Award for Technology Transfer.

Sarah McCloughry FRSA, co-founder of STEMM Commercial Ltd, trains innovative scientists, technologists and engineers to become more commercially shrewd. Clients typically highly intelligent and original thinkers, look to advance their enterprise to win stakeholder support and buy-in. Whilst she trains doctoral students at Oxford University's Institute of Biomedical Engineering, senior researchers at Stockholm Environment Institute, leaders in Cisco, MapiGroup and Skanska, she specialises in training leaders and teams in small to medium sized enterprises to grow their business into healthy and prosperous concerns.

Gary McGonagle is a founding partner at Howman Solicitors and has specialist knowledge in Corporate and Intellectual Property law. He was previously a partner in a city law firm and a media and entertainment law firm in London. He can draw on a wide range of commercial experience having also worked as an "in-house" lawyer for a FTSE listed, international fashion company. Howman Solicitors is a Mayfair based firm of solicitors, with an ethical and modern approach. We build strong and long lasting client relationships and help our clients achieve and develop their business strategy.

Allison McSparron-Edwards is Managing Director of Consultrix Ltd and began life as a Chartered Accountant before training to become a business psychologist. She works at board level, and has invested in numerous companies of varying sizes and backgrounds using finance, strategy and psychology to improve commercial returns. Allison combines a shrewd business sense with the ability to understand the human issues involved in leading and managing companies; honest and forthright, she tells it how it is. Consultrix Ltd works with both creative and knowledge-based companies speeding up growth, improving profits and enhancing capital values.

Dr. Dirk Mersch is a co-founder and Managing Director of Cambridge Innovation Consulting (CamIn). His speciality is identifying clients' science and technology needs and locating academic experts with the specific expertise required to solve their problems. He has worked with universities around the world regarding their processes, infrastructure and regulatory hurdles in order to connect academic experts with clients in industry, law, finance and consulting. Dr. Mersch holds a PhD degree in Chemistry from the University of Cambridge and a Diploma in Physics from Ruhr-Universität Bochum in Germany.

John Moetteli, J.D., M.A., BSME, P.E., founder of Da Vinci Partners LLC, is a US and Swiss patent and trademark attorney, and a registered European Trademark & Design attorney with more than 20 years total IP experience. He's admitted to practice before the United States courts and is a registered Professional Engineer, currently on inactive status. Since 1997, Mr. Moetteli has been based in Europe and represents individuals as well as U.S., European and Asian corporations, both small and large. He holds an Engineering degree, a Doctor of Jurisprudence degree, and a Masters in International Management. He is particularly specialized in preparing freedom to operate, invalidity and unenforceability opinions on US patents, as well as preparing US and International patent and trademark applications. He's been inducted into the honorary fraternities Tau Beta Pi, Pi Tau Sigma, Order of the Barons and Order of the Coif, graduating law school magna cum laude. He's lectured for the Da Vinci School of Intellectual Property, the Swiss Patent Office, WIPO (as a WIPO Patent Expert) and the European Commission, and has served as IMD faculty for the Program for Executive Development (PED). He's published several articles on the subject of intellectual property law as well. Prior to his legal experience, Mr. Moetteli was a senior design engineer at NASA and was featured on the Smithsonian Institute's Invention Series program. He speaks fluent English, French and German.

Prof. Paul O'Brien graduated from Liverpool University in 1975 and obtained a PhD from the UC Cardiff in 1978. A lecturer at Chelsea College 1978-1984 he transferred to Queen Mary in 1984 and in 1995 moved to Imperial College. Notable awards include the Kroll (2007) and Platinum Medals (2014) of IoM3, the Gold Medal of the Society of Dyers and Colourists (2015) and the first Peter Day Award and the Longstaff Medal (2016) RSC. He holds honorary degrees from: the University of Zululand, South Africa (2007), Liverpool (2013), Aveiro Portugal (2015) and QMUL (2016). Paul has lectured widely to the public, especially young people and received the Sir Colin Humphries Award of IoM3 for outreach activities in 2011. In 2002 he co-founded Nanoco, subsequently listed on the LSE, and at present chairs the board of Sci-Tron, a University of Manchester spin-out. In 2016 his work in science and engineering was recognized by the award of a CBE.

Keeley Patten joined Miller insurance Services LLP in 2009. She began her insurance career in 2002 with Aon and then Mitsui Sumitomo Insurance Group. Keely specializes in assisting small to medium sized companies from all sectors who hold Intellectual Property Rights (including patents, trademarks, designs, copyrights, trade secrets and domain names), identifying the risks they may face and endeavouring to mitigate these through IP insurance. Keeley specialises in arranging insurance coverage for the defence and pursuit of IP infringement claims, which include legal costs, damages, settlements and counterclaims, as well as any disputes arising out of contractual obligations.

Jonathan Reuvid is an editor and author of business books and a partner in Legend Business. He has edited all eight editions of 'The Investors' Guide to the United Kingdom' and has more than 80 editions of over 30 titles to his name as editor and part-author including 'The Handbook of International Trade', 'The Handbook of World Trade', 'Managing Cybersecurity Risk' and business guides to China, the 10 countries that joined the EU in 2004, South Africa and Morocco. Before taking up a second career in business publishing Jonathan was Director of European Operations of the manufacturing subsidiaries of a Fortune 500 multinational. From 1984 to 2005 he engaged in joint venture development and start-ups in China. He is also a founder director of IPR Events, the quality exhibition organizer and President of the charity, Community First Oxfordshire.

Prof. Graham Richards CBE served as the Chairman of the Department of Chemistry at Oxford. Throughout his career he has been involved in the commercialisation of technologies. He was a founder and for 20 years a director of the University's technology transfer company. He co-founded Oxford Molecular group Plc which was its first spin-out, going from s £350,000 start-up to a £470 million public company. The deal which he did to fund the new Chemical Research Laboratory grew to become IP Group Plc, now a FTSE250 company and of which he was at one time chairman and now Venture Partner.

Guy Robinson is a Deputy Director in the Innovation Directorate at the Intellectual Property Office. He heads up policy teams that help people to make informed choices about IP, to derive value from IP that they own and to mitigate risks around IP ownership. Guy has 17 years of IP experience both in policy and operations. He began his career at the IPO as a patent examiner in 1999. The Intellectual Property Office (IPO) is the official UK government body responsible for intellectual property (IP) rights including patents, designs, trademarks and copyright. The IPO is an executive agency of the Department for Business, Energy & Industrial Strategy.

Will Steele is an economic Advisor for the UK IPO, working in the Economics, Research and Evidence team. His work involves ensuring that IP policymaking is supported and underpinned by an up to date and robust research and evidence base. He has experience as an economist across government and the private sector having worked previously in the department of Business Innovation and Skills, the Department of Health and the pharmaceutical industry.

Olaf Swanzy is the PNO Group's Managing Director and sector specialist for innovation who has close working relationships with all of the principal funding bodies in this sector. He joined the PNO Group in 2004 to help establish the UK operation with an initial focus on technology development within the Environmental Sector. Over the past 9 years, Olaf has worked with an extensive range of SMEs and large companies across all industry sectors and academia to advance research and innovation activities through the procurement of government funding from national and EU sources. Since 2008, he has been involved in the delivery of training to SMEs in the areas of government funding for innovation investment activities. In 2009 alone, he secured in excess of £15 million of grant support for clients.

Jeremy Tear has worked extensively in a number of technology sectors, in many industries including Agrochemicals, Pharmaceuticals, Petrochemicals, Television, video and digital, and Construction. He has a wealth of experience in manufacturing for the Agrochemical, Engineering, Electronics and non-food retail markets. Jeremy has a wide and varied global business experience having spent 10 years working for Sumitomo Corporation of Japan, involved in numerous merger, acquisition and joint venture programmes around the world. He has founded a number of advisory businesses over the last 10 years involved in recovering state benefits for industry and, in particular, the SME sector. To date this has secured in excess of £125 million for clients.

Claire Vane set up Integrated Services eleven days before the Twin Towers fell in 2001. After several senior roles in HR she felt that there was a gap in the market for top quality HR expertise, across all functions and sectors, but at affordable fees. The business focuses on the whole employee lifecycle from recruitment and employment law, through performance management, compensation and benefits to training and development, coaching and the application of psychometrics. Headquartered in Cambridge and London, the organisation provides bespoke blue chip interim and consultancy services to clients throughout the UK and Europe. Claire's passion is in releasing potential, whether from individuals or within a client organisation. The team puts great store on first-rate communications as a critical aspect of its work. A Cambridge graduate in Classics and Modern Greek, Claire uses her other great passion, the piano, to perform for her favourite charities.

Jim Watson is senior director, innovation and enterprise at Scottish Enterprise. In April 2008 Jim was appointed senior director of company growth and in February 2009 took on the additional role of senior director financial services. He served as National Director company growth from 2010 to 2013.

Charlie Wilson OBE is a coach who specialises in teamworking and leadership under pressure. Executives come to him when they want to develop the disciplines they need for consistent performance in challenging conditions. His first career was in the Royal Navy in which he was a successful leader in a wide range of situations and an integral member of a variety of high-performing teams.

Aaron Wood is a Chartered Trade Mark Attorney and European Trade Mark and Design Attorney, and is the founder of Wood IP (www.wood-ip.com). A member of the executive council of the Chartered Institute of Trade Mark Attorneys (CITMA), he is one of a small number of Chartered Attorneys also having full rights of audience before the UK courts and so is able to provide a one-stop shop for intellectual property disputes.

INTRODUCTION

We are all exposed to innovation in our daily lives as consumers and members of the public. We are the passive beneficiaries of new technology, mostly to our benefit, from medical diagnostics to faster broadband speeds or safer motor cars. Sometimes, technological advances, particularly in IT, leading to privacy intrusion such as unwanted emails or telephone sales, are less welcome. However, this book is for innovators rather than consumers, those who are proactive agents of change, the businesses in which they are thought leaders or senior managers and those who stimulate and support them.

Innovation comes in all shapes and sizes from steady processes of improvement in business practice to spectacular breakthroughs in technology. Whatever its form, innovation needs nurturing and the first and final parts of this four part book includes chapters from authors who are themselves innovators and service providers who offer their experience-led advice.

Intellectual property (IP) is at the heart of most innovation, both a by-product and its handmaiden. IP when registered becomes a marketable asset in its own right which may be included as an intangible asset in a company's balance sheet. Indeed, in some cases, it is nor unknown for the value of a company's IP portfolio to be more than the rest of the business.

The central parts of the book are focused on all facets of IP management including its registration, protection and defence, competitive activity and the issue of reserving rights without registration In the final part of the book further aspects of innovation are articulated and we address the opportunities for releasing value by monetising established IP.

I take this opportunity of thanking all those who have authored this first edition of *Growing Business Innovation*. The next edition is already planned. My appreciation also to Tim Ross, Chief Executive of UK Intellectual Property Office for his Foreword and Professor Graham Richards for the Preface.

Jonathan Reuvid
Editor

Part One

Preparing for Innovation

1.1 BUSINESS STRUCTURES

Gary McGonagle, Howman Solicitors

INNOVATION

With the advent of artificial intelligence, the world is currently on the brink of a new industrial revolution. This will further bring to the foreground intellectual property law and the ability of business entities to develop, exploit and protect their intellectual property. In order to accomplish their aims, business entities must choose the correct business structure to allow their innovation to flourish and be protected.

CHOOSING THE RIGHT STRUCTURE

In order to help you identify the correct structure you should consult with your accountant and lawyer to look at the various options that are available to you. The correct option for you will depend on a number of variables, for example:

- the size of your business;
- your tax structure;
- whether you wish to seek external investment;
- whether you wish to form a joint venture with another person; and
- your appetite for risk.

Tax

The tax benefits/pitfalls of each business structure are outside the scope of this chapter; however, taking tax advice should be one of the pre-cursors for launching your products, setting up your business structure or analysing how best to exploit your innovative intellectual property.

HOW TO DECIDE WHICH STRUCTURE IS CORRECT

Currently, there are a great variety of business structures to choose from. They provide flexibility in management and budget, although some options may be immediately discounted as it would be unlikely that you would choose to exploit intellectual property through some of those structures. For example, Charitable Incorporated Organisations (available for charities or charitable groups) or Community Interest Companies (intended for social enterprises that want to use their profits and assets for the public good) are unlikely to be utilised for exploitation of intellectual property unless, it was specifically for a charitable purpose or the public good.

In this chapter we will therefore concentrate on the more familiar business structures and consider the benefits or drawbacks of each. In order to be able to draw a fair comparison between the various business structures we need to utilise the same comparables. In my experience, the following comparables are the main driving factors behind deciding which business structure to choose:

- **Speed & Costs**
  How quickly can you get up and running? Will there be large set-up costs and ongoing costs?

- **Liability**
  If the business structure is sued or gets into financial difficulty, who will be potentially liable for the losses?

- **Finance**
  Can the business structure easily raise finance? In the intellectual property sector research and development is a necessity and can be very costly. Therefore, the more options you have to finance, the better.

- **Confidentiality**
  Under this heading we will consider what filings and disclosures are required in relation to each business structure. This should not be confused with the disclosures that you will be required to make in relation to the intellectual property that you are seeking to exploit. For example, if you are exploiting a patent then you will be required to have disclosed details of the invention when you made your application for a patent.

- **Potential for investment**
  If third parties can invest into your business structure then you can use the money that they invest to research, grow and develop. If you need a lot of research and development then this will be a key factor for you to consider.

- **Business perception**
  Under this comparable we will identify how your competitors, suppliers and clients will perceive your business structure.

TYPES OF BUSINESS STRUCTURE

Sole trader

This is trading on your account (i.e. as an individual although, you may adopt a trading name).

Speed
Very quick, there are no legal formalities to comply with.

Costs
To start, there are no costs involved and ongoing costs will be basic accountancy charges.

Liability
You are fully liable personally, so this is a big negative.

Finance
You can borrow but you cannot offer security above your personal liability (i.e. you cannot create charges over your business structure to enable borrowing).

Confidentiality
No disclosures are required outside your basic tax return.

Potential for Investment
No potential.

Business perception
Other businesses are likely to view you as a young/basic business.

General Partnerships

The Partnership Act 1890 defines a partnership as, 'the relation which exists between persons carrying on a business in common with a view to profit'.

Speed
You can start a partnership without a partnership agreement and be governed by the Partnership Act 1890. However, this out-dated piece of legislation should be avoided unless you want business uncertainty. Therefore, it is advisable that you put in place a partnership agreement before you set up. This may lead to a delay in getting started.

Costs
Start-up costs are limited and ongoing costs will be basic accountancy charges although that can vary depending upon what sector you are operating in. That said, you should engage a lawyer to draft a partnership agreement to avoid uncertainty.

Liability
Partners are fully liable personally, so this is a big negative.

Finance
You can borrow but you cannot offer security above your personal liability (i.e. you cannot create charges over your business structure).

Confidentiality
No disclosures are required outside your basic tax return.

Potential for Investment
No potential.

Business perception
With the advent of Limited Liability Partnerships the general partnership was seen to have had its day. It seems that in recent years this viewpoint has now been rejected as people still consider that the confidentiality benefits offered by a general partnership can be attractive, if they wish to keep their success, or otherwise, under the radar.

Limited Liability Partnerships (LLP)
Members of an LLP have limited liability, which is very attractive. The LLP is a separate legal entity but is taxed as a partnership and it has the organisational flexibility of a partnership.

Speed
You will need to incorporate the LLP at Companies House and put in place a limited liability partnership agreement, which can lead to a delay in set-up.

Costs
Initial costs will be a registration fee with Companies House and a limited liability partnership agreement. Ongoing costs will be preparation of accounts and making basic filings of a confirmation statement at Companies House.

Liability
Members' liability is limited to their capital share, therefore they are not personally liable above that sum (except in limited circumstances).

Finance
You can borrow and can create floating charges rather than be restricted to having to offer personal liability as per a sole trader or a general partnership.

Confidentiality
You must file with Companies House your accounts, registered office details, members' and designated members' information. Any limited liability partnership agreement between members is a private document that is confidential to the members and does not need to be registered at Companies House.

Potential for Investment
You cannot raise money by issuing shares, although there is the potential that an investor could invest capital and become a member/designated member. That said, this is a pretty inflexible investment route.

Business perception
Although LLP's have been very popular with the professional services sector, for example, solicitors, they have not had the same popularity with intellectual property rich companies. Therefore, business perception may be neutral.

Limited Company

A limited company is probably the most commonly used and flexible business structure. A limited company has its own separate legal personality and has shareholders and also directors, the latter who direct the company's day-to-day activities.

Speed
You will need to incorporate the limited company at Companies House. This can be done on the same day, for an additional fee. Additionally, you may wish to have tailored articles and a shareholders' agreement, although this is not a legal requirement.

Costs
Initial costs will be a registration fee with Companies House and, ideally, tailored articles of association and a shareholders' agreement (i.e. regulating how the shareholders conduct themselves). However, if you are setting up a company on your own you can rely on the model articles and would not need a shareholders' agreement. Ongoing costs will be preparation of accounts and making filings at Companies House.

Liability
Shareholders' liability is limited to any sums unpaid on their shares. The share capital should also be available on a winding up. Therefore, it is always better to ensure that a limited company's overall share capital is fully paid up and that the total share capital

is not an excessively high figure (for example, you can have 10,000 shares with a nominal value of 0.01 pence each, that would amount to a total issued share capital of £100).

Finance
A limited company is the most flexible method for raising finance. You can borrow, create floating charges and issue loan notes.

Confidentiality
This structure requires the most disclosure. You must file with Companies House your accounts, registered office details, director and shareholder information and certain information regarding shareholder resolutions.

Potential for Investment
A limited company can, within certain legal parameters, allow you to seek investment or take investment from certain individuals or other entities. This is a well worn path with investors looking to invest in a company for shares. This can clearly be greatly beneficial for an intellectual property rich company as intellectual property companies can require large sums of capital to develop and exploit their innovative ideas.

Business perception
A well known business model which will be viewed as standard.

OTHER INFLUENCING FACTORS

Retaining talent
The core of any business is its employees. In intellectual property rich companies the key employees are the developers and exploiters of their intellectual property. Competition to retain and develop these talented individuals has never been higher and, given the ever expanding global job market and the United Kingdom's exit from the European Union, British based businesses will always have to work hard to retain talent. A limited company does offer the business a way of incentivising those individuals to stay. For example, you can incentivise by issuing share options or a creating an EMI Scheme (i.e. a tax-advantageous employee share scheme). These types of incentives will allow individuals a share of equity now and/or in the future.

It is true that LLPs and general partnerships also offer the option to incentivise and retain talent; however, they are less flexible. Additionally, offering individuals partnerships in a general partnership may also be counterproductive as they may be intimidated by the prospect of becoming personally liable for any losses.

Ring fencing

Ringfencing an asset describes a procedure whereby you identify an asset in a business structure that you want to protect and you structure your business to protect that asset. For example, you could ringfence an asset by deciding to transfer that asset, for an appropriate value, to another entity in order to separate the asset from another area of the business. This can be a sensible step to take however, it is only worthwhile taking with the correct business structure. Ringfencing would be most beneficial if used by a limited company or an LLP. An example of ringfencing would be if a trading entity owns a patent and wants to diversify into another area of business. This alternative area of business may be more risky, in which case the business could set up another limited company to start the more risky area of business or, alternatively, transfer the more valuable patent to another limited company. Therefore, if the "risky business" limited company entity fails then, it reduces the risk of the patent being lost in a potential liquidation scenario.

THE PITFALLS

The majority of problems occur where a business rushes to adopt a business structure without any consideration of its ultimate future aim or without taking appropriate advice (tax or accountancy). This can lead to tax problems, potential personal liability or curtailed expansion. Some of the potential pitfalls are:

No written agreement

Businesses that are a general partnership, an LLP or a limited company may require their main protagonists to organise themselves and sign up to an agreement that determines what should happen if, for example, someone wishes to leave, they die or they wish to sell. Without such an agreement in place that specifies how this should be done the parties may find themselves in disagreement, the business may stagnate or the parties may, at worst, find themselves in court seeking a resolution.

Compromised intellectual property

If the main asset of your business is its innovative intellectual property, then to lose control of it is a disaster. This can happen if: -

- you enter into a business structure with third parties who do not share your vision;
- you do not have appropriate agreements in place to control the business structure, the individuals or the usage of intellectual property; or
- you do not ringfence the intellectual property and protect it from insolvency or bankruptcy proceedings.

Summary Table

Structure	Benefit	Negative
Sole trader	Low cost. Easy to set up. Basic financial reporting.	Full personal liability. Lacks business credibility in market.
Partnership	Low cost. Easy to set up. Basic financial reporting. More potential to raise finance.	Full personal liability. Can lack business credibility in market. Can reduce expansion due to personal liability risk.
Limited liability partnership	Less personal liability. LLP is a separate limited entity and can enter into contracts.	More ongoing costs. More disclosure (e.g. partners must disclose income in accounts).
Limited company	Less personal liability. Better market perception. Better ability to seek finance and raise investment.	More ongoing costs. More disclosure (e.g. annual accounts and financial reports must be placed in public domain).

1.2 MASTERING BUSINESS PLANS

Allison McSparron-Edwards, Consultrix Ltd

DOES WRITING A PLAN MAKE YOU AND YOUR BUSINESS SUCCESSFUL?

Some directors create business plans because they have been told to by advisors and investors rather than because they truly believe they need one. They create plans to please other people, not because they believe in the process or because they intend to adhere to its content. Such plans are often based on internet or book based formats, use a lot of spreadsheets and rarely involve quality analysis, goals or strategies; they tend to remain, once produced, unread on a dusty shelf.

Much has been written about the efficacy of business plans. Indeed, on examining Babson graduates in the USA in 2006, William Bygrave and his team found that entrepreneurs who began with formal plans had no greater success than those who started without them. His main concern about such plans was that often they were all "talk". Bygrave does believe, however, that all businesses need a plan whether it's a mental construction (never committed to paper) or a more advanced description jotted down on the back of an envelope.

On the other hand, Clemson University Entrepreneurship Professor, William B. Gartner, believes business plans are essential. "The importance of a comprehensive, thoughtful business plan cannot be over-emphasized." In contrast to Bygrave, who thought plans were all talk, Gartner emphasises that business plans are all about "walking the walk". To create a meaningful plan planners must do "stuff" such as researching markets and preparing projections, all of which increases the chances that an entrepreneur might follow through and be successful.

THE BENEFITS OF CREATING A PLAN

Many books have been written on the benefits of creating business plans but it often helps to understand why it's necessary from an owner's perspective. As an example, Richard Merrin (45), a Londoner, had the opportunity to complete an MBO of a technical PR agency (Spreckley PR) in 2015 and develop it into a larger, more profitable business. The business, which employed 20 people, had provided a lifestyle to its previous owner but was seen to be old fashioned and run in a paternalistic manner with a restricted offer, a poor culture and limited profitability.

By 2015 Richard had been MD for four years but, lacking a controlling share in the business, had been unable to push through the changes he knew needed to be made to make the business more profitable. He was first and foremost a 'PR Man' whose focus was client centric, sales oriented and results driven. While an acknowledged expert in PR, data centres and Cloud based technology, he would be the first to admit that when confronted with Excel spreadsheets, monthly management accounts and balance sheets he'd run a mile!

Richard knew the business had to change dramatically to take advantage of broader changes taking place within the communications sector but, after a decade of conservative management (and one obsessed with keeping financial planning secretive), he wasn't sure how to go about it. He knew he needed to develop growth strategies, work on the business rather than in it and to create an exit strategy for himself (the new key shareholder). He'd never created a formal business plan before so was unsure what he needed to do to create one. In effect, "He didn't know what he didn't know". Indeed, until the MBO, all management and financial planning was driven solely by the lifestyle needs of the former major shareholder so, as Richard said, "Even looking further ahead than a quarter's finances was a new and daunting experience for me".

Richard and his advisors recognised that what he needed to address were issues common to many businesses regardless of their size and included:

Table 1

Typical Business Issues

Shareholders
- No clear exit strategies for shareholders

Business
- Lack of a Vision, Mission and Goals
- People
    * Management teams focused on tactical delivery rather than strategic goals
    * No clear successors and too much reliance on one key individual
    * Senior management team not being empowered or rewarded to take on additional responsibilities
    * A culture driven by individual egos and secrecy around financial data

- Finance
    * Low profitability
    * Lack of liquidity

- Narrow product offering
- Poor generation of new business opportunities or conversion
- Inadequate processes and management controls causing over servicing
- Threats to client retention

STRENGTHS, WEAKNESSES, OPPORTUNITIES AND THREATS MATRIX (SWOT)

Richard set about creating a plan that would address similar issues and provide him with strategies and solutions. He realised he and his business needed clear goals so the first thing he did was to clarify what he, as an employee and shareholder, wanted out of the business in terms of lifestyle, income, capital return and over what time period. This meant a degree of soul searching and asking the questions many of us avoid in the flurry of day-to-day life. He forced himself to sit down and evaluate what he and his partner wanted to achieve and work out what had to be done to do that. For many – and Richard was no exception – that also meant spending time understanding other financial aspects of his life including pensions, investments, property and household running costs.

It also meant some difficult discussions and conversations with the senior members of the management team and, as for many small business owners like Richard, this was a difficult and sometimes fraught process.

Having understood his own goals, he spent time collecting and analysing data to understand what the business might be capable of achieving and its strengths and weaknesses using a SWOT Matrix.

Table 2

SWOT Matrix*	
Internal Strengths	Internal Weaknesses
• Accreditations? • Proposition? • Capabilities? • Competitive advantages? • Cultural, attitudinal, behavioural? • Experience, knowledge, data? • Financial reserves, likely returns? • Innovative opportunities? • Location? • Talent: Management team / succession plans? • Marketing - reach, distribution, awareness? • Price, value, quality? • Processes, systems, IT, communications? • Physical resources? • USP's (unique selling points)?	• Accreditations? • Capabilities? • Cashflows; cash cow or start up? • Continuity, supplier robustness? • Effects on core activities, distraction? • Financials? • Known vulnerabilities? • Lack of competitive strength? • Leaderships, morale, commitment? • Management cover, succession? • Processes and systems? • Proposition? • Reliability of data, predictability, sensitivities? • Reputation, presence and reach? • Timescales, deadlines and pressures?

External Opportunities	External Threats
• Business/product development?	• Competitor intentions?
• Competitors' vulnerabilities?	• Economy - home, abroad?
• Geographical, export, import?	• Employment market?
• Global influences?	• Environmental effects?
• Industry or lifestyle trends?	• Financial and credit pressures?
• Information and research?	• Insurmountable weaknesses?
• Major Clients, contracts?	• IT developments?
• Market developments?	• Legislative effects?
• Market need for new USP's?	• Market demand?
• Market volume demand trends?	• New technologies, services, ideas?
• New markets, vertical, horizontal?	• Obstacles faced?
• Niche target markets?	• Political effects?
• Partnerships, agencies, distribution?	• Seasonality, weather effects?
• Seasonal, weather, fashion influences?	• Vital contracts and partners?
• Technological development and	
• innovation?	

* Adapted from Businessballs.com

The SWOT, and all the supporting data, enabled Richard to set himself a BHAG (A Big Hairy Audacious Goal) which he believed would change the nature of his business (See "Built to Last: Successful Habits of Visionary Companies" by James Collins and Jerry Porras). The BHAG and SWOT provided the foundation for the business plan he subsequently wrote, ensuring that he understood its impact on resources, financials and processes. The plan had to ensure that it maintained, built on or leveraged the business's strengths; prioritised and optimised opportunities; remedied or removed weaknesses and countered any threats.

CONTENT OF THE BUSINESS PLAN

Richard's plan, and yours, needs to address and articulate the following:

Table 3

Business Plan Content
• Executive Summary
• History
• Key Players
• Positioning and offer
• Sales and marketing
• Clients and client development
• Talent and talent management
• Culture
• Business model
• Processes and IT infrastructure
• Property
• Capital and working capital requirements
• Financial summaries

Plans need to be robust, comprehensive and realistic and the planner should consider the following:

1. Objectives of the plan

Who and what is the plan for: is it for founder/shareholders, directors, corporate owners, a funding body or the bank and/or are you trying to support an initial investment; secure funding for growth or working capital requirements; or support a shareholder led exit strategy?

Establish this early on as it will influence the language you use, the content and your strategies.

2. Typical length

Bygrave notes that the modern trend is for shorter plans as they have a better chance of being read (rather than old fashioned strategic plans which could be up to 50+ pages!). Make the plan understandable and easy to read and ensure that, if written, it is less than 20 pages long, including the summary. In the 21st century many plans are summarised and presented in a digital format e.g. PowerPoint, making them easy to read and distribute to others.

Many modern plans have become padded out with complex financials that are often based on guesses and assumptions. Nowadays investors and directors want fewer, but better-documented, financials. Good plans probably only devote a few pages to income, cash flows and balance sheets with numbers that are capable of being explained instantaneously (remember the failure of individuals on The Dragons Den who couldn't explain their financials to the Investors?). Keep your financials short and to the point!

3. *Shareholder and Senior Management Goals*

All companies have investors and it is important to understand both their motivations and those of the senior management team. Explain what key individuals hope to gain from the business (capital, income, a career, a challenge, peer recognition?) and whether you think the plan provides them with the strategies to achieve these goals.

It is important to ensure that all these interests are aligned when considering dividends, capital growth and remuneration scenarios. Management should be rewarded on the achievement of goals e.g. short term bonuses and/or long term share incentives, of which a summary should be noted in an Appendix. An unmotivated management team is unlikely to be successful – a fact which investors are acutely aware of.

4. *SWOT*

Having created a SWOT, management must decide and articulate whether the subsequently derived goals are realistic or not. Show that decisions are based on reality not wishful thinking; clearly documented risks; explain how the biggest opportunities can be achieved and the biggest weaknesses overcome.

Directors need to be honest because otherwise all planning will be based on false premises.

5. *BHAG, Vision, Mission, Strategic Goals*

Show how you have turned your BHAG into clear, unambiguous statements including a Vision supported by Values, a Mission and strategic and financial goals. Whilst these must be stretching they must also be realistic; having a BHAG gives the business a sense of purpose, something to challenge them and to work towards.

6. *Talent and the psychological characteristics of your leader and the Management Team*

Investors want to know whether the management team can deliver the goals and whether continuity can be maintained. Outline your succession plans, identifying the next generation and, if this is not possible, how you intend to develop and/or recruit successors.

Industry and management experience is of course immensely important but can't always guarantee success. Personal and group dynamics are equally impactful. Utilise psychological profiling to establish what drive, social skills, ability to cope with pace, change and strategic thinking leaders and their supporting management team have. After all, different scenarios require different leaders and teams. When goals require rapid change (3-5 years) a driven, innovative and networked team may be required, whereas extended time frames may mean a less driven but well-motivated team could still be very successful in the long run. Explain the current dynamics and how they need to evolve.

Create mini CVs in an Appendix for key players in your business.

7. *Culture*

Even if the senior team is driven and motivated, an unsupportive culture can still impede strategic success. Summarise your assessment of your culture and how you intend to evolve it over time (cultures take time to change e.g. 2-3 years in larger organisations).

8. *Business Model*

It is important to understand not just what your client's problems are but what your solutions are and how you cost and make profit from them. Explain whether you provide unique one off solutions or volume based commodities and implications for the future of the business based on these assumptions.

9. *Client Development*

Keeping clients is the surest and cheapest way of growing your business. Show the reader that you understand this and comment on whether your clients are satisfied. Explain how you measure satisfaction and retention now and/or will do so in the future. If your client turnover is high, explain what you intend to do to increase retention levels.

Provide a brief analysis of current client profitability and client development plans, outlining the greatest opportunities for enhanced profitability and growth and what resources will be needed to achieve the goals.

10. *Product development*

Explain what the key elements of your current product, services and offer are and how you intend to develop them in the future.

11. Premises and location

Identify lease terms as they are often an important planning and risk factor. For example, too long a lease might inhibit a business's ability to acquire larger premises when growth does occur or an acquirer might not want to commit to taking on the burden of a long lease.

Your location could be a help or a hindrance as being remote might reduce costs but equally might inhibit talent recruitment. Explain your thinking on location and its impact on the business.

12. Sales and promotion

It is important that you can demonstrate clear marketing messages; that you can demonstrate the strength of your new business pipeline and current conversion rates. Explain, briefly, who you are targeting and why and the size of the market, the opportunity and who, on the board, is responsible for managing this important activity in your business.

13. Creation of financial plans based on the above goals

Ensure you include integrated and summarised financial plans that link strategic goals to long term profit and loss accounts, cash flows, balance sheets and KPIs. List the key ratios and how they will be changed over time.

Explain what working capital you need to support your plans and why; how you think it should be sourced and what you think the terms should be e.g. reserves, rights issues, overdraft, loans etc. Include sensitivity analyses as they show that you understand inherent risks within the business and that you have already thought about the consequences on profitability and cash should they arise.

14. Strategic goals and KPIs

It is important that you identify, throughout the plan, the strategies that you will need to achieve your goals. It is worth summarising the strategies, as well as their SMART objectives, including timings, named individuals and teams responsible for their delivery and the KPIs that will be used to measure their success or otherwise.

15. Monitoring, reviewing and amending

No plan should remain fossilised and put in a drawer. Your plan should be reviewed on an annual basis or when there is a major political, economic, technical change that may impact on future goals. Amendments will need to be made and communicated as appropriate.

DO PLANS WORK?

Richard thought the creation of his plan enabled him to better understand the status quo, to clarify his own personal goals as well as those of the business and to create an exit strategy with clear timings and financial goals. He felt that it helped him to see the bigger picture and enabled him to see the connections between the disparate parts of his short, medium and long term plans.

At the same time as deciding what the future profitable products and services of the business were going to be, Richard also clarified his own role and those of the senior management team. When the plan and its objectives were communicated to the management team and the wider business it had a big cultural impact. People felt excited, motivated and empowered; staff and client retention improved and future "stars" were recruited to support growth. Aligned with better processes, new products and services, profits and cash reserves have also increased in line with the strategic plans.

In summary Richard Merrin says, "It was vitally important that I gave myself time and permission to look at my business as an 'outsider', that understanding what I didn't know was infinitely more important than focusing only on what I did know. When you are running a small business, people look to you to take decisions on everything from the colour of the logo, through to where to buy the coffee cups from. Every small business owner will recognise this but carving out time, developing the plan and sharing as much as I could with my team has given not just me a sense of direction but everyone in the agency as well. Staff retention levels have soared, client retention levels are higher this year than last, business costs have been contained and we have even opened a satellite office in Scotland. And how? Because we were able to identify the issues facing the agency during this process and address them constructively.

"Creating a business plan has enabled me to look at the business with renewed confidence, to reposition it in the market based on quantifiable data and to plan for an exciting future that I believe in. In summary I feel that it was worth the time and effort that I put into it and am looking forward to achieving the longer term goals outlined in my plan."

Table 4

Key benefits of a business plan

- Challenges the status quo
- Enables the exploration of the unknown
- Creates challenges
- Creation of linked short and long term action plans
- Holds the board to account to the shareholders
- Creates clear corporate goals
- Identifies issues with succession plans
- Crystallises the offer and matching financial business model
- Clarifies an exit strategy for the shareholders

1.3 THE PROS AND CONS OF UNIVERSITY INNOVATION AND EXPLOITATION

Paul O'Brien, The School of Chemistry and The School of Mathematics, University of Manchester

1. INTRODUCTION

I decided to use this short article on the pros and cons of the development and exploitation of innovation from universities in terms of:

* potential benefits to society in general;
* the perspective and drivers of the universities/their employees and other individuals/investors involved.

The views here are based on my experience over the last 20 years or more, which have involved founding a company which is now listed on the LSE. I have also tried to help numerous academics in developing business ideas, notably discussing and understanding the problems of IP, its costs, ownership and division. I have also served on a number of groups advising on/or supporting translation research and finally lectured widely on the subject. The view presented is personal but tries to explain how such spin-outs are viewed by: the university, their technology transfer offices (TTOs) and inventors/academics. Strengths, weaknesses and points of issue and difference are discussed, together with their impact on the nascent company. This view might help academics and others to understand themselves and others involved, hence to gain insight into how they can work to make the activity truly successful. I will also discuss what governs the readiness of early stage investors to get involved, and in conclusion provide some thoughts on how the partners could work together more effectively.

The dichotomy between academia and business is quite easily encapsulated by a quote (*https://www.imperial.ac.uk/alumni/imperial-alumni/alumni-stories/geoffrey-nicholson*) from Geoff Nicholson, one of the 3M Post-it team who described:

"Research as the transformation of money into knowledge and innovation as the transformation of knowledge into money."

This quote provides a simple platform to explain much of what I will discuss in what follows. It gives a working idea as to where academics sit in their university and what inventors achieve in successful corporate research. The article will essentially delve into the middle ground, in which academics can be helped to start to think that their research may have a use, and how this might become developed as an exploitable reality with the help of others.

Universities exist, in my opinion, for three reasons:

- To preserve knowledge and transfer it to the next generation – broadly speaking, education;
- To create new knowledge and understanding of research; and
- To benefit society more widely through vocational training and transferable ideas and/ or technology.

These were formalised by the 3 mission concept of universities' work in the UK which has only been reinforced by the introduction of impact as a performance criterion in the UK. Innovation and entrepreneurship were first given a higher profile in the time Margaret Thatcher was Prime Minister (for a synopsis and references see *http://www.rsc.org/aboutus/news/pressreleases/2013/baroness-thatcher-science-entrepreneurship.asp*). This was an essentially deregulated model in which IP generated on government grants was made available for PIs/universities to exploit, on a no royalty basis, the results of government funded research (*http://www.eua.be/eua/jsp/en/upload/lambert_review_final_450.1151581102387.pdf*)

This is somewhat in contrast to the USA where the Bayh-Dole ruling is a bit more prescriptive (*http://www.nature.com/nbt/journal/v24/n3/full/nbt0306-320.html?foxtrotcallback=true*) and inserts more specifics into the position. The US Model has often been followed e.g. in India and South Africa, but there is some evidence that the UK approach is more effective. The impact of technology transfer from universities is generally agreed to be a significant factor in economic growth, well appreciated by the Obama administration. However, the dependence of state/general economic benefit on the nature of the arrangement for academic technology transfer is less clear.

2. THE PARTIES INVOLVED

2.1 The Inventor(s)

The idea will most likely originate from an academic(s) at any level. Most typically, ideas originate with an individual academic or a grouping. It is important that if a group of people venture forward in this way that their ownership (of IP) is defined as early as possible and written down on a terms sheet. These groups may broadly be identified/typified as:

- Academic(s);
- and or plus student(s) (usually a research student);
- and or plus other university employees e.g. a postdoctoral employee working for one or more academic and experimental officer or technician.

This specifically excludes parties sponsoring work owning i.e. having paid for the right to exploit or an option on exploitation/IP.

There are, it seems to me, three fundamental universal reasons why an academic might be interested in IP/technology transfer:

- to change the world, or interest or creativity driven;
- to make money;
- to enjoy the process.

A fourth reason also exists: self-interest. Success in this area is often now a necessary criterion for promotion per se; in my view a bad idea. This final motivator is a poor one as it encourages people without a real interest in the area to get involved. In some ways this encouragement by universities is an overreaction to academic prejudice against useful innovation, which was rife until the 1970s.

My analysis of the general ideas is at odds with my perception of many of my colleagues.

To change the world: How will your idea/ invention have influence? How will it find its way to the market place? What will it cost to reach the market place? Where will it fit into a supply chain? What are the regulatory requirements? These are questions academics need to think about but it is a good reason to get involved. Many great inventors/innovators have been driven to some extent by this desire: Edison, Ford, Land, Gates, Jobs and Wozniak provide very different examples. Academics need to appreciate the difficulty of exploiting ideas: publishing a book is easy – a computer programme is more complex (both principally copyright issues); designing an article to be third party manufacture, e.g. a toy or food product, is a little harder (IP, licensing start-up); manufacturing a diagnostic more difficult again (tens of millions of dollars to pass regulatory hurdles) and a drug to market regulation > one billion dollars). Some inventors of exploitable technology waive rights to personal income in favour of research money e.g. from the Gates foundation; this is laudable as many important projects, especially those benefitting the third world, are not intrinsically attractive as profit making exercises.

To get rich: There is nothing wrong with making money. If you succeed it can be a good consequence. Many academics react with horror at the idea of contaminating their purity, a very limiting approach but perhaps not as reprehensible as only being interested in the money. If you make money it can be used to do good things.

To enjoy the process: On average you will find it tough to work through to success – at some stage you will have problems and maybe wish you hadn't bothered. I would suggest 'simply for pleasure' is not a good idea.

2.2 The Technology Transfer Team

Universities in the UK all have some kind of grouping managing technology transfer. The normal arrangement is as a fully owned limited company. This route helps with compliance and simplicity of management as universities are charities, and although other large charities do trade, it does make things simpler. However, as TT groups are most often fully owned they tend to follow the current fashion in university politics rather than take a business based position based on seeking success. Pay in these groups is also low and not bonus incentivised so highly motivated entrepreneurs are not generally attracted to them. It is a shame because working with academics gives an opportunity to work close to a fecund source of new projects.

If we analyse this as a customer client relationship, the academic is always pretty free to develop or not develop an idea and they can also often progress the idea without the use of the TTO. If both sides want the idea to progress and be successful what might they aspire to in concert?:

- To be successful;
- To satisfy university performance criteria – often statistical driven numbers of patents, spin-outs, licensing agreements etc.; and
- To be good at technology transfer i.e. causing ideas and inventions to be exploited and usually make money.

This view presents a common conundrum in life, business and even sport. If we are successful in exploitation then criterion one will be met. The reverse is not true – if we produce without value we will have statistics but no value, score lots of goals and never win a match or big trophy.

Benevolence is also possible in this area, where commercialisation processes are protected, but e.g. in the area of orphan drugs extensive free licensing is made available.

2.3 The Investors

There are many different routes to early stage funding and the availability of such funding varies with the culture at the time and the national and international economies. Funders include:

- Universities themselves, although they often prefer to fund research within the confines of the university;
- Business angels;
- Schemes, often government sponsored, providing early stage investment. These were rife around 10 years ago, often involving RDAs, but much less common now; and
- Venture capitalists, usually in a limited partnership or a company.

Family and friends are often listed as a first option, but for the majority of university spin-outs the amounts of money may be too great for an individual. That said, universities seem remarkably unprepared for the idea that academics might want to invest in their own company.

One dichotomy in the area is what people define of or think of as research; academics have a clear perception of where research ends and development starts. They err on the side of caution in defining research as that which has great academic impact influencing other research and originality is key in determining quality and perceived academic value. On the other side of the coin, investors and others in TT will try and get academics to fund development through research funds. This situation can produce a Catch 22 position when linked to peer review processes, which will either tend to view an application as one or the other. It is common, in my experience, for academic peer review to undervalue development and on exploitation to call things research so as to put off funding, or only consider it when risk has been reduced. There is room for much more clear and specific advice from funders in this area.

3. CONCLUSIONS

At present we are in a time of change in this area in the UK, with the influential Dowling Report (*https://www.gov.uk/government/publications/business-university-research-collaborations-dowling-review-final-report*), a recent publication, coming into play and serious consideration of the future of such activities in hand with a consultation on patient capital active as I write (*https://www.gov.uk/government/publications/patient-capital-review*). In conclusion, to understand this interface we can look at common divergences based on the key perceptions of the parties involved by using a series of topics: Value, Innovation, Risk and Exploitation on which the various parties (e.g. all shareholders in a spin-out) need to agree on for success, and harmony.

- **V**alue: Academics are poor at understanding valorisation and universities can badly affect the value by strategies to diminish their risk. Investors, myself included, diminish risk by maximising the equity return on investment. Investors are often over keen to define money making exit strategies, based on a good valuation.

- **I**nnovation: Academics tend to think of disruptive ideas as intrinsically valuable. Universities want success criteria to be compatible with academic objectives and impact metrics;investors often poorly understand the nature of innovation and the landscape. A new innovation will occupy disruptive space; new entities without a product are difficult for investors to understand, value and invest in.

- **R**isk: Needs to be understood by all parties as it will exist. It may be perceived differently – academics may be blind to risk, universities over adverse to it and investors mitigate risk in valuation and by market research.

- **E**xploitation: Academics like the idea but perhaps are not knowledgeable on the process that leads to success; universities want to see this happen (metrics, to make money), and investors want to see innovation but also focus on money.

This divergence of views can be frustrating to all parties and a holistic view is needed. I think groups need to be more aware of this problem and agree what success will look like. It could, for example, be at the extremes of:

- To make money e.g. a trade sale, sale of company wholesale, licensing, listing and sale of shares.
- To see a profitable company employing in a few years' time a company listed on a main market with a strong future.

Nobody knows the future but it is important to understand each other to successfully form deals that lead to start-ups or IP transfer. An ex-oil trader friend of mine, the late Julian Walsh, once told me that good deals are ones with which everyone is happy. I leave the last word with him.

4. ACKNOWLEDGEMENTS

I would like to dedicate this article to my great friend Julian Walsh, who amongst others, encouraged me in the 1990s, before it was fashionable, to take an interest in entrepreneurship.

1.4 DEVELOPING AN INNOVATIVE MINDSET IN LEADERS AND TEAMS

Sarah McCloughry, STEMM Commercial Ltd and Charlie Wilson, Bosideon Consulting Ltd

THE ISSUE

In 2014, Hermann Hauser, the technology entrepreneur responsible for the introduction of Catapult innovation centres to build UK economic growth, was genuinely surprised at how well these were progressing[1]. However, he also said the UK was still playing catch-up with Germany in supporting growth and innovation in science and engineering. By the time of the referendum in 2016, things were looking far bleaker. Paul Nurse (Nobel Prize-winning head of Europe's biggest biomedical research centre in London) said that Britain's vote to leave the EU was worrying his European employees and would hit "extremely important" funding[2]. As a result of the vote, industry faces challenges in funding and personnel. According to universities, UK international students created £10.8 billion in export last year. Already we are seeing a reduction in students from the EU. This has implications for research and discovery and the decline will only worsen as the 2019 deadline approaches.

Innovation is more likely to be successful where there is a diversity of employees of gender, ethnicity and culture: 45% of companies are more likely to report a

1. The Guardian Nov 2014

https://www.theguardian.com/technology/2014/nov/05/hermann-hauser-science-catapults-more-innovation-uk

2. EURACTIV.com Sept 2016 "Funding, staffing woes after the Brexit vote"

https://www.euractiv.com/section/uk-europe/news/funding-staffing-woes-for-uk-science-after-brexit-vote/

growth in market share and 70% more likely to report success in capturing new markets. When a member of the team shares traits in common with the customer, either through gender or ethnicity, they are 152% more likely to understand the needs of the customer[1]. Workplaces that are successful in fostering innovation inspire employees with a sense of connection to the work. They are willing to give extra time and effort and are 8 times more likely to say they want to stay longer term. This ensures stability and long-term growth in what is necessarily a fast-changing industry that involves shifts of landscape, executives and internal operational structures.

Innovation builds economic growth. However, it involves risk and leaders need to be ready to take those risks. To do this they need to have leadership strategies that support innovation as well as the backing of their organisation to make it happen. This is especially important where it is likely to be a longer-term investment.

WHAT NEEDS TO BE DONE ABOUT IT

Gallup Organisation conducted a 30-year global study into 1 million work teams with 20,000 face-to-face interviews with leaders and 10,000 face-to-face interviews with team members. The research indicated team members need four conditions in order to collaborate successfully and happily: trust, compassion, stability and hope.

Trust: Trusted leaders win better output, morale, retention, loyalty and revenue. But one of the biggest mistakes a leader can make is to assume that they are trusted by virtue of their title. Leaders win trust by demonstrating consistent respect, integrity and authenticity. They acknowledge their flaws and admit mistakes, particularly in delivering difficult news. They commit themselves to their followers. The chances of employees being engaged at work when they do not trust leaders are just 1 in 12. When they trust them, that engagement increases six-fold. Because trust needs time to develop, employee retention is critical.

Compassion: Mounting evidence shows that a caring manager means that people stay with their company longer, are more productive and produce more profit. By listening, taking interest and supporting followers' happiness and wellbeing, leaders demonstrate that followers matter to them. As a result, the leader (and their ambitions) matter to their followers.

---

1. Fortune (Tech) "Why Diversity and Innovation Play a Role in becoming a Great Tech Company" by Lewis-Kulin and Rohman:
http://fortune.com/2017/01/17/best-tech-workplaces-innovation-diversity/

Stability: When teams are taking chances in developing their innovation they need a leader they can count on to buffer them from external threats while maintaining discipline and consistency. As Simon Sinek asserts in his TED Talk "Why Good Leaders Make You Feel Safe", "When we feel safe within an organisation we naturally combine our talents and our strengths and work tirelessly to face the dangers outside and seize the opportunities."[1]

Hope: Leadership is not to be found by avoiding mistakes. An innovative leader is necessarily making best guesses so is often at the boundary of their competence. Inevitably, mistakes are part of the process. It is how quickly leaders recover that makes them outstanding as leaders. The key to a resilient team is how the team themselves engage in the strategic vision, inspiring themselves with hope in the future of the project. Everyday reversals and mistakes then become mere trifles. Leaders can often fail to realise how deeply followers need something to look forward to that helps them see a way through the chaos and complexity. Knowing things can and will get better is a powerful motivator. To keep on being the best they can be, followers need to believe in a brighter vision of things to come. One leader is known for building in periodic "champagne points" on long projects – moments of celebration at the conclusion of different stages to maintain morale and increase hope. She takes care of herself and her team to ensure continued hope so that everyone weathers the storms with enthusiasm intact.

Together, trust, compassion, stability and hope foster a sense of psychological safety for team members. Google invested a lot of resources in research into what made an effective team. One of the things they did was to measure "team intelligence"[2]. It soon became clear that there was no direct link between the average intelligence of the team members (which tended to be quite high at Google) and the intelligence displayed by the team as a whole, as measured by the decisions they made and how well they implemented them. The most important difference between smart teams and dysfunctional teams was the sense of psychological safety experienced by team members. Innovation requires people to think of new ideas and to think in different ways. They will be reluctant to share those ideas, some of which will appear ridiculous to start with, if they think that they will be ridiculed. Google also found that building that sense of psychological safety came down to something as simple as how members

---

1. TED Talk by Simon Sinek, "Why Good Leaders Make You Feel Safe":

https://www.ted.com/talks/simon_sinek_why_good_leaders_make_you_feel_safe

2. Duhigg, C (2016). What Google Learned From Its Quest to Build the Perfect Team, New York Times Magazine, 25 Feb 16:

http://www.nytimes.com/2016/02/28/magazine/what-google-learned-from-its-quest-to-build-the-perfect-team.html?_r=0 of the team treated each other. Key to this was that everyone was allowed to speak and everyone was listened to. This does not mean that there is a stopwatch and everyone gets equal amounts of time to speak, it means that everyone is heard. Nor does this mean that everyone has to agree about everything. It is quite possible to have stand-up, blazing arguments in a productive team as long as the arguments are always about the ideas, never about the people. When people feel that it is safe to voice an idea (however crazy), that even if their idea is genuinely crazy and is never adopted that their status in the team is not threatened by ridicule, then the one crazy-but-great idea that will change everything has a much better chance of seeing the light of day.

Leaders need to ask genuine questions and sincerely listen to the answers to build trusting relationships with subordinates. This will confirm good upward communication to give them the safety they require. Without that communication, organisations are neither effective nor safe. Edgar Schein says in "Humble Inquiry"[1] that the art of questioning becomes more difficult as status increases. Leaders in our culture are supposed to be wiser, set direction and articulate values which predisposes them to 'telling' rather than 'asking'. Effective leaders cultivate humility. Because they ask good questions, the whole team gains valuable shared intelligence and engages in independent and creative thought. By having a hand in the decision making, they have a stake in the outcome.

HOW TO DO IT

Smart teams don't just happen. If you want to create a smart team, it requires investment of resources and effort. One framework to direct that effort is Peter Hawkins' model, "The Five Disciplines of Teams"[2]. The Five Disciplines are:

- **Commissioning**: A team is brought into existence by someone to do something; it has been given a purpose. It is surprising how many teams are not aware of this. It is quite possible that the person who created the team will also be a member of that team. Although of course they are closely linked, these are two different roles and must be kept separate. Keeping them separate can be a challenge.

- **Clarifying**: The team-members do not just accept their commission, they internalise it. They disassemble it, examine all the parts and then put it back together in a way that makes sense to them. They might need to ask some questions to make sure that what they have reassembled is still what is wanted. They might have come up with a better idea.

---

1. "Humble Enquiry: The Gentle Art of Asking Instead of Telling" by Edgar Schein

2. Hawkins, P (2014). Leadership Team Coaching (second edition), London: Kogan Page Ltd. See also https://www.youtube.com/watch?v=tl-soMKuyYg

- *Co-creating*: The team puts into practice the values, vision and processes that have been "clarified". They notice what is happening when the team is functioning well and do more of it; they notice what is happening when the team is functioning badly and do something about it.

- *Connecting*: Having a great team is one thing but it is not enough on its own. In order to get things done, that team will have to connect to its stakeholders. One of the measures of an effective team is that if a stakeholder talks to one member of the team on one day and another on another day, they will get the same message. One of the products of the first three disciplines is that this is more likely to happen.

- *Core learning*: The team needs time collectively to reflect on its performance and processes, both individual and collective. This is a key part of creating that sense of psychological safety that is essential to creating a smart team.

These are things that all the team members need to do. There are things that the leader of such a team can do to encourage them.

- Develop a 'questioning' rather than 'telling' approach. Ask open questions (ones that don't just have yes/no answers) to get as much of people's input as possible. Your questions can be tough and direct but they must always be with the aim of moving the project along and solving problems.

- After you've asked a question, keep quiet and really listen to the answers. If you have your own answer to the question you have posed, give it honestly but acknowledge that it is only one possible answer and does not have extra value just because it is yours. You do not have a monopoly on good ideas.

- Ask questions of yourself. Leaders must ask themselves what they could do better or differently. Understand your own motives and scrutinise yourself for bias.

- Question the organisation. Review your practices, processes and structures, asking, "Why do we do things this way?" "Is there a better approach?" "What's the point of this?"

- Cultivate sincere interest in others. People know when you fake it. Positive engagement generates positive regard.

As companies strive to increase productivity, new ways of thinking and doing will become urgent. Innovation means challenging current thinking, taking risks and making mistakes. Innovative teams confront the status quo, are willing to take problems in their stride and continually learn from their mistakes. Creating such teams requires a culture of psychological safety throughout the organisation, starting within the leadership. This guarantees a successful and rewarding economic future.

1.5 NEW INNOVATION PROGRAMS FOR UK INDUSTRY: URGENT IMPERATIVE

Jeremy Tear, GovGrant Ltd and Karren Brooks

The UK Government's stated intentions to invest significantly in innovation and to develop the UK Research Institute are a bold and positive step forward; these initiatives will become urgent imperatives if Britain is to compete in a post-Brexit world.

However, the track record of UK Government initiatives to stimulate industry and the small and medium enterprise sector (SME) in particular have been mostly unsuccessful, often because of a lack of understanding of the target markets and how to reach them effectively. Other program failures can be attributed to an inability to operate within timescales appropriate to those markets because of tedious risk/compliance requirements employed by the Government to ensure their funding is placed in the right hands.

A notable exception to the litany of failed initiatives is the success of the Research & Development tax credit scheme. It is well documented that this R&D programme has reached far more SME companies in comparison with other Government initiatives distributing state investments. This is due, in no small part, to the accountancy profession and advisory businesses acting as guides to the legislation and developing confidence in passing the compliance requirements and scrutiny, which invariably comes with accessing Government funding.

The masterstroke for this success, however, is for the Government to use an existing infrastructure with a significant number of skilled financial staff to carry out the effective risk assessment i.e. Her Majesty's Revenue & Customs (HMRC). Every other initiative using either national, regional or local quango structures has either been "unsafe", poorly focused or too long winded: wrapped up in time consuming bureaucracy and red tape.

This use of HMRC as more than a tax collector has proven to be such an effective way of assessing the risk investment on a project-by-project basis that they have now introduced the Research and Development Expenditure Credit scheme (RDEC). This is a clear demonstration that the process has moved from simply tax rebating to actual expenditure investment, using HMRC to perform the risk assessment.

The use of tax rebates and credits has significantly more appeal to industry because of the mitigation of the cash "leak" when Corporation Taxes (CT) are paid on non-cash assets under the Generally Accepted Accounting Practices (GAAP) tax accounting system, which is the fundamental process through which business accounts are prepared for tax purposes. There is a great deal of focus on tax mitigation by business because of this "cash drain" effect where tax payments are not simply based on the free cash in the business and working capital can be damaged because of this liquidity outflow. All the assets that are generated in any period carry a tax liability, which includes increases in debtors, work in progress and stock. Cash balances can often be a small part of the assets.

These R&D schemes have wider implications for business as this process strengthens balance sheets and improves working capital. All the benefits fall through to the balance sheet. The incentive to invest in innovation with this backdrop of support becomes obvious and may mitigate the post-Brexit negatives.

Some consideration should be given to simplification of the schemes in respect of the compliance rules, as there remains a large degree of subjectivity by the HMRC inspectorate when trying to assess claims against the legislation.

Looking beyond R&D at the other "innovation tax" initiatives there is some optimism with the potential of the UK Patent Box Scheme, originally introduced in 2012, which had obvious benefits for large technological organisations that had already built some scale to their operation. This scheme has been revised and relaunched more recently as it was rejected by the EU in its original format because of EU state aid restrictions:

- The initial scheme (vetoed by Germany) was relatively straightforward; however, the re-worked legislation has substantially increased the developmental burden of proof and introduced complex adjustment factors, which will prove difficult to quantify or justify for all concerned.
- The UK government may decide to revert to the original, simpler Patent Box scheme as we exit the EU, but the fundamentals are as follows:
    * The structure of the scheme is to reward innovation at the point of real commercial success, i.e. when the patent is approved and significant income is being generated from its success.
    * Such an approach is only likely to appeal to large well-funded businesses that have a developed process that includes the need for patenting as a global protection mechanism, such as those in the pharmaceutical industry.

* If the scheme is purely to tempt large multi-national technology business to move their tax paying head offices to the UK – then the scheme may have some merit. It is unlikely, however, that the tax regime differentiation will be significant for wholesale migration of international business with the proliferation of similar schemes from competing governments.

A DIFFERENT TYPE OF PATENT BOX REGIME

The gap between early development and market launch has always been the area where financial support from any source is limited. The cost of taking a developed idea, service or product through to a successful launch can only be achieved with high risk capital, which is invariably limited. This scarcity of funding is the biggest factor in the lack of investment in Intellectual Property (IP), such as patenting. The damage from early competition for unprotected successful products and services is a large factor in British failures in international market development and legislation should be rewritten to encourage innovators' ideas.

Most SME businesses struggle to find the funding to develop an idea. Adding a further burden of the cost of protection is often beyond their financial capabilities. The global intellectual property protection laws are clear on disclosure pre-protection – it is generally assumed that patent investment is prior to any disclosure of invention, never mind generation of commercial income from the invention.

KEY CONSIDERATIONS FOR SUCCESS FROM THE UK GOVERNMENT INNOVATION INITIATIVE

- *Timing*: The most critical time for the UK Government to invest is at the beginning of the process, at the VC1 stage. This would lead to more companies considering the use of patenting to protect their intellectual property. Early stage government funding could be promoted with reduced risk by a straightforward benefit share. An alternative protection for the management of risk for government investment can be achieved using similar principles to the UK student loan scheme. Additional taxes could be placed on the benefiting companies when they are demonstrating improved profits from the patent investment. This way the government could act as an early investor (like "patient" capital but around a more tangible patent investment) with a beneficial part assignment in the success of the intellectual property.

- *Cost*: It is not only the cost associated with the initial local patenting process but the "roll on" effect once the requirements to internationalise the process begins. Through the European Enterprise network, the Government already offers grant support of up to £3000, with a contribution from the business of £400, for an expert assessment of any intellectual property, based on feasibility for patenting. This process is registered through the Intellectual Property Office. Such a process could be refined to ensure the support offered under the early investment above could be risk assessed. In addition, any successful UK patents could receive international roll-out IP investment from Government to create global positions, where the recovery of investment is through patent part assignment to the state vehicle.

- **_Disclosure Protection_**: The view of many SMEs is that the publishing of the local patent gives their competition direction for development before granting, thus enabling disruption tactics: "Better to just keep the inventive step a secret." The Germans have a better idea.

   The German Patent Office issues what are called utility models, (Gebrauchsmuster) – these are granted immediately without a search on assessment by the German Patent Office. They give immediate protection, and are generally used by companies as part of their patent strategy whilst the patent is pending, as they cost only c€300. Such instruments exist in France, Italy, Spain, Austria, and the Netherlands, but not the UK or US. They're also popular in Australia and China but as there is currently no international filing treaty, unlike regular patents, they must be applied for country by country. The UK Government should consider such a solution.

- **Defence Litigation**: The costs of obtaining a patent pale into insignificance in comparison to litigation costs for defending the IP rights. As part of the trade negotiations that are going to take place across the world as we move into Brexit it will be necessary for the government to demonstrate a level of commitment to agreeing best practice with each trade partner. Areas to be considered are:
  * Establish a strong patentability standard, with appropriate limitations drawn from international commitments;
  * Adopt strong copyright protections drawn from international norms;
  * Consider utility models to facilitate rapid introduction;
  * Close loopholes used by counterfeiters and make enhanced penalties available for particularly serious cases;
  * Ensure the availability of mechanisms to effectively enforce intellectual property rights, including the recent introduction of mediation services by the IPO; and
  * Consider financial support and supported insurance solutions for assistance with litigation.

- *Value*: There are no clear guidelines, valuation models or recognised markets for trade in I P. Cash flow is often closely connected to a company's IP and intangibles. Despite this, and good evidence to show that high growth IP-rich businesses are more resilient and perform better than others over time, IP and intangibles are rarely considered in mainstream lending practice. Balance sheets do not represent the value of these assets, and current regulations actively work against consideration of IP and intangibles as an asset class. There are plenty of examples of faster growing economies taking steps to understand this issue and make knowledge assets bankable:
    * Malaysia and Singapore are introducing guarantees to facilitate IP-backed lending;
    * Denmark and India are supporting the development of IP marketplaces;
    * Germany has sought to articulate the 'Wissensbilanz' (knowledge scoreboard) to assist financial analysis of individual firms;
    * Brazilian banks are experimenting with IP audits prior to lending;
    * China has publicly set out its policies to make the country a world leader in technology by 2050, which has included the establishment of targets for the creation of "indigenous IPR"; and
    * Hong Kong set up an Innovation and Technology Fund targeting IP-rich businesses with a $5bn injection as long ago as 1999.

The UK Intellectual Property Office commissioned a report from Martin Brassell and Kelvin King in 2013 entitled *"Banking on IP"*, which we have cited throughout this note.

One of their conclusions is that:

"The most important step in harnessing IP value is to realise that this value is not nil, and therefore requires active consideration. Robust approaches to determine the value of intangibles exist in the same way as for tangible property and are now included alongside them within the Royal Institute of Chartered Surveyors' Red Book, regarded as a banking industry reference."

UK GLOBAL RANKINGS ARE NON-EXISTENT

The lack of success in developing Intellectual property through Government institutions in the UK is borne out by the Thomson Reuters Report on the Global top 25 Government institutional Innovators:

Table 1: The top 25 Global Innovators - Government

Organization	Country/Region	Rank
CEA	France	1
Fraunhofer Gesellschaft	Germany	2
Japan Science & Technology Agency (JST)	Japan	3
Department of Health and Human Services (HHS)	US	4
Centre National de la Recherche Scientifique (CNRS)	France	5
Korea Institute of Science & Technology	South Korea	6
National Institute of Advanced Industrial Science & Technology (AIST)	Japan	7
United States Department of Energy (DOE)	US	8
Agency for Science Technology & Research (ASTAR)	Singapore	9
Institut National de la Sante et de la Recherche Medicale (Inserm)	France	10
Helmholtz Association	Germany	11
US Department of Veteran Affairs	US	12
RIKEN	Japan	13
National Research Council Canada	Canada	14
Max Planck Society	Germany	15
Chinese Academy of Sciences	China (Mainland)	16
Le Reseau International des Instituts Pasteur (RIIP)	France	17
National Institute of Materials Science (NIMS)	Japan	18
US Navy	US	19
Commonwealth Scientific & Industrial Research Organisation (CSIRO)	Australia	20
Consejo Superior de Investigaciones Cientificas (CSIC)	Spain	21
Academia Sinica	Taiwan	22
US Army	US	23
National Aeronautics & Space Administration (NASA)	US	24
Russian Academy of Sciences	Russia	25

Source: Thomson Reuters Derwent World Patents Index, InCites and Web of Science

What is of greatest concern is that 32% of the top 25 are from Europe, our closest competitors, and whilst France has 4 organisations on the list, the UK has none.

CHINA'S IP STANDARDS AND INNOVATION STRATEGIES

China has only the Academy of Sciences, ranking them 16th on the previous table. The preponderance of counterfeiting and skirting international patents and treaties is slowly changing to align with global policies and this trend is expected to accelerate, as more Chinese technology requires protection. China has used US academics to advise them on legislation and standards and is now looking to initiate global policy rather than follow the developed West.

With the impending Brexit, the UK has a unique opportunity to both assist and collaborate with China in the development of trade agreements and IP norms and practices. In a recent report, *Standards, Stakeholders, and Innovation*, co-authored by Chinese and US academics, Su, Kennedy and Suttmeier, the professors stated, "China is making a long-term commitment to the development of Standards as part of an effort to promote domestic technological innovation and make China an 'innovative society'." The UK will necessarily be re-writing its own innovation norms and policies and can partner with China in various initiatives to our mutual benefit.

CONCLUSION

If success in innovation is to become an effective strategy in the UK, it will come from the SME sector, and the Government must find a way of helping and supporting this group by protecting the innovation that they already generate.

The existing approach of using HMRC to risk assess investment by Government should become the preferred route. This will require investment in the infrastructure of HMRC but the foundations for an effective national processing regime are already in place.

The Government must avoid falling into the same trap as before in creating expensive untested infrastructures that fail to deliver funding where it is needed and simply become self-fulfilling institutions that forget that the objective is to incentivise innovation and regain the United Kingdom's competitive reputation.

1.6 CRACKING OPEN THE WORLD'S FINEST ACADEMIC MINDS TO DRIVE INNOVATION IN BUSINESS

Dirk Mersch, Cambridge Innovation Consulting Ltd

INTRODUCTION

Nowadays, innovation seems to be something that everyone desires. Governments invest billions into research and development, an investment that spurs innovation and drives economic growth. Companies often spend a considerable percentage of their revenue on developing new products and processes in order to stay competitive. Finally, consumers and businesses enjoy the end results of innovation in the form of better, cheaper and (in some cases) revolutionary products and services.

However, there are still substantial inefficiencies in the knowledge transfer from the area of innovation creation to the area of innovation demand, which significantly slows down the pace of innovation overall. This is apparent in cases where academic innovation is not investigated further because no immediate application or use is apparent—while, at the same time, businesses sometimes fail to improve their products and services, or try to keep solving technical challenges that have already been solved by academics.

In the past, the innovation process was simple enough to allow a company to innovate internally. However, today's technological advancements are extremely diverse, and no company can be expected to comprehend and be involved in all types of innovation. For that reason, many large businesses that rely on innovation have started to form ties with universities, research institutes and individual researchers who assist in their innovation processes. Such industry-academia relationships have primarily been driven by long-term research and development (R&D) goals where the aim is for technology research to become commercial in 5 to 10 years, in order to ensure the company's future market competitiveness. However, until today, large corporations have been almost the only industrial players who have the resources and ambition to penetrate the academic bubble, whilst smaller businesses around the world lose out on such access to important academic intelligence. But even for large companies, collaborations with universities are usually limited to a small number of research projects, and there is little communication between university researchers and the company outside the scope of the collaboration.

In addition, businesses in the legal, financial and consulting sectors are still unaware of the opportunities that academic researchers can provide for their technology activities—whether that may be conducting technology due diligence for an investor in disruptive technologies, assisting a lawyer on technology dispute litigation, or helping a consultant develop an industrial technology roadmap.

All this means that the majority of researchers, consultants, managers, partners, directors and other decision makers within businesses are often unaware of information, known within academic circles, that is highly relevant to (and potentially lucrative for) their business. In this article, we will outline how all types of businesses can engage with academia, and how they can benefit from such engagement.

ACADEMIC CONSULTING AS THE SOLUTION

Consulting is commonplace in the business world. Companies such as McKinsey, PricewaterhouseCoopers, Deloitte, Bain and others have long been assisting their clients in a wide range of corporate challenges — from understanding the industrial

Coventry University

Enterprise and Innovation – Supporting Business, Driving Growth

The Enterprise and Innovation team acts as the gateway to business services at Coventry University, being awarded the Queen's Award for Enterprise in 2015. We have a range of ways we engage with businesses from working with entrepreneurs and small organisations to partnerships with multi-national giants of industry.

These include:

- Student internship programmes lasting from a few weeks to longer - depending on requirements
- Opportunities to work with a research graduate to explore new products, new markets and new solutions
- Flexible CPD courses
- Start-up and small business support including free networking events, consultancy and funding advice
- Professional venues and catering for all sizes of meetings and events
- Access to our academic expertise and research
- Office and business incubation space on our award-winning Technology Park

Contact us to find out more about how we could work together:

T: +44 (0)24 7615 8258
E: ei@coventry.ac.uk
www.coventry.ac.uk/business

THE QUEEN'S AWARDS
FOR ENTERPRISE:
INTERNATIONAL TRADE
2015

 @CovUni_business

 Coventry University

Consultrix

Specialists in developing people and growth strategies

Today your business is successful but will you achieve tomorrows goals?

Our objective is to help you understand, not just where you are now, but where you want to be and how to get there.

We can help you:

- Identify and develop corporate (and personal) goals and strategies

- Plan to maximise profits and capital growth

- Be more creative in tackling challenges

- Attract, develop and motivate talent

- Win and develop more business

Our consultants understand what it is like to be entrepreneurial and enjoy working with businesses, wherever they are in their life cycles. We delight in offering fresh insights and impartial advice, especially when it leads to success!

Contact us:

For more information please contact Allison McSparron-Edwards (Managing Director) or Niki King (Operations Director)

Head Office: 01793 726128
London Office: 020 7409 7398
Email: enquiry@consultrix.co.uk

www.consultrix.co.uk

TRANSFORMING INDUSTRIES WITH
SCIENTIFIC INTELLIGENCE

Cambridge Innovation Consulting (CamIn) provides consulting and expert network services related to emerging technologies. We provide expert advice on innovation strategy, technology due diligence and other activities related to R&D, commercialisation and transformation.

Businesses have to innovate to stay competitive, a process that is complex and is constantly disrupted by emerging technologies. Scientific and industrial experts have an excellent understanding of new emerging technologies and how they will affect an industry, but locating such experts is a challenge. This is why CamIn was created.

OUR UNIQUE SELLING POINTS

With strict due diligence, we hand-pick and recruit world-class scientific and industrial experts on a per-project basis, tailored to your needs.

We work exclusively with scientific and industrial experts in the full technology spectrum, and select people who already have a deep understanding of our clients' challenges.

We fully take over the management of the recruited experts and provide our clients with a clear high-impact deliverable.

OUR PROPOSITION FOR CLIENTS

INDUSTRIAL
Through CamIn, industrial organisations can make their innovation process much more efficient and therefore increase competitiveness, secure future revenue streams, expand market share, and diversify into lucrative opportunities.

CONSULTING
Through CamIn, consulting firms can expand their science and technology knowledge-base to grow technology-related practices and gain more industrial clients.

FINANCE
Through CamIn, financial services companies and investment firms can conduct technology due diligence to reduce risk on their investments in innovative companies.

LEGAL
Through CamIn, legal institutions can develop strong and concise cases related to technology disputes and commercial litigation and increase their chances of successfully representing their clients.

+44 (0)1223 926 926   info@camin.com

CAMIN
www.camin.com

Imitation isn't always the sincerest form of flattery!

Intellectual property (IP) describes a multitude of rights, including patents, trademarks, designs, copyrights, trade secrets and domain names and for many businesses their IP constitutes a growing proportion of their business wealth.

How would your business cope if your IP was disputed?
Any business can be adversely affected by IP disputes. IP litigation can be disruptive, expensive and even ruinous. If rights are infringed, it is important for IP owners to seek resolution.

Protecting against IP disputes
Specialist IP insurance will not only provide cover for legal expenses incurred in defending or enforcing IP rights but also reassurance that your business is backed by a team of specialist underwriters, brokers, lawyers and approved experts.

Miller Insurance Services LLP is a leading specialist insurance broker and our IP experts can advise on all aspects of IP insurance.

For more information about protecting your IP contact:

Keeley Patten
T: +44 20 7031 2725
E: keeley.patten@miller-insurance.com

Melanie Mode
T: +44 20 7031 2313
E: melanie.mode@miller-insurance.com

miller-insurance.com

Financial and professional services

Advanced engineering and manufacturing

Land-based industries

Digital and information and communications technology

Swindon and Wiltshire an area of growing industry and business

Low carbon economy

Health and life sciences

Visitor economy

Creating wealth, jobs and
new business opportunities in
Swindon and Wiltshire.

swindonwiltshire
Local Enterprise Partnership

www.swlep.co.uk

markets of foreign countries to drafting strategies for market penetration. Businesses engage with consulting firms because this allows them to obtain intelligence they do not possess for a fraction of the cost and time that would be required to directly employ someone to do the same research. A one-hour phone consultation with an expert or a comprehensive report can save businesses weeks or even months of work. For the same reason, consulting is a powerful way to connect businesses with university researchers, who can provide similar services to help businesses understand scientifically challenging fields.

Academics are the ideal consultants for innovation and technological development. Their daily job is to push the boundaries of the scientifically unknown and to be aware of any relevant research in their fields. Because of the long duration of their research and the associated uncertainty of success, they have to think years ahead and shift their research focus based on advancements in their fields or related disciplines. Many technological challenges have to be solved on a daily basis as part of their research, which sharpens their problem-solving skills.

Even though R&D collaborations within academia and industry have increased significantly in these past decades, consulting activities remain miniscule, even though academic institutions could heavily capitalise on this great potential. However, the benefits to the researcher from such an engagement reach far beyond simple monetary incentives. The experience that researchers receive by being exposed to and solving real-life problems can be very valuable to them. By understanding shifts in technological demand and challenges in the industry, researchers can better adapt the angle of their research to attract additional funding through industrial partners for their long-term collaborations.

ACADEMIC CONSULTING AT EVERY STEP OF THE INNOVATION PROCESS

The term "innovation" is often used in the context of technological innovation, because nowadays most of the innovations are technology-driven. However, innovation in the broader sense covers the following four areas:

- **Product/Technology Innovation**: A new product that is different from its predecessor (e.g. Apple iPhone);
- **Process Innovation**: A new approach to providing the same or similar service (e.g. Ford's Model-T and McDonald's);
- **Position Innovation**: A new business model under which the company operates (e.g. low-cost airlines);
- **Paradigm Innovation**: A ground-breaking innovation that delivers something completely new (e.g. Spotify and Netflix).

Even though innovation does not always require scientific or technological innovation, it mostly directly or indirectly relies on it. Therefore, the key to enable all types of innovation is to support technological innovation.

Technological innovation is a process that is comprised of three key sub-processes:

1. Research (idea creation): This step is dominated by the academic world and, to a lesser extent, by R&D departments at large companies. This is not surprising, since governments spend billions on academic education and encourage idea creation, making the output publicly available.
2. Development (idea testing): This stage is driven, to the greatest extent, by industry and, to a lesser extent, by university spin-outs. Industries utilise ideas from the public domain and their own research, and develop those concepts into working prototypes. Spin-outs originate from a university idea that was valuable enough to develop.
3. Commercialisation (monetisation of the idea): Ideas that have passed the development stage are good enough to be commercialised. In many cases, the spin-outs are bought out by larger businesses or, in rare cases, try to commercialise the idea themselves. Large industrial firms buy ideas that have passed the development stage or commercialise their own developed ideas.

In the following section, we will show how academic consulting can assist business and industry at every stage of this process. Even though vast amounts of information on new technological developments are publicly available, the sheer amount of it makes it difficult to know where to look and what to focus on. This becomes further complicated when there are different viewpoints present, making it difficult for non-specialists to distinguish between credible and non-credible information.

Idea creation

Before idea creation can begin, a business has to select the technology area that it wants to develop a new technology in. This depends on what the purpose of this idea is and what problem the business wants to solve. The best way to address this challenge is to identify what industry/application/market one is interested in, and then develop a roadmap of technologies in this sector. This is something that researchers with industrial experience (e.g. professors) can do, because they have a very good overview of the current state of technologies in their fields (and related fields), and they understand where the development is headed and what impact it will have on a given industry.

Businesses, through open innovation programs, have begun turning to universities for idea creation where random academics are assembled to brainstorm. However, more targeted workshops are needed with purposely selected academic researchers, where they are confronted with a challenge and then use their complementary skills to solve it.

Idea testing

This stage of technological development is very research-intensive, and, as in university research, many technical challenges have to be overcome on a daily basis. Because of the similarities with academic research, PhD and postdoctoral researchers who are confronted with such challenges on a daily basis are the perfect candidates to tackle them. Furthermore, it is likely that there are already university researchers who have faced similar challenges, and their insights on how to overcome them can be valuable. Even though researchers publish very detailed procedures of their research that are publicly available, these reports rarely discuss the challenges faced during development.

Commercialisation

Any final commercial product rarely contains only one technology. For that reason, companies often have to acquire other technologies through licencing or acquisition to complement the technology they have developed. That means they have to understand what functionalities they need and which companies offer the best technology for this functionality. This is what experienced academic researchers can identify. They can assess companies that another company wishes to acquire—not based on a flashy website or how well the marketing department of that company describes the technology, but based on the underlying technology. Furthermore, they can compare it to competing technologies, and can also comment on whether this technology is future-proof and whether there are better technologies on the horizon that can make this technology obsolete. All these insights are extremely valuable to any executive who has to make a purchasing decision.

Academic expertise for other sectors

Undoubtedly, businesses in the financial, legal and consulting sectors are often confronted with lack of technical knowledge when they seek to provide a service to their clients. This is now becoming increasingly apparent, due to increased technological integration in many aspects of our lives, which makes understanding technologies and their evolution essential. Therefore, all these sectors would benefit greatly if they had a direct communication line to a technology/industry expert on-demand who could quickly answer their questions.

CHALLENGES OF WORKING WITH ACADEMIA

In most cases, when a company seeks academic advice, the company's representatives approach a university close to them, where they are introduced to a local professor working in a vaguely relevant field. By doing so, the company is not speaking to the most suitable scientist. They are contacting a university without knowing whether the person who can help them with their particular problem is actually at this university.

Therefore, locating a person who can answer a particular question can potentially become time-consuming and unfeasible.

Asking one academic researcher a simple question is very straightforward. However, complex problems require working with a group of researchers with different scientific backgrounds and levels of seniority, who come from different universities and countries. Such engagements can become difficult from a managerial perspective, because one has to understand, collate and analyse the researchers' output, and since the researchers are university employees, their other commitments must be respected.

We at Cambridge Innovation Consulting understand these challenges and have developed methods and procedures that allow us to utilise all the advantages of working with academia with no disadvantages.

CONCLUSION

A century ago, academia underwent a revolution. More and more graduates stayed at university after the completion of their degrees in order to conduct scientific research. Academic institutions have been historically considered teaching organisations rather than research institutions, which started to change after the enormous potential of academic intelligence was recognised. This transformation made universities the innovation powerhouses they are today. Now, it is time for yet another transformation, where the knowledge of researchers can become available on demand, wherever it is needed.

1.7 THE LEAN STARTUP PHILOSOPHY

Andy Hill - Fieldridge Limited

INTRODUCTION

In the aftermath of the dotcom bubble in the early 90s, a number of researchers, entrepreneurs and academics began to explore why so many start-up and early-stage businesses were failing. Though now widely dismissed as a myth, a story emerged that 80% of technology businesses in Silicon Valley failed in the first eighteen months after start-up and the majority of the remainder within five years.

Research into the reasons for this apparently disastrous failure rate strongly suggested that a lack of 'fit' between the technologies being developed and the needs of customers was a significant factor.

The Lean Startup movement evolved from this research with the aim of establishing a more scientific, more rigorous approach to creating businesses – one built on objectively identifying customer needs, developing and validating solutions targeted at those specific needs, and testing the myriad assumptions that normally underpin the 'classical' business plan.

ORIGINS OF THE LEAN STARTUP MOVEMENT

The Lean Startup movement had its genesis in the work of Steve Blank, a serial entrepreneur and academic from Silicon Valley. Blank formulated his key ideas around customer-focused product development in the mid-90s and published his influential book The Four Steps to the Epiphany in 2005. Blank's Customer Development process is regarded as the foundation upon which the Lean Startup movement is based.

Eric Ries, an entrepreneur, start-up mentor, venture capitalist and academic built upon Steve Blank's scientific approach to entrepreneurialism. Ries developed his ideas through observation and personal experience of a failed start-up. Marrying his thoughts to concepts underpinning the lean manufacturing philosophy, Ries developed the Lean Startup methodology, publicising his views and the approach in a blog he started in 2008. Ries published his book The Lean Startup in 2011.

Further building on the work of Eric Ries, in 2004 Alex Osterwalder, a Swiss PhD student, under the supervision of Professor Yves Pigneur, completed his thesis *The Business Model Ontology - a proposition in a design science approach*. This work led to the creation of Strategyzer, a management consultancy, and the publication in 2010 of *Business Model Generation: A Handbook for Visionaries, Game Changers, and Challengers* by Osterwalder, Pigneur and some 470 collaborators. To date this book has sold a million copies in 30 languages.

Business Model Generation: A Handbook for Visionaries, Game Changers, and Challengers provides a framework and language for discussing the key components of a company that are easily grasped whether or not the reader has prior knowledge of business practice and its associated jargon. The approach aims to define a consistent set of terms to describe aspects of a business model and how they interrelate to generate value for the customer and profit for the business.

The key tool from this handbook, the Business Model Canvas, provides entrepreneurs with a framework for developing, testing and validating their thinking, based on the Lean Startup methodology.

As use of the Business Model Canvas grew, it became apparent that practitioners needed a further tool to more deeply explore the needs of customers and the value generated by a business through satisfying those needs. In 2014 Osterwalder et al published *Value Proposition Design: How to Create Products and Services Customers Want*. This book effectively joined up the work of Eric Ries and the Lean Startup movement, the work of Steve Blank on Customer Development and Osterwalder's philosophy on business model generation.

In the years since its founding in 2010, Strategyzer's blog, its webinars, workshops and its growing range of tools have increasingly become the cornerstone for those entrepreneurs seeking a different and (many might argue) potentially better way to formulate and test their business ideas – whether in the context of a spin-out, a start-up or larger multiproduct companies seeking to better manage and create value in their product portfolios.

IMPACT AND ADOPTION OF THE METHODOLOGIES

The methodologies described above have been adopted across the world, particularly in the setting of business incubators and accelerators – physical or virtual spaces, independently run or corporate-sponsored, where entrepreneurs can seek advice, funding and mentoring to develop their ideas into businesses.

One of the leading UK-based health technology incubators/accelerators claims that more than 90% of the businesses that have passed through its programme in the 14 years since its inception are still active – a remarkable survival rate compared to the

61% reported in the health technologies industry as a whole[1]. This programme has at its heart the Strategyzer toolset and Lean Startup approach.

University technology transfer offices are also increasingly employing these method-ologies to undertake detailed feasibility testing, in conjunction with their academic entrepreneurs, of any intellectual property they are considering for licensing or spin-out.

Strategyzer claims that more than 5 million practitioners use its products and services globally. The organisation regularly hosts training workshops and seminars around the world for users and provides a wide range of on-line resources to practitioners.

THE STRATEGYZER CANVASES - SUPPORTING THE LEAN STARTUP APPROACH

It is not the purpose of this chapter to provide more than a very high-level introduction and overview of the Lean Startup philosophy. If reading this sparks your interest you will find a host of resources listed at the end and I would recommend that you go 'back to the source' to learn more and decide whether the approach is for you and your business at www.strategyzer.com.

The Strategyzer Canvases – Overview

1. The Value Proposition Canvas

© Strategyzer AG

The Value Proposition Canvas has two halves: the value proposition (the left-hand side) and the customer segment (the right-hand side).

A value proposition is that combination of products and services that a company offers to its customers to satisfy their needs. The value gained by the customer should be perceived to merit the price charged by the company to deliver its offering profitably.

The first step in using the Value Proposition Canvas is to describe the profile of the customer segment in terms of three domains: Jobs (what they need to get done – e.g. problems, needs and tasks); Pains (those things that they would like to avoid or remove from their day to day work – e.g. costs, risks and negative emotions); and Gains (those positive outcomes and benefits the customer is seeking – e.g. positive emotions, cost savings and reduced risk).

The second step in using the Value Proposition Canvas is to describe the value proposition map, that is those products and services the business is planning to offer to customers. Three domains are used here too: Products and services (those things that help the customer get their jobs done); Pain relievers (those aspects of the product or service that address specific customer pains); and Gain creators (those aspects of the product or service that provide specific customer gains).

Bear in mind that pains and gains are not all equal and that the merits of addressing them are proportionate to their respective perceived downside and upside. There is greater perceived value to the customer in the relief of a severe pain and the creation of a significant gain compared to that generated by addressing lesser needs.

The aims of the Value Proposition Canvas are twofold: (1) to understand and articulate the customer segment profile in terms of jobs, pains and gains and (2) to create a set of products and services that address those customer jobs, pains and gains as closely as possible to achieve the best 'fit' between the company value proposition and its customer.

The value proposition is the first step on the road to building a viable business model. The Business Model Canvas is the tool that allows an entrepreneur to create a business model to deliver the value proposition effectively and profitably.

1. The Business Model Canvas

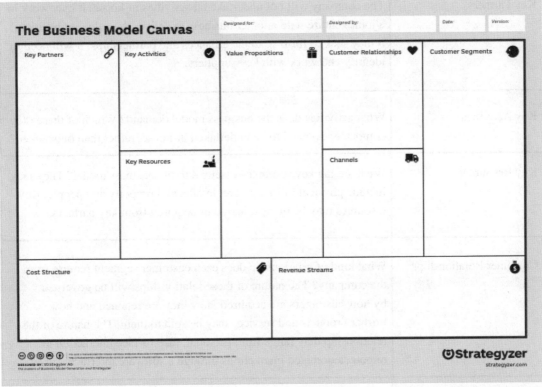

©Strategyzer AG

The Business Model Canvas is a visual representation of a business's key functions. The canvas is divided into 9 sections (two of which are the value proposition and customer segment – these are 'imported' directly from the output of the Value Proposition Canvas). The remaining seven sections are:

Key Partners	The company will not undertake all activities in-house. It may work in a joint venture with another business to deliver the value proposition; it may seek to form strategic alliances and partnerships; it will need to identify and work with key suppliers.
Key Activities	What activities does the business model demand? Which of these (key competences) need to be undertaken in-house, rather than outsourced?
Key Resources	What are the key resources essential to the business model? They may include physical infrastructure, intellectual property and people. Key resources may be owned, leased or acquired from key partners.
Customer Relationships	What kind of relationship does each customer segment require from the company? The nature of these relationships will be governed by how customers are acquired, how they are retained and how further products and services may be sold to them. The nature of the relationship may range from personal, face-to-face interaction to remote, automated interactions through a software interface.
Channels	How will the company communicate with and reach its customers to deliver its value proposition? The channel may be direct (by company employees) or indirect (through a distributor) or a hybrid of the two. The channel structure needs to encompass: customer awareness raising; customer evaluation of the value proposition; customer purchasing; product and service delivery; post-sales support and, for example, in the case of medical devices, mandatory post-market surveillance.
Cost Structure	The specific configuration of the business model will generate a cost structure. The cost structure needs to be supportable at an acceptable level of profitability (eventually, at least) by the revenue streams arising from sales of products and services.
Revenue Streams	What is the structure of the revenues that the business model will generate – one-off or recurring revenues? What is the sales model – sale of an asset; fee per use; subscription; leasing or similar; licensing; other? How will the product be priced?

These seven categories need to be designed and structured to create a business model that can support the profitable delivery of the company's value proposition to the chosen customer segment (as captured by the Value Proposition Canvas).

ASSUMPTIONS

The exercise of populating the blank canvasses is the first step to describing the proposed business.

Great value can be derived from the canvasses before product development begins, as they can highlight potential structural faults in the business model design that may render it non-viable.

The use of the canvasses needs to be iterative; that is, they are of necessity packed full of assumptions that need to be tested for validity in the real world. It is essential that entrepreneurs seek to validate, as far as is feasible, the assumptions upon which they plan to build their business. Learning early that a proposed value proposition or business model is not viable, before too much hard cash has been spent, and 'pivoting' the plan to address structural faults is a key mantra for the Lean Startup movement.

The Lean Startup approach advocates a series of exercises to drive assumption testing through a process of validated learning, employing concepts such as the minimal viable product and the build-measure-learn loop to validate or invalidate assumptions – quickly, cost-effectively and early.

Though not the subject of this chapter, the Strategyzer Progress Board is a useful tool for systematically prioritising and testing the assumptions underpinning the business model being considered. The key to testing assumptions is to "get out of the building" and speak with potential customers, suppliers, advisors and other entrepreneurs. It is an effort that is always worthwhile.

Eric Ries' book The Lean Startup and his blog provide an accessible and practical overview of these concepts and how to get the best from them.

SECTOR-SPECIFIC ADJUSTMENTS

The Lean Startup methodology was originally developed in the context of technology (i.e. software-based start-ups). The concept of the Minimum Viable Product (MVP), used for customer validation, and the ability to shorten product development cycles to account for customer feedback is rarely so straightforward or easily applied in the context of a highly-regulated industry, for example, like that governing healthcare technology or where engineering cycles are long.

There are, however, simple adjustments that can be made to the techniques described that enable entrepreneurs in other industries to derive great value from the Lean Startup approach and the Strategyzer canvasses.

An example of one area for confusion around the Lean Startup philosophy relates to the concept of the MVP and how it translates from the relatively unregulated world of software development (where short development cycles can allow multiple iterations of a product to be evaluated with different customers simultaneously) to the much more regulated world of, for example, medical technology (where engineering and regulatory requirements mean product design cycles may be measured in years).

This is the view I offered to a questioner about what an MVP is:

"A Minimum Viable Product (MVP) is a means to test certain assumptions about the planned product or service. An MVP can be as simple as a series of questions for a customer to answer about the planned product's use or as complicated as a prototype of the product. The idea behind an MVP is to validate an assumption or number of assumptions or invalidate them to drive a change in the proposed product in order to ensure better product/market fit. An MVP is not the final product; MVPs are a means to refining and optimising the design of the final product."

And, quoted from the original source[1]:

"A minimum viable product (MVP) helps entrepreneurs start the process of learning as quickly as possible. It is not necessarily the smallest product imaginable, though; it is simply the fastest way to get through the Build-Measure-Learn feedback loop with the minimum amount of effort."

"Contrary to traditional product development, which usually involves a long, thoughtful incubation period and strives for product perfection, the goal of the MVP is to begin the process of learning, not end it. Unlike a prototype or concept test, an MVP is designed not just to answer product design or technical questions. Its goal is to test fundamental business hypotheses."

And, from the same source:

"The minimum viable product is that version of a new product a team uses to collect the maximum amount of validated learning about customers with the least effort."

My view and that of many entrepreneurs involved in the creation of new business models is that the Lean Startup philosophy can reduce the risk of wasting time and precious cash resources on the creation of badly configured business models that are doomed to failure.

---

1. Ries, Eric: The Lean Startup, Portfolio Penguin (2011)

This approach is not at a panacea, nothing ever is; and the value derived is clearly proportionate to the time, effort and energy put into the process, especially that time spent face-to-face with potential customers.

Good luck in all your entrepreneurial endeavours.

SOURCES AND RESOURCES

www.strategyzer.com

Strategyzer has a range of tools to make working with their canvasses easy and efficient. The organisation also runs workshops around the world to educate practitioners and promote its products and services.

- The Lean Startup - Eric Ries
- Value Proposition Design - Alex Osterwalder et al
- The Business Model Generation - Alex Osterwalder et al
- Four Steps to the Epiphany - Steve Blank
- The Startup Owner's Manual - Steve Blank & Bob Dorf

Part Two

Focus on Intellectual Property

2.1 THE IMPORTANCE OF PATENTS – UK INGREDIENTS FOR A SUCCESSFUL PATENT REGIME

Will Steele, Economic Adviser, UK Intellectual Property Office

All businesses and inventions start with an idea. Intellectual property rights, like patents, are the expression of that idea. What role do patents and play in supporting and encouraging innovation? And what role does this play in driving economic growth? The answer to these questions is not simple and straightforward. To unpick a little bit, it is worth going back to basics.

The UK's IP regime, with patents at its heart, is a system that is designed to enable firms and individuals to protect, share and exploit their ideas and inventions. Formally the system dates back to the 1850s but the practice of granting a time-limited monopoly of the rights of an invention or new inventive step dates back several more hundred years than that. In fact, the UK has the world's oldest continuous patent system which dates back to the 15th century.

In its modern form a patent provides up to 20 years of protection. You can use a patent to protect yourself from others making money out of your invention without your permission, but you have to enforce patents yourself if infringement occurs. It also provides a basis on which you can share your idea for financial gain, by licensing its use. It is a practical way that protects a business investment and allows you to bring a new invention to market. It is also a way to share new ideas for the wider benefit of society, thereby encouraging new ideas and further inventive steps in products and services.

But the link which ties the patenting of an invention to supporting and encouraging innovation and, by extension, economic success, is not straightforward. Reducing much of the respected academic work on this area down to a single point, the simple fact is that there are a multitude of factors which contribute to an innovative business environment and economic growth. Consequently, it is difficult to isolate the specific impact of patents.

It is clear that patents play a hugely valuable role in a number of key sectors in the UK economy. Foremost of these are industries where the invention can be well defined in a patent and involve large upfront investments in R&D. Pharmaceuticals are a notable example where patents are vital in ensuring the incentives that allow companies to invest in the expensive R&D that provides the future innovations that improve our lives. But in many other sectors other strategies can be much more important than patents in bringing a product to market, such as being the first to market, secrecy or superior sales and service.

However, patents can carry a hugely strong brand in themselves. They are often held as a badge of honour as they may be seen as conferring the value of an originator of an idea or concept on an individual. At the Intellectual Property Office, we know they have huge appeal. The number of private applicants, those who apply without the support of professional legal support, has historically been very high. The image of the lone inventor is a strong one. It is also a truism that, when pitching an idea on the hugely popular BBC programme *Dragons Den*, the Dragons will routinely quiz the hapless victim whether they have patented their invention.

It is an easy trap to fall into that patents can automatically confer value or importance on an idea and its creator. Too often the number of patent applications is used as a proxy for innovation. Countries with large and increasing numbers of patents are seen as innovative, an image they are all too eager not to dispel. There are significant issues with this, not least because there is no clear definition of what constitutes innovation. But in an increasingly complex marketplace, with long supply chains and continual variations on products and services, a microscopic analysis of patent applications would be required to make a confident extrapolation. Not all patents are equal and one high value patent could be worth a thousand other patents. For example, if you take a single and apparently simple product like a car windscreen wiper, it could contain multiple patents for individual components. Multiplied across many thousands of patents in any given year, it would be impossible to draw conclusions without considering a myriad of other factors, including date of grant, the state of the art in the field of technology, varieties of names and nationalities on a patent application and, most important of all, economic success of the product. These may be affected by a whole range of non-economic factors. And when you consider that there are other methods to protect inventions, for example trade secrets, you cannot hope to draw a meaningful analysis.

Patent application numbers are useful in painting pictures of other aspects of economic activity and market attractiveness. If we look at the UK patent system, not only it is long established but it is well regarded too. We have among the lowest application and renewal costs and, aside from the issues of backlogs which most IP offices suffer from, our customers feel our services represent good value for money.

We offer a range of tailored services, including online application and renewal and accelerated application, and the quality of our search and examination is seen as very high. Our customers have praised us for our approachability and the satisfaction rating they give us has remained consistently high.

Having disclaimed a causal link between application numbers and an 'innovative' environment, it is worth describing the UK patent landscape in more detail. The UK does tend to have relatively high numbers of patents. Judged by plain numbers of applications alone the UK ranks sixth in the world (including application to the UK through the European Patent Office), behind China, the US, Japan, Germany and South Korea. If you choose to adjust this and consider it against a country's GDP the UK jumps to fourth overall. Furthermore, when compared to numbers of applications against population size the UK jumps to second place. This basic analysis of numbers proves nothing but certainly suggests an effective operating regime and the popularity of the UK as a place to patent.

If we look at the pattern of applications in the UK it reveals that 93% come from applicants based outside the UK. While in a complex global economy it may be more difficult to pin a single nationality on a company, such a high level raises a few questions. It is reasonable to suggest that foreign firms invest in patent protection in the UK because they are active in this market, since IP rights are territorial. Firms patent where they sell, manufacture, or develop their products, and the UK's open and global economy encourages firms to patent in the UK.

But this analysis raises the issue as to why UK companies do not have a high propensity to patent. The data suggests this is particularly evident among the smallest firms. This, in itself, is no huge surprise. Investing in patent protection, taking into account the timeline and overall costs, favours bigger firms with better resources. Looking at the international and domestic picture it is clear that there is a higher level of patenting across certain sectors, such as manufacturing, and a lower level across services-based sectors. The UK's relatively smaller manufacturing sector and strengths in the business and services sector – an area less naturally suited to patenting – may go some way to explain lower levels of patenting among UK firms. The technologies in which UK firms patent most are the pharmaceutical and computing technology sectors.

The key issue to consider here is making sure you do not look at patents and the patenting system in isolation. The quality of the UK's regime is held in high regard by our customers but there are many more elements that demonstrate the overall health and strength of a complex and interdependent system. The remainder of the UK's IP rights landscape is equally robust. The popularity of trademark registration continues to grow with new records for applications having been set in both 2015-16 and again in 2016-17. Numbers of registered design rights are also rising. Both are supported by accessible and low cost systems that the IPO is committed to improving continuously. Over the past few years we have introduced more effective online application and renewal services and increased the range of accelerated services we provide.

But a right has little value if it cannot be defended, and the UK continues to be a world leader in the area of enforcement. We have made sure we have an accessible and relatively low cost judicial process which supports those that need to defend their rights from infringement. Changes over the last few years to the IP Enterprise Court have seen caps put on claims and fees with an emphasis on handling cases quickly. The Taylor Wessing sponsored Global Intellectual Property Index (2016) in particular cited the competence, reputation and specialisation of the UK's judges alongside the consistency and reliability of predicting decisions and the influence they have in other jurisdictions.

At the same time, we have made sure that rights holders are not open to speculative or vexatious attacks from others claiming infringement. Our recent work with the Law Commission saw the Unjustified Threats Bill pass into law which will provide additional clarity for businesses and legal advisors alike. And it will create an environment that supports negotiation and settlement rather than conflict and litigation. These measures are complemented by an IPO-supported mediation service, and a wider and developing mediation marketplace, that aims to resolve disputes in less costly and more practical ways.

In addition, as part of the contribution to stimulating a business environment that supports and promotes innovation, the UK Government provides a tax incentive through the Patent Box scheme. As a way of encouraging high value growth and supporting UK research and development from conception to commercialisation, firms are offered a lower tax rate on profits derived from products that incorporate patents. So far more than 700 companies have benefited from this relief in the first full year of operation.

More widely, looking at the international scene, there has been a consistent move over the past decade towards increasing patent harmonisation. IP rights are territorial and each national system has its own unique features and approaches. But as with increasing economic interdependence, IP offices around the world have been puzzling about what can be done to make national systems work more effectively together. The B+ group, previously chaired by our last Chief Executive John Alty and now under the leadership of Ms Patricia Kelly, Director General of IP Australia, has been concentrating on efforts to streamline global arrangements including developing and extending initiatives such as the Patent Prosecution Highway. This scheme works on the basis that, if granted in one of the recognised IP offices, a patent will be considered more quickly in other participating offices. This obviously helps accelerate the process for the applicant but, through information sharing, can also help IP offices cut their backlogs too. There are a range of technical issues that the group is working on, recognising that efforts towards greater harmonisation reflect the importance of patent protection in an increasingly global marketplace.

Coming back home, this attractive environment is further complemented by the IPO's work to reach out to businesses, especially small firms, to help them understand

and better manage their IP. We have a well-established team that travels the length and breadth of the UK, talking to businesses. We provide a range of simple tools to boost understanding and undertake a range of activities to support the central message that IP should become a core part of any business strategy.

In addressing the role patents play in creating an innovative environment and supporting economic growth, it is clear that an effective IP regime, and patent protection in particular, is a consistent ingredient in a mature and successful economic framework. The patent system in the UK is held in high regard and used extensively by foreign-based applicants which reflects on the attractiveness of the UK to market goods and services. It is a key tool for certain sectors such as pharmaceuticals and high value manufacturing, which rely on extensive research and development of products. Their use of the patents system reflects their desire to see a return on substantial levels of investment. The patent system works well for the economic actors for whom it works and this virtuous circle reinforces its reputation. It is no mistake the UK's IP regime is consistently viewed as one of the best and we lead the way on key issues, like patent harmonisation and enforcement, which help strengthen and add value to already effective systems.

2.2 STRATEGIC IP MANAGEMENT

Dr. Nicholas Acham, Stratagem IPM Limited

Whether your company is large or small, technology or non-technology based, it is essential to consider the role that intellectual property can play in achieving and furthering its business objectives. As intellectual property encompasses numerous rights such as patents, utility models, trademarks, designs, copyrights, confidential information including trade secrets and know-how, database rights, and domain name rights, it is plainly apparent that companies need to consider the impact of more than one type of intellectual property right on those business objectives. Furthermore, each right cannot be considered as existing in isolation but rather as inter-related, forming a complex web both with other intellectual property rights but also with the business objectives of your company.

Thus the objective of this short article is not so much to provide the answer on how to manage intellectual property in your company, but the rather more modest goal of stimulating a discussion on the subject of strategic IP management. More specific advice on how the various types of intellectual property rights set forth above can play a role in achieving and furthering the business objectives of your company can be sought from your patent and/or trademark attorney, or from a lawyer specialising in managing intellectual property rights.

Consideration is now given to the role each of the intellectual property rights previously mentioned can play in your business.

PATENTS

Patents protect inventions of a technical nature by providing a monopoly for, typically, up to 20 years preventing, without the consent of the proprietor of the patent, third parties from using the subject matter of the patent. Therefore, consideration must be given to patents when devising a product, whether it is tangible or in the form of a service which your company is planning to sell. This should include whether the product can and should be patented, and whether you are free to sell the product.

In regard to whether the product can be patented, as the subject matter of a patent must be new, that is to say not previously disclosed anywhere to the public whether by written or oral means, on the date an application for the patent is filed, consideration should be given to searching published disclosures in the technical field relevant to your product before significant funds are invested in the development of that product. Furthermore, measures should be put in place to prevent public disclosure of the details of your product before any application for a patent is filed. This can include checking that employment contracts include a confidentiality clause, and putting in place a system whereby any exhibition material, scientific or conference papers are first checked by a patent attorney for inadvertent disclosure.

A more general issue to consider is that of entitlement to a patent as lack of entitlement is a ground for revocation of that patent in Europe. Whilst national laws can provide that entitlement to an invention created by an employee lies with their employer where that invention is made in the course of their normal duties of employment, employment contracts should nevertheless be checked to ensure inclusion of a specific clause relating to ownership of inventions. Inventorship should also be determined, recorded with reasons, and communicated to the relevant inventors for their comment, thereby providing a written record should inventorship be later challenged in a court. Ensuring entitlement and inventorship is even more important when one or more inventors is not an employee. In this situation, a contract needs to put in place between the company and the third party before their involvement in creating the product, setting out clearly which party owns what.

Turning now to whether the product should be patented, the mere fact that a product is potentially patentable does not, of course, mean that a patent should be applied for that product. For example, existing patent protection may be sufficient, the product may be short lived, a granted patent might be vulnerable to attack, or the patentable subject matter might be difficult to police; that is to say, it may, for example, relate to a method of manufacture which does not leave a signature on the resulting product.

As for ensuring you are free to sell the product, it should be borne in mind that you are not free to sell a product simply because you have patented it. As you may recall, a patent prevents, without the consent of the proprietor of the patent, third parties from using the subject matter of the patent. However, patents owned by third parties may still prevent you from selling your product. Therefore, there is a need to carry out a freedom to operate search. There is, however, a balance to be struck between carrying out a search as early as possible so that any problem patents are flagged up early to management, but not so early that the product upon which the search is based is subsequently substantially changed thereby invalidating the search. One option is, of course, to carry out more than one search.

Utility models are available in some countries and are very similar to patents but have a shorter duration and, in some countries, a lower standard of patentability, and thus should be considered alongside patents. As they can generally be obtained very quickly, they can prove very useful when considering litigation.

TRADEMARKS

Trademarks protect unauthorised use of your brand. In order to register a trademark, it must meet certain requirements, the most important being that it must function as a trademark; in other words, the sign must be capable of distinguishing your goods/ services from those of another company. Thus it is important to carefully select your trademark so that, for example, it does not consist exclusively of a sign which indicates a characteristic of the goods/services, or is generic. Furthermore, a trademark may not be registered when it is identical with or similar to an earlier mark that has rights in the territory in question. Thus consideration should be given to carrying out a search for prior rights in the sign which is proposed for trademark registration in the territories of concern.

Registered trademarks are registered for specific goods and/or services. It is normally a requirement of registration that the mark as registered is used and therefore it is important that measures are put in place to ensure that the form of the trademark actually used corresponds to the form as registered, that usage is in relation to the same goods or services as registered, and, furthermore, that the legal entity using the trademark is the same that is registered as the proprietor or with its consent. If these requirements are not met, then the registration may be at risk of being revoked for non-use.

If your trademark is a word mark and you have a business in non-English speaking countries, consideration should be given to how the mark might be perceived abroad. This is even more important in countries where the Roman alphabet is not used, such as in China or Japan. In these countries, you may need to consider an alternative form of your trademark such as a transliteration or a translation. Alongside registration of trademarks, consideration should also be given to obtaining the corresponding domain names.

If your trademark has been created by a consultant, it is, of course, essential that there is an agreement in place assigning all the rights in the design of the sign to you.

DESIGNS

A registered design in Europe protects the appearance of the whole or part of a product, including its surface decoration, provided it is new and has individual character; that is to say, the overall impression the design produces on an informed user differs from the overall impression produced on such a user by any other design which has been made available to the public before the filing date of the registered design application. Registration cannot be obtained for purely functional designs, nor for designs which subsist in features of appearance which must necessarily be reproduced in their exact form and dimensions in order to permit the product in which the design is incorporated or to which it is applied to be mechanically connected to or placed in, around or against another product so that either product may perform its function. An example of the latter design would be a design for plug pins. Furthermore, any registration cannot be enforced where the design constitutes a component part of a complex product used for the repair of that complex product so as to restore its original appearance. An example of such a design would be that of a car panel.

Registration is relatively simple and fast compared to patents, and consequently less expensive, and therefore registered designs are particularly suitable for short-lived products. The term of protection of registered designs in Europe is up to 25 years, therefore they can usefully extend the protection of products beyond the expiry of patents and, where applicable, registered designs should be considered alongside patents.

In the UK it is also possible to have unregistered designs. Whilst they are of shorter duration, they do cover functional designs. However, because there is no registration, subsistence of the right must be proven and furthermore infringement is by copying. There is also an unregistered Community design right which is of extremely short duration and suffers from the same drawbacks as UK unregistered designs.

If an external consultant is used to create your design, it is essential to have an agreement which assigns all the intellectual property rights, including of course design rights, to you.

COPYRIGHT

Copyright protects the expression of ideas in tangible form and infringement of this right requires, as its name suggests, actual copying. For infringement to be found, it suffices to copy a substantial part rather than the whole of the copyright work. As copyright is an unregistered right in Europe, any management of copyright tends to be focussed more on licensing rather than registration.

The database right is a sui generis right available in the European Union protecting databases and which is similar to copyright.

CONFIDENTIAL INFORMATION

Know-how and trade secrets are both forms of confidential information, normally of a technical nature. The difference between know-how and a trade secret is that the latter tends to be considered of more importance. As the value of confidential information is lost once it is no longer confidential, it is important to identify company confidential information and mark it as such. You may additionally wish to password protect particularly sensitive documents. The circulation of all confidential information must be controlled both internally and externally. In the case of trade secrets, circulation is limited to only a highly select small group of persons.

It is also important to identify and track any confidential information owned by third parties that is in your possession. This can be onerous and is one reason why you should try to avoid accepting any or at least minimise exposure to confidential information from third parties. Another reason is that the confidential information might cross-contaminate any development work being conducted in-house. One way to prevent disputes over ownership of developments and possible cross-contamination is to accurately record all your internal development work including the results of any brain storming sessions before engaging with third parties.

If you are planning on sharing any company confidential information with a third party, it is essential to mark that information as confidential and put in place a non-disclosure agreement before exchanging the information. Putting in place such an agreement can sometimes take longer than you think so this should be planned well before exchange.

It is important that any collaboration agreement with a third party adequately addresses the ownership of confidential information as well as other forms of intellectual property.

CONCLUSION

From the foregoing overview of various forms of intellectual property rights, it is apparent how varied they are and that not all forms will be relevant to all businesses to the same degree. However, it is also apparent that many of the rights are complementary and therefore all need to be considered as to their relevance to company business objectives.

2.3 COST-EFFECTIVE HANDLING OF INTELLECTUAL PROPERTY

Ilya Kazi, Mathys & Squire LLP

The costs associated with protecting your own IP and managing the risks posed by third parties' IP can quickly add up, regardless of the size or maturity of your business. Therefore it is increasingly important to develop a focused strategy that is in line with your commercial goals whilst providing the best possible value for your budget. This chapter looks at fundamental considerations behind a cost-effective IP strategy.

MANAGING YOUR OWN IP

Why are you protecting your IP?
There are a multitude of reasons why IP protection is sought. For example, critical protection may be sought for a well-defined, high-margin easily reproducible product, as part of a cumulative web of protection for an evolving product line, for licensing revenue, for defensive purposes to cross-license or deter competitors from picking a fight, to build up value for sale or acquisition, or to qualify for funding or investment or for tax incentives. The reason(s) for seeking protection are fundamental to the strategy that should be employed, whether that informs what, where or how protection is sought.

What to protect
It would be near impossible, and financially unviable to gain protection for everything everywhere. Key products and brands should be protected, particularly where it is commercially important to keep competitors or counterfeiters out of the market. Where a particular component is present in multiple product lines, gaining even narrow patent protection covering the particular component may be most valuable since profits made on all those products may qualify for tax incentives (e.g. Patent Box in the UK).

If an innovation is likely to be interesting to competitors, it may be worth protecting even if there are no plans to commercialise it; this can provide useful licensing revenue or protection in terms of cross-licensing collateral.

Where innovations are in clearly technical fields[1] and seem clever and different from what everyone else is doing, a patent application may sail through without much difficulty and is normally worthwhile.

However, in some cases the decision may be taken not to file a particular application for a seemingly clearly patentable improvement because an earlier patent has claims which cover the product for its foreseeable lifetime. Where obtaining protection is likely to be difficult, it may make sense to take a pragmatic approach and not to file, or to withdraw at an early stage. Costs saved could be better spent by the business on another matter, for example protecting something else in another territory, as a fighting fund for an expected difficult battle, or even on something other than IP.

A similar consideration applies to branding. Subsidiary brands which are likely to be short-lived, or only used with a key brand, may not warrant protection and the budget saved could be used to obtain better protection for a core brand (e.g. covering more goods/services or more territories). The commercial focus of the business (and competitors) should be what informs budget and strategy concerning what is filed, where it is filed and how it is prosecuted.

Occasionally the best form of protection is simply keeping the innovation secret. This only works where competitors could not discover how the product works or is made by obtaining one on the open market. Famously, the formula for Coca-Cola® has been kept secret for over 125 years, far longer than any IP right would last. However, it is very important to ensure that the importance of keeping the secret is impressed on employees and collaborating companies, and that they know exactly what they can and can't disclose and to whom. It is essential that anyone who is going to have knowledge of the secret has signed a water-tight confidentiality agreement, and it is worthwhile spending time and money getting this right.

Unregistered rights, such as unregistered design rights (UDRs) and unregistered trademark rights are also available in some jurisdictions. As the name suggests, no registration is required so no legal costs are incurred to gain protection. These can be enough for small-scale products or brands that are likely to be short-lived. However, the scope of protection and remedies available are normally less extensive than for registered rights.

How to protect it

Patents are used to protect new technological innovations – inventions. A patent can only be granted for inventions which are new and non-obvious when the patent application is filed. Therefore it is essential to file a patent application before an

---

1. As opposed to fields such as business methods or software.

invention is disclosed publicly. Once an application has been filed, information cannot be added and therefore it is worthwhile investing in the initial application to ensure the invention is fully described; this can reduce costs in the long-term as prosecuting a "thin" application across various territories can be extremely costly and result in sub-optimal protection. Where there are budget constraints it may be preferable to file one application that is likely to succeed and that the business can afford to prosecute properly, rather than filing two with insufficient budget. Conversely, having a portfolio that protects a product can discourage a competitor from entering the market or encourage them to take a licence. Filing a further application to enhance your position is a tiny fraction of the expense of litigating.

Design applications cover the look of products, such as the shape, rather than the technical features; designs can also be used to cover intangible things such as user interfaces. Designs tend to be much cheaper than patents as they are relatively simple to file (normally requiring simply a few line drawings and/or photographs) and in most jurisdictions are not examined. Conversely this can mean their protection and validity are less robust. Whilst it is not normally recommended, it is possible to apply for a registered design within a 12 month period after the first public disclosure of the design, so you can apply even if your product has already been disclosed (unlike for patents). The International Hague design registration system allows an international application to be registered in various countries across the world, which can further reduce costs[1], and make an international design portfolio affordable. For a business with a broad array of evolving consumer products, taking the time to plan a design strategy can provide an effective web of protection for the range, and reduce costs whilst ensuring all products and features are protected.

Another option for potentially patentable innovations at a lower cost is a utility model; this is cheaper and easier to obtain as it is not examined. However, it is not available everywhere, tends to have a shorter term and may be less likely to withstand invalidity proceedings.

Use of copyright is often overlooked as a useful tool in IP protection. In most jurisdictions, no registration is required and the length of protection is far longer than for other IP rights (e.g. author's life plus 70 years, compared to 20 years for patents, 25 years for registered designs and as little as 3-15 years for unregistered designs). In some territories, such as the US, actively registering copyright can have advantages.

Where to protect it
Whilst many consider simply protecting their products and brands in their active markets, it is worthwhile taking a step back and looking at other factors before

---

1. However, if objections arise it may become necessary to employ local attorneys; therefore if taking this route it can be worth investing more in the initial filing to get it right first time.

launching into such a strategy. The cost of gaining protection in multiple countries can dwarf the initial filing cost.

Some territories are less friendly to certain types of technology, such as business methods, medical methods or software, which could make gaining protection, at best, a long, expensive slog, and at worst, impossible. In others, a positive indication from a well-respected patent office can clear the way for a speedy grant, e.g. using the patent prosecution highway.

Competitors should also be considered; where filing has potential for cross-licensing or deterrence, obtaining protection in territories where your competitors sell or manufacture can be key, and could end up being even more valuable than protection in your own markets.

Whilst for trademarks a cost effective strategy could include delaying filing an application until preparations to use the mark in the relevant territory have begun (particularly since a registered trademark can be cancelled if it is not used for a certain period of time, on average five years), this is not the case everywhere. For example, if planning to manufacture in China in two years' time it may be worth beginning the application process in China now, even though there is a three year non-use period, due to the time it takes to register a trademark in China.

One strategy can be to prioritise registering IP where unregistered rights are not available, although it should be borne in mind that such protection is often restrictive.

How to defer costs

It is not necessary to file applications everywhere you may eventually want protection on day one. Most countries have signed up to the Paris Convention, which allows an applicant who has filed a first application in one Paris Convention country a certain period of time (known as a "priority period") to file subsequent applications for the same subject-matter in other Paris Convention countries; the subsequent applications will be treated as though they had been filed on the day of the first application. The priority period is 6 months for designs and trademarks, and 12 months for patents.

This means that any disclosure of the product, or application for IP protection by someone else, between filing the first application and the subsequent application cannot be used against the grant of the patent, design or trademark. This gives time to launch a product and see how successful it is, which can inform whether it is in fact worthwhile pursuing global protection, which markets to seek protection in and where key competitors may be operating. Official searches can also be completed in this time to provide some idea of how easy it will be to obtain protection.

For patents, the decision on where to apply can be delayed by a further 18 months by filing an international application under the Patent Co-operation Treaty (PCT) system[1]. A PCT application will not result in an international patent that is enforceable

---

1. A PCT application can be used to obtain protection in most countries, but notable exceptions include Argentina and Taiwan.

worldwide, but it provides the option of filing national applications up to two and a half years from the initial filing. This can be a very effective way of deferring costs. Furthermore, if the search (and examination, where requested) is positive this can make getting subsequent national applications granted easier, quicker and cheaper because many local patent offices trust the international procedure. On the other hand, if it does not look from the international file as though the prospects for protection would be commercially useful, e.g. if prior art very close to the invention has been found, then costs have not been wasted on filing and prosecuting applications across the world.

MANAGING RISKS POSED BY THIRD PARTIES' IP

There is a fine line to tread between looking for all IP that could potentially be infringed and accepting it is not possible to find everything that may be relevant to commercial activities. At one extreme, an almost limitless amount of money can be spent searching for and analysing third parties' IP. At the other, a strategy to do nothing may result in being surprised by something that really should have been caught before and may have had a simple work-around, had it been identified before full commercial launch of a product or brand.

In-house searching may save costs, and has the advantage of developing a lot of in-house knowledge about IP in the industry. However, done badly it can cause other issues; once a third party patent document has been identified as relevant by a technical team there is a risk of "wilful infringement", e.g. in the US.

One effective strategy is to look at the IP of only a few carefully selected companies, which may include direct competitors, those with large market shares or who may want to move into the market, or those known to be litigious.

Once third party rights have been identified, an effective way proactively to avoid litigation is to use third party observations, oppositions or invalidation actions, pre- or post-grant, to invalidate competitors' IP before the proprietor brings infringement proceedings. For European patents, third party observations and oppositions (both of which can be filed anonymously) tend to be much more cost effective than litigating in national courts. The European Patent Office has also recently brought in a streamlined opposition procedure to bring the length of cases down to 15 months, which should provide the added advantage of early certainty. In the US, the new *Inter Partes* review procedure can also be used to invalidate patents post-grant without the expense of a court action.

Another very useful strategy, briefly touched on above, is to gain protection which may interfere with competitors' commercial activities, even if such IP does not directly cover your own. This can provide a disincentive for competitors to assert their own IP, and can provide something useful to negotiate with, and potentially cross-license, should they still decide to do so.

ENFORCING IP

Once IP has been obtained, there are many ways of ensuring third parties don't infringe it. Some can be as simple as marking your products with "®", "patented" or "patent pending", the idea being that this can be disincentive enough for would-be infringers and courts may be more likely to award damages if they do infringe. Exactly how this is done should be considered, e.g. providing the address of an up-to-date webpage detailing patent rights covering the product can greatly improve the effectiveness.

If you find out a company is likely to infringe, simply writing to them to point this out can also be effective. However, great care should be taken in doing so since this can put you at risk of a groundless threats action if approached incorrectly; you should always consult your attorney before doing this.

It is almost always worth trying to settle a dispute out of court, as litigation can be vastly expensive and always comes with the risk that it will go the wrong way. By being aware of what the other side may want commercially, and by thoroughly understanding the litigation process, it is possible to make offers at strategic times in order to come to an advantageous agreement. Other avenues include formal mediation and alternative dispute resolution. Even if it is necessary to go to court, showing a willingness to make a reasonable settlement early can have beneficial results in terms of costs.

However, if litigation seems inevitable, the Intellectual Property Enterprise Court (IPEC) is a little-known, but effective and fairly low-cost forum for bringing infringement or revocation actions in the UK. Costs awards are capped at £50k, which reduces exposure and can make it worthwhile fighting a case, while damages are capped at £500k. The procedure is shorter and less complex than a High Court action and parties are encouraged to narrow the issues early, which brings costs down. I recently represented British Gas in *Meter-Tech & VanClare v British Gas (2016)*. When Meter-Tech (as exclusive licensee) threatened VanClare's Patent against British Gas's installation program of 16 million utility meters and refused to come to a reasonable settlement, British Gas brought a revocation action in the IPEC in the hope of resolving the matter quickly and cost effectively as the Patent seemed clearly invalid. The revocation action was subsequently transferred to the High Court following Meter-Tech bringing a £30m infringement action there . In the end the High Court ruled the Patent was invalid on the grounds of obviousness. Had the Claimant been willing the case could have been quickly and efficiently dispensed with in the IPEC at a fraction of the costs to both parties.

The Unified Patent Court, assuming it does at some stage come into effect, although at the time of writing this still appears uncertain, will open up another forum for quick, efficient and cost effective invalidation and infringement proceedings, with the added advantage of pan-European effect.

CONCLUSION

Approached naively, it is possible to spend vast amounts protecting IP and searching for risks posed by third party IP, without providing any real value. However, with some forethought and a strong understanding of the commercial roadmap it is possible to gain effective protection, mitigate risk and create value in IP, even on a small budget.

2.4 KEEP INFORMED ABOUT IP RIGHTS

Margit Hoehne, patentGate GmbH

A lot of technological knowledge is published only in patent applications and not in other sources like journal articles. It is necessary to use patent information as a source of technical developments.

Every year duplicate inventions and R&D activities cause unnecessary costs for companies. Products or procedures cannot be used if they are already patented by competitors, who can claim injunctions and damages based on their IP rights.

Knowledge about current IP rights helps avoid these problems.

The main aspect of patent monitoring is to inform R&D and the engineers about new technical trends and what your competitors do.

They should keep in touch with current developments and give feedback to the patent department if they deem legal actions like opposition are necessary.

Knowledge of patents gives freedom to operate and shows licensing opportunities.

You can show that you work with due diligence and have taken reasonable steps to satisfy legal requirements if you:

- have or plan to have a regular patent monitoring workflow in your company;
- inform users about current technological developments from patent databases on a regular schedule and have access to the history of that workflow;
- want to reduce the number of patents to delegate and review based on patent families;
- wish to link other internal documents like examination reports to a publication; and
- keep data related to research like search queries, users and groups involved in patent information, classifications and comments in-house then a patent monitoring tool can support you.

Depending on your expectations, some resources may be stored in-house and others linked to external sources. These can be legal status information, citations and translations, patent term extensions and different sources for open or linked data. There are interfaces to access these ressources and to export data to transfer to other applications (statistics / report tools or spreadsheets).

Figure 1: Number of patent publications per year

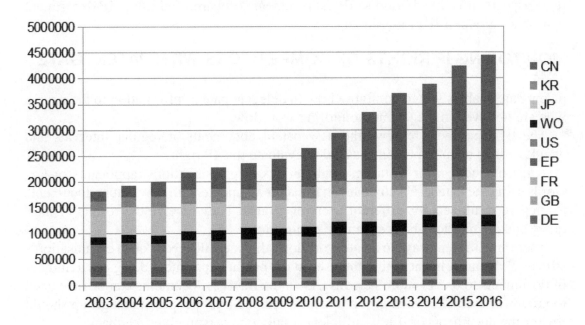

The number of patents published worldwide increases yearly. While patent applications in industrial countries of Europe or the Americas have grown moderately, the number of patents published in Asia is increasing exponentially. Therefore it is a challenge for worldwide selling companies to be informed about all markets.

The number of Chinese publications was 7 times higher than the sum of all British and European patents in 2016.

PLATFORM TO COMMUNICATE WITH INVENTORS ABOUT IP RIGHTS

Patent monitoring applications like patentGate accompany you through the full life cycle of an IP right: users will be informed periodically about the state of the art in the patent monitoring workflow. They then have access to new ideas that can be developed into a patent application. Further documents will be added when an application has been filed but is not yet published, for instance from the search and examination procedure. After some years the question will be answered whether an IP right is still in use and if so, in which products or procedures. This informs the decision as to whether the annual fee for the patent will be payable for the next year.

The two most important uses are the monitoring of competitors or technology trends and the communication with inventors about their inventions.

The patentGate application is accessible for an unlimited amount of users in a company and focuses more on the technical aspect of patent information and less on legal aspects. It is an addition to IP management software used in the IP department by a small group of IP professionals.

MONITORING IP RIGHTS OF COMPETITORS WITH PATENTGATE

patentGate enables you to configure how to delegate patent information to the people who are involved in the patent monitoring workflow.

The IP department reviews the new patent documents at regular intervals and decides which team or person is asked to evaluate this IP right.

A list of queries, for instance combinations of classifications, applicants or key words using the database's content can run after an update with new patent documents to prepare result sets for different users or groups. They receive the results of their query and are notified about each new publication.

There are different ways to create workflows that meet the needs of an organisation's structure: the most linear is that the user in the patent department delegates a number of documents to one or more persons. As an alternative, documents can be delegated to groups of users. For each group it can be decided if all people in that group should review the documents or if it is sufficient if only one person gives feedback.

In larger organisations the delegation can comprise multiple levels – first a contact person in a R&D department and then this person can decide who within their department is the best to evaluate the IP right.

The distribution of the patents can be done manually: after reading the bibliographic data, like title or applicant, users or groups are selected as recipients for that document. The number of documents delegated to a user is visible and can be limited individually.

Figure 2: A sample monitoring workflow

If it is possible to decide by search criteria who is responsible for commenting on a patent, then distribution can be done automatically, so that an engineer receives all results of the query without the manual selection of the IP department.

If there are many results and the recipients would receive too much information, the more time consuming manual distribution increases the chance that the engineers will take the time to read, evaluate and comment.

Sharing of information is a parallel process – groups of people can be informed at the same time, independently from each other.

To enhance the quality of a patent in-house archive a customer can assign a set of descriptors or an internal classification to the documents.

This allows division of the IP rights into categories that correspond with the company's structure or product portfolio. Often classifications like IPC (International Patent Classification) or CPC (Cooperative Patent Classification by the EPO and USPTO and successor to the US classification) are too broad or too narrow and don't fit exactly to the projects or products.

The hierarchical structure of the descriptors can also be used as a subscription service: people can access all documents that have one or more descriptors to match their interest. In this case the patents are not delegated to specific users or groups. Instead, the subscribers of the descriptor receive the IP rights that have been assigned to that descriptor.

Descriptors can also be used to search in the in-house database.

The tasks for the engineers doing the monitoring should be as convenient as possible. They tick one of 3 or 4 boxes based on importance: is legal action necessary? Should the document be monitored or is there nothing further to do and the IP right will not be monitored in the future?

Figure 3: User feedback form for monitored patents

If the engineers decide that an IP right concerns their work, they are required to give a comment on how the document affects the company. They can delegate the document to another person for a second opinion and their feedback is returned to the IP department.

Companies active in the US market often ask to separate in-house information for different subsidiaries so that a user of daughter company A is unable to access comments made by users of subsidiary B. This can be realised with one single database for the holding company in patentGate, where all workflow related information is separated based on user groups.

CHALLENGES

Are R&D users required to give feedback? Can the patent department compel them to take part in the patent monitoring process?

Do the users have the time to read and understand the patents provided for them? What basic knowledge about patent law is required to make informed decisions?

UK patents can be revoked within 2 years from the grant of the patent. In European and German patent law there are deadlines for a possible opposition procedure within 9 months after grant. These deadlines are calculated and displayed in patentGate on the patent for every user to see. When they expire, it is more difficult to take legal action against an IP right. Do users understand the impact of these deadlines?

Are they able to understand the legal text and translate it to the technical solution described in it? Often the patent's claims are not easy to comprehend for an engineer because they are formulated by patent lawyers.

The number of patent documents published increases every year. With the internationalisation of the market new countries come into focus.

Language barriers make it more difficult to understand the scope of a patent – more than one third of all PCT applications in 2016 were published in an Asian language. More than 75% of these have no patent family members other than national (Chinese, Japanese or Korean) publications. To access the full text of these documents you can't use patent family members, but have to use translations or a native speaker.

Even with more detailed classification systems like the CPC these documents are not more accessible. That is because for these applications the CPC is assigned with a concordance between CPC and IPC, so that the benefits of the more detailed CPC notations can't be used.

It is impossible to monitor an unlimited number of technology fields – the goal is finding a practical solution to work with due diligence and limit the IP rights to circulate.

FOCUS ON THE COMPANY'S OWN IP RIGHTS

If inventions are made by employees the inventors have the right to be kept on track about the status of patent applications based on those inventions.

As these inventors are often involved in the patent monitoring process the monitoring application can be used to provide these details. The first step is to collect ideas and improvement suggestions that may be developed into a patent application. All information necessary for filing an application will be collected and documented. This includes data to calculate inventor compensation for service inventions.

When a patent application is the result of such an idea then it is linked to the invention and later to the patent document as soon as it is published.

The next step is the communication with inventors to inform them of the current state of their invention. Documents from the patent office regarding the application will be linked to the invention. Inventors will be informed about documents cited by the patent examiner in the search and examination procedure. These documents – as well as other state of the art patents – will be added to the monitoring database so that they are available to review and respond to.

Later in the IP right's life cycle a request is made as to whether the invention described in the patent application is still in use as a procedure or product. This information is used to determine if the annual fee should be paid for the next year. It also gives an overview of the connection between products and IP rights.

IDEAS AND UNPUBLISHED PATENT APPLICATIONS

This module collects 'early bird' information about a patent application and makes it available to the users involved in the invention. The IP department can share all or selected unpublished files.

The access to these files can be restricted before the official publication, so that only the inventor(s) and IP professionals can view the current documents attached to the invention, for example the claims that have been filed. The structure is similar to published publications with front page drawing and linked documents.

There can also be questionnaires about the invention and forms to notify inventors about the filing process and assignments as well as to gather details to calculate inventor compensation.

When the patent application is published by the office there will be links between the internal file and the patent document.

INFORMATION FROM THE SEARCH AND EXAMINATION PROCEDURES

Backward and forward citations of the document and patent family show references cited by the applicant and examiners. If the citations are imported to the in-house archive they can have the same descriptors as the document where they were found. This association connects IP rights with a similar scope.

The same principle is used when material from a state of the art search is linked to a patent or topic. Documents mentioned in the patent office's search report with their relevant paragraphs and/or drawings make it easier to respond.

Searches for a topic or an IP right support the decision making process. These searches can be linked to each other. A basic invention that is referenced in more than one search reports can be used to show connections between themes.

IS AN IP RIGHT STILL IN USE OR COULD IT BE ABANDONED?

Later in the life of an IP right it is decided if the annual fee should be paid. Depending on a company's policy, this decision process is carried out every year or every couple of years (for instance, parallel to the due date of fees for US patents after 3.5, 7.5 and 11.5 years).

In patentGate a list of patent applications where the payment is due can be circulated to the inventors to answer questions about the invention's usage: is the invention still in use? If not, is it planned to use it? If those answers are positive the annual fee should be paid again. Otherwise, the solution to abandon a patent right can be justified.

WHY USE PATENT MONITORING?

Patent information is a comprehensive source of technical knowledge. Using patent monitoring to be informed about competitors' inventions and having an overview of the company's own patent portfolio helps a business avoid unnecessary conflicts and stay competitive.

2.5 BUSINESS AND MAKING THE MOST OF YOUR IP

Guy Robinson – Deputy Director – Innovation, Intellectual Property Office

All businesses have some intellectual property (IP), whether they realise it or not. For some, it is the very cornerstone of their business; for example, the hugely successful British company ARM which licensed the manufacture of its silicon chips. For others, it can be incidental to their core activities.

Since the early 2000s levels of investment in intangible assets, that is ideas and knowledge, have outstripped investment in tangible assets such as buildings and machinery. Our research shows that in 2014 UK firms invested £133 billion in intangible assets, 7 per cent higher than investment in tangible assets (£121 billion). Of this investment, more than £70 billion (53 per cent) was protected by IP rights. It is clear that the knowledge-based economy is of increasing importance to the UK, but business knowledge of IP does not meet these growing demands.

Our business surveys tell us that knowledge of IP, throughout UK businesses, is generally very low. For example, nearly 80 per cent of companies surveyed did not know that telling people about your invention could lead to an unsuccessful patent application. Fewer than one in ten firms has any formal IP training for staff and, unsurprisingly, 96 per cent of them had not valued their IP. However, of real interest to us was that 94 per cent of businesses we spoke to thought protecting IP was important and one in five firms licenses its IP for others to use for a fee.

At the Intellectual Property Office (IPO) we want to help businesses, of all shapes and sizes, to understand their IP better so they can make informed and strategic decisions to support the running and development of their business.

IP is an investment and, like any investment, a business needs to weigh up the pro and cons of spending money on one thing and not another. The resources required to apply for an IP right, need to be considered in the context of all of the other decisions that need to be made to keep a business running. We routinely direct firms to seek expert advice when applying for IP rights, especially patents, to help to navigate the technical and legal processes. We know that of the unrepresented individuals that apply for patents only around 5 per cent of their applications are granted. And, despite the great advances improving access to low cost and effective justice, a business should still consider the impact of having to defend its rights. On the other hand a lack of understanding about the value of your IP assets and how to exploit them may mean many a firm might be missing a trick.

So, how do we go about changing this situation? Over the last decade the IPO has developed an increasingly sophisticated business outreach programme. We have chosen to focus our efforts on face to face engagement mainly because engaging firms on IP is not simple and straightforward. We attend around 300 events a year, from conferences to seminars, working in partnership with other government organisations such as Companies House, where we meet and speak to around 60,000 people annually. In addition to that we have built a business advisers network, providing them with information and training including our successful IP Masterclass. We know that increasing the understanding of IP among the professional community that directly supports businesses will always reach more people than we can alone.

However, we are always alive to new ideas and the latest developments in the way we communicate. As our face to face work has matured, so we have developed our digital content and social media activities in parallel. We have built a suite of online tools that aim to build more detailed knowledge and its application, IP Equip, available on the GOV.UK website as well as downloadable as an app, takes you through basic learning modules to help you understand the different IP rights, whether they are relevant to your business and how best to access them. Our IP Healthcheck is a more thorough questionnaire-based tool that produces a tailored, confidential report for your business. It makes specific recommendations, provides guidance on how to implement them and points you to useful sources of further information.

We support this offering through a range of other rich content to get a complex message across. We have a series of video case studies of companies that have had a positive business experience by making informed decisions about their IP. We have also produced a series of animated films called IP Basics, accessible on YouTube, a series of podcast discussions, a highly regarded blog through GOV.UK and LinkedIn and Facebook Live events to cater for the widest audience possible on as many aspects of IP practice as we can manage. We are taking on the challenge of trying to bring IP to life, making it relevant to everyday business practice. We want to get creators, companies and investors to think about IP as part of their whole approach to business, as an integrated business process just like planning an investment strategy.

Year on year we know we are reaching more businesses; in 2016-17 we estimated that we directly and indirectly reached more than 200,000 businesses across the country. In the coming years we will build our understanding about what decisions businesses take after we engage with them so we can improve our offering further.

Engaging with firms, assisting them to identify, understand and better manage their IP, does not sit in isolation. By drawing insight from our existing customers and our well established stakeholder community we have a well-developed and strategic approach to business support. This support is also integrated into the Government's wider approach to making the UK the best place to start and grow a business by focusing on driving growth across the whole country, encouraging investment in research and innovation and supporting trade and inward investment.

At the heart of this is helping firms understand the value of their IP and then providing hands-on tools to help them commercialise it. Your IP could be as valuable as your plant, premises or stock. It could even be your single most valuable asset which you could use to secure finance for company growth. You may also need to know the value of your IP assets when looking for more funding, thinking of joint ventures, mergers and acquisitions and, in the worst case, during bankruptcy. But not all IP is valuable. Unless your IP assets help to create, maintain or increase cash flow they may have no financial value.

But valuing IP is not an easy task. How much is your brand name worth after years of marketing? Does your patent protect your product or is it redundant?

IP rights might change in value for a variety of reasons. A patent may begin its life as a unique solution to a problem, but in time other solutions to the problem may be found which reduce its worth. Alternatively, successfully marketing your product can ensure your patent is very valuable. Trademarks generally gain value as they become better known.

There are a number of ways to value IP rights. They all have their limitations and no method is appropriate in every case. The stage of development of the IP rights, the availability of information and the aim of the valuation all have a bearing on the method used. We provide some detailed information on methods that can be used, such as the cost, market value and income or economic benefit methods, and support this with a useful checklist and skeleton licence to guide you through the process of exploiting your IP.

Being able to easily value IP may well lead to better commercialisation and trade, but unfortunately there is no universally agreed methodology . We know that IP rich businesses struggle to secure lending against their IP due to the opaque nature of the asset and this can be one of the things preventing them from scaling up. Over the past few years we have been working closely with the investment community to help them understand better the nature of IP as an asset and facilitate the development of the market in IP. For a number of years we have worked with partners across government to identify high growth potential businesses and offer them IPO part-funded IP audits. This has helped them get a better grip on the value of their IP assets and support the development of a proper business strategy to develop and exploit their value to the business.

This work has a knock-on beneficial effect in supporting better collaboration between research institutes and businesses and, in turn, driving innovation. In 2016 we reviewed and refreshed a set of tools, known as the Lambert toolkit, designed to help facilitate negotiations between potential partners and reduce the time, money and effort required to secure agreement and provide examples of best practice. The toolkit consists of a decision guide, model agreements and guidance notes to walk you through the process and address a wide range of situations.

Closely tied to better valuation and commercialisation of your IP is better protection. Setting up and running a business can be a risky business. In the same way you can protect your physical assets from a variety of risks you can also insure your intangible assets. Much of this insurance (but not all) is aimed at businesses who have already secured IP rights. However, you can also protect yourself against inadvertently infringing the rights of others. We provide a range of information on types of insurance that are available and how they can be used to protect your investment. As with all other aspects of business decision-making, expert advice should be used to help make the best choices for your circumstances.

In the same way we work with business advisors to help spread our message through our outreach activities, so we work with other business representatives and support organisations to extend and improve our reach. We are putting increasing emphasis on driving growth across the whole of the country by putting IP representatives in key regional areas to enhance existing regional networks. By the end of 2017 we will be running pilot approaches in the North West and West Midlands.

As the trend for greater investment in knowledge and ideas continues to grow it is apparent that the ability to use your IP more effectively is a key business advantage. By bringing together our efforts to help businesses, through targeted information and support and a creative approach to outreach and engagement, we are building a better informed business community ready to face the challenges of a more complex and challenging global marketplace.

Guy Robinson
Guy is a Deputy Director in the Innovation Directorate at the Intellectual Property Office. Guy heads up policy teams that help people to make informed choices about IP, to derive value from the IP that they own and to mitigate risks around IP ownership. Guy has 17 years of IP experience both in policy and operations. He began his career at h the IPO as a patent examiner in 1999.

The Intellectual Property Office
The Intellectual Property Office (IPO) is the official UK government body responsible for intellectual property (IP) rights including patents, designs, trademarks and copyright. The IPO is an executive agency of the Department for Business, Energy & Industrial Strategy.

2.6 USING TRADEMARKS, DESIGN RIGHTS AND COPYRIGHT TO PROTECT INNOVATION

Gregor Kleinknecht, Hunters

THE ROLE OF BRANDING AND DESIGN

Branding and design are key to turning innovation into marketable and commercially successful products. Branding and design, and the associated IP rights, enhance product awareness, quality perception and customer loyalty, and help to distinguish new products from those of competitors. As the value and importance of brand rights have increased for businesses in a rapidly changing global economy, so are brand protection challenges and threats to brand integrity becoming ever more demanding for brand owners. For products originating from or targeted at customers in the United Kingdom, the need to prepare for a post-Brexit environment adds an additional layer of complexity.

OPTIONS FOR PROTECTION

In simple terms, different IP rights protect different aspects of a product. Patents are dealt with in detail elsewhere in this compendium, and this chapter will therefore focus principally on the value of trademarks in protecting innovation, as well as the role of design right and copyright. A trademark is essentially the name or sign placed on or used in connection with a product to distinguish it from other products. Registering a trademark protects that name or sign from infringement by others although under English law unregistered trade names are also in certain circumstances protected at common law. By contrast, design right is concerned with the appearance of products. Again, design rights can be registered or unregistered. Finally, copyright can also be used to protect aspects of design and aims to prevent others from reproducing a protected work. In the United Kingdom, copyright protection arises without the need for registration (indeed, there is no copyright register). New products will generally be protected by a combination of these rights, in addition to any patents that protect the innovation underlying the new product.

TRADEMARKS

Trademarks defined

Section 1(1) of the Trade Marks Act 1994 ("TMA") defines a trademark as any sign capable of being represented graphically which is capable of distinguishing goods or services of one undertaking from those of other undertakings. A trademark may, in particular, consist of words, slogans, designs, letters, numerals or the shape of goods or their packaging. More recently, smells, sounds, colours, gestures and moving digital images have also been considered in principle as being capable of registration as trademarks. Trademark lawyers typically speak of word marks, device marks, shape marks and olfactory marks, etc. The key function of a trademark is to distinguish the products of different traders and to serve as an indication of origin; this is known as the "guarantee" function.

The legal framework

Trademarks are essentially national rights, i.e. they provide protection only in the country where they are registered. In the United Kingdom, registered trademarks are dealt with in the TMA. The TMA implemented European Council Directive 89/104/EEC, which harmonised national trademark laws across the EU, and was later supplemented in 2008 by the Trade Marks Directive (2008/95/EC). The current law will in principle be replaced in accordance with a new Directive (EU) 2015/2436, which must be implemented into the national laws of member states by January 2019.

A notable exception from the principle of territoriality are EU trademarks, which were in themselves an important innovation when first introduced as Community Trade Marks, because upon registration they provide trademark protection in all 28 EU Member States. EU Trade Marks are dealt with by the EU Trade Mark Regulation (207/2009/EC), which is directly applicable in all EU Member States although it will be replaced by a new Regulation as of 1 October 2017. National and EU trademark registrations provide parallel systems of protection.

Registering a trademark

Trademark registrations are generally best made at a relatively early stage in the product development cycle to ensure that the preferred mark is validly registered by the time the product is ready to be launched in the market. Before a trademark application is filed, it is prudent to obtain trademark clearance advice on the question of whether a proposed candidate mark is available for registration and use across the territories in which it is likely to be marketed. Possible delays and conflicts (in particular as to third party rights) can often still be avoided or resolved at that stage, for example, through a coexistence agreement, challenge of the validity or subsistence of the conflicting mark, or simply through acquisition of the conflicting right.

Trademarks are registered for use in respect of specific of goods and/or services which are categorised in some 45 international "classes". The specification of the trademark should be drafted by an IP professional.

The UK national trademarks register is administered by the UK Intellectual Property Office ("IPO"); EU trademarks are administered by the EU Intellectual Property Office ("EUIPO"). Upon receipt of a trademark application by the competent trademark office, an examiner will review the application to assess whether there are any "absolute" grounds on which an application must be rejected. These grounds include, for example, that a mark is devoid of distinctive character and does not have acquired distinctiveness through use, or that the mark is descriptive of the goods or services to which it relates. If the examiner finds that there are conflicting registrations of identical or similar marks, it will notify conflicts to the applicant and to the owner of the conflicting earlier trademark applications and registrations.

If the application passes this stage, it will be publicly advertised in the Trade Mark Journal or the EU Trade Mark Bulletin respectively. This stage provides third parties with an opportunity to oppose the registration of a mark on "relative" grounds – basically, on the ground that the application conflicts with rights that already exist in respect of some or all of the goods and services to which the application relates. If the application is not opposed, or an opposition is successfully resolved in favour of the applicant, the mark will proceed to registration and a certificate of registration will be issued.

Trademark registrations must be renewed periodically (currently every 10 years) but are renewable indefinitely for successive ten year periods upon payment of a renewal fee.

Nature and scope of trademark protection
A trademark registration confers on the proprietor the exclusive right to use the mark in connection with the goods and services for which it has been registered. The proprietor may prevent others from using the same or a similar mark in the course of trade in connection with identical or similar goods without consent and can sue for trademark infringement where this occurs. Unless an identical mark is used for identical goods or services, the proprietor must show that use of the mark causes, or is likely to cause, confusion on the part of the public.

If a trademark is well known and has a reputation, it enjoys a wider scope of protection than if the mark is used without due cause and such use takes unfair advantage of, or is detrimental to, the distinctive character or the repute of the trademark. This applies even if the infringing use of the mark is in relation to goods or services which are not similar to those for which the trademark is registered.

EU trademarks have the same effect as national marks in the UK but with wider territorial scope. Importantly, in economic terms, a trademark registration of course also enables the proprietor to exploit his IP rights commercially, for example, by granting trademark licences to third parties, or by selling and assigning the rights to a third party.

Extending protection internationally
If an innovation is to be commercialised outside of the UK and the EU, the Madrid Protocol enables trademark registrations to be extended to designated signatory countries based on the "home" registration.

Passing off
The owner of goodwill in an unregistered trade name may be able to protect that trade name against infringements through the common law tort of passing off, provided that he can produce evidence (i) of his ownership of the goodwill in the name; (ii) that the unauthorised use of the trade name by another person amounts to a misrepresentation (typically in the form of evidence of actual confusion or likelihood of confusion); and (iii) that this misrepresentation causes, or is likely to cause, damage. Establishing the necessary evidence to the required standard of proof can be difficult and costly; in particular, in the case of new trade names which may not yet have built up sufficient goodwill in the market place. Relying on trademark protection at common law is therefore no effective substitute for registered trademark protection.

DESIGN RIGHT

The legal framework
The (external or internal) appearance of a functional product or of part of a product can be protected through registered or unregistered design rights if the statutory requirements are met. Unregistered designs are protected at a national level through the Copyright, Designs and Patents Act 1988 ("CDPA"), and registered designs through the Registered Designs Act 1949 (RDA) as amended first through the CDPA, then by regulation in 2001 and 2006, and more recently by the Intellectual Property Act 2014. At EU level, designs are protected by the Council Regulation on Community Designs (6/2002/EC).

Requirements for unregistered design right protection
In order to be protected a design must:

- consist of the shape or configuration of the whole or part of an article;
- be original (which means that it must not be commonplace in a qualifying country in the design field in question at the time of its creation);
- be recorded in a design document or an article must have been made to the design; and
- have been created by a qualifying person.

If reliance is to be placed on unregistered design rights under the CDPA, it will be essential for detailed records to be kept of when the design was first created and when articles made to the design were first marketed so as to be able to establish existence of the design right in any subsequent infringement proceedings. In order to assist with legal action against infringers, design documents should be signed and dated. Products made to the design should be marked with the words "Design Right", the name of the design right owner and the date when the right came into existence.

The CDPA specifically excludes design right protection where the design:

- is a method or principle of construction (as opposed to the finished article); or
- comprises features of shape or configuration of an article which enable the article to be connected to, or placed in, around or against, another article so that either article may perform its function ("must fit" exception); or
- are dependent upon the appearance of another article of which the article is intended by the designer to form an integral part ("must match" exception); or
- is a design for surface decoration.

The scope of the European unregistered design right (described in more detail further below) is somewhat wider in that it protects designs of the appearance of the whole or part of a product resulting from the features of, in particular, the lines, contours, shape, texture and/or materials of the product itself and/or its ornamentation.

Nature and duration of unregistered design right protection
The owner of a design right in a design has the exclusive right to reproduce the design for commercial purposes by making articles exactly or substantially to that design, or by making a design document recording the design for the purpose of enabling such articles to be made, and can prevent others from infringing his design right by interfering without the design right owner's consent with those exclusive rights (these acts are called "primary" infringements). Design right is aimed at preventing

copying; importantly there will therefore be no infringement if the alleged infringer has independently created the same or a similar design.

A "secondary" infringement occurs when a person imports into the United Kingdom or has in his possession for commercial purposes, or deals in the course of a business with an article which is, and which he knows or has reason to believe is, an infringing article, without the licence of the design right owner.

Design right lasts the lesser of 10 years from the end of the calendar year when articles made to the design were first marketed or 15 years from the end of the calendar year when the design was first recorded in a design document (or, if earlier, when an article was first made to the design), subject to a licence as of right during the last 5 years of the term.

Registered design protection

The RDA as amended defines designs as features of lines, contours, colours, shape, texture or materials of the product or its ornamentation. In order to be capable of protection as national registered design in respect of the whole or part of a product, the design must be new and have individual character. These criteria are subject to an examination procedure by the registrar at the application stage. Registered designs can protect both three-dimensional and two-dimensional designs. There is a "must-fit" exemption but the "must-match" exemption does not apply to registered designs. Designs are protected as such and protection is not limited to the product to which the design was originally applied. Applications are made to the IPO and the registration process is relatively short and inexpensive compared, in particular, to that for obtaining a patent. The period of protection is a maximum of 25 years. Registered design right protection can be extended to other countries under the Paris Convention regime. International design registrations are possible pursuant to the Hague Agreement. Products made to a registered design should be marked with the words "Registered Design" and the corresponding registration number.

European design protection

The Council Regulation on Community Designs (6/2002/EC) established a framework for protecting industrial designs throughout the EU, mirroring the EU trademark regime, by creating a registered Community design administered by the EUIPO. Registered design protection lasts for 5 years and may be renewed for subsequent 5 year periods up to a total of 25 years.

In addition, the Regulation introduced an unregistered Community design right, which comes into existence when products incorporating the design are made available to the public in the EU and lasts for a period of three years. There are detail differences between the regimes for protecting unregistered designs under the CDPA and under European rules and an assessment must be made on a case by case basis as to which regime proves more beneficial in the particular circumstances.

COPYRIGHT

Basis of protection

In the United Kingdom, copyright is an unregistered right protected through the CDPA. It arises automatically for any work that has been recorded in any form and meets the statutory requirements to qualify for protection, including that it has been created by a qualifying person. Earlier legislation still applies (with some amendments) to works created while the earlier legislation was in force.

Nature and duration of copyright protection

In the context of protecting innovation, copyright is of relevance principally with regard to original design and technical drawings and computer programs and code.

In contrast to some other IP rights, copyright is intended to prevent copying of the whole or a substantial part of a protected work and certain other restricted acts but does not provide monopoly rights where another author has independently and without reference to the protected work created a similar or even identical work. Famously, copyright seeks to protect the expression of an idea but not the idea itself. The CDPA also seeks to prevent "secondary" infringements through importing, possessing or dealing with infringing copy.

Copyright usually lasts for the lifetime of the author plus 70 years from the end of the calendar year of his or her death. In the case of computer-generated works, copyright protection lasts for 50 years from the end of the calendar year in which the work was made.

Relationship with registered and unregistered designs

There is some overlap between the scope of design right and copyright, in particular, since amendments to the CDPA now extend the benefit of copyright protection to industrially exploited artistic works. Where an action for copyright infringement is possible, an action for infringement of an unregistered design may not be brought.

THE IMPLICATIONS OF BREXIT

As matters stand, the UK will cease to be a Member State of the EU on 29 March 2019. The UK's withdrawal from the EU will have significant implications for IP rights and rights holders. It is not yet known, for example, whether the UK will implement the new trademark Directive (EU) 2015/2436 into national law. At a European level, EU trademarks will cease to extend to the UK and rights holders who have relied to date on an EU registration to provide trademark protection in the UK are well advised to apply for a national UK trademark now to avoid gaps in protection. While the principle underlying the European Union (Withdrawal) Bill envisages that the EU Trade Mark Regulation will be incorporated into domestic law, it is difficult to see how this is intended to work on a practical level if the UK is no longer part of the EU trademark system administered by the EUIPO. Similar considerations will apply to European design right protection.

The harmonisation of copyright law has traditionally been driven by international treaties rather than by European Community law. However, EU law has been gaining in importance in a number of areas related to copyright, for example, though the Information Society Directive and in the area of collective rights management. One of the principal implications of Brexit in the copyright field will be that the UK will no longer form part of the project to create the digital single market.

BRAND MANAGEMENT AND PROTECTION

The effective management of an IP portfolio is key to a successful brand strategy and to maximising the value of IP rights. This includes not only the maintenance of registrations, and a watching brief to monitor third party applications to register potentially conflicting rights, but also an effective enforcement program to prevent, identify and pursue rights infringements. What form that enforcement action takes will depend on the circumstances of each individual case, on the rights involved, the type and seriousness of the infringement, and the identity and location of the infringer. The available options range from administrative proceedings before the trademark registry, or the involvement of police forces and customs or border agencies and the instigation of criminal investigations, to domain name dispute resolution procedures and enforcement action in the civil courts, including interim and permanent injunctions, claims for damages and/or an account of profits, and an order for the delivery up or destruction of infringing articles.

2.7 PROTECTING AGAINST IP DISPUTES

Keeley Patten, Miller Insurance Services LLP

Intellectual property (IP) describes a multitude of rights, including patents, trademarks, designs, copyrights, trade secrets and domain names. IP rights constitute a growing proportion of business wealth, especially due to the expansion of industries within the knowledge-based economy.

IP rights create a value of their own. They are often a catalyst for investment, and can be traded in the same ways as other business assets. However, regardless of the strength of IP rights, they are vulnerable to challenge by competitors and need to be protected.

Any business can be adversely affected by IP disputes. IP litigation can be disruptive, expensive and even ruinous. If rights are infringed, it is important that IP owners have the financial resources to protect their asset and their business. Here are four case studies showing how IP litigation insurance has been able to help and support businesses. The companies involved have taken steps to protect themselves, by purchasing insurance, against any potential challenges to the ownership, validity or title of their IP rights and ensure they have appropriate financial resources in order to pursue infringing third parties.

TRADEMARKS

'Company A', a web-based company offering online education, training and qualifications, wanted to protect its IP rights. Most notably, it wanted to safeguard the company logo, which was used to distinguish its services from other companies, and to protect its trademark against infringement. Company A appreciated that a trademark could not be an idea or a concept – it had to be something that could be "put on paper", or be capable of being "graphically represented".

Company A was concerned that the legal costs in pursuing an action against infringement of its trademark would have a significantly detrimental financial impact on the company. In addition, it was aware from past incidents that its customers could believe there was a connection between the company and a third party infringer, which would be damaging to its business.

The insurance solution

An insurance policy was sought to provide a substantial amount of cover for legal expenses incurred by the company if it had to pursue legal action in the UK and Europe in the event of an infringement, giving the company confidence that it would have the financial resources necessary to protect its business. In view of the nature of the intellectual property and Company A's competitive environment, it was established that the amount of cover required should be £500,000. In addition, to reduce costs the company was happy to pay a fixed amount of costs relating to any individual claim as an excess and also a proportion of any amounts claimed under the policy.

The outcome

Company A purchased the cover at a fixed cost which gave it the resources necessary to defend its brand. The protection ensured that, if any competitor copied the company's website and/or logo designs, Company A could take immediate legal action by instructing specialist lawyers to demand that the offending company "cease and desist" using its intellectual property. Any such action would also deter other companies from IP infringement.

LICENSEES

'Company B', a small but innovative audio products company, owned a large portfolio of intellectual property, including several design and utility patents, granted in the UK, EU and USA. Global licensing represented 10% of its income, and Company B granted licence agreements to manufacturers and suppliers of its products. One of the key issues faced, in relation to the company's licensee(s), was the potential for allegations of patent infringement from a third party and, in turn, the licensees were looking to Company B to provide them with protection from any resulting claims.

The insurance solution

Company B investigated the purchase of intellectual property insurance to safeguard their patents and reinforce their contractual position with the licensees. Crucially, the policy granted the same level of protection to the company's licensees, with licensee details recorded under the insurance policy. For example, if a "cease and desist" letter were received by a licensee, detailing Company B's intellectual property as an alleged infringement, the licensee could claim costs and/or damages from Company B, as owner of the intellectual property. Company B could then in turn make a claim under its own insurance policy to defend the allegations made against the licensee.

The outcome

Company B was able to reassure any potential licensees that, in the case of any allegations of infringement being made against them, Company B would be able to reimburse the licensees for any costs incurred in their defence. Therefore, both Company B and the licensees had peace of mind that insurance would be available to cover the substantial costs arising from allegations of patent infringement claims, court costs and damages. In addition, Company B purchased pursuit costs coverage, to enable it to take offensive action against any entity it believed to be infringing its patents.

CONTRACTUAL REQUIREMENT

Company C, a medium-sized spectacles manufacturer, was contracting with a large US manufacturer to supply its designs and license the use of its patented products. The US manufacturer as licensee required full indemnification, with a minimum financial limit of USD 10,000,000, for claims arising against it, due to the use of Company C's designs, patents and product. The licensee also stipulated contractually that insurance be purchased to protect the licensee's financial exposure to IP litigation.

The insurance solution

Insurers were able to provide coverage to meet Company C's contract obligations, including intellectual property litigation costs for any claims for alleged infringement directly against Company C. In addition, the insurance was extended to provide protection for legal costs incurred in connection with any contractual dispute, including non-payment of royalties, between the two parties.

The outcome

Company C was able to sign up to the commercially profitable agreement and earn considerable royalties from its licensee. The insurance fulfilled the contractual requirement and gave both parties reassurance that their legal costs and any resultant damages, up to the policy limit of USD 10,000,000, would be covered in the event of any third-party allegations of infringement.

Company C and the licensee also gained the benefit of advice from expert insurance brokers and insurers, who could instruct patent attorneys on their behalf. These industry experts were experienced in the intellectual property field, saving Company C the time and expense of locating and appointing appropriate experts itself.

GENERAL PROTECTION

Company D, an innovative company involved in the development of new building material products, was seeking to export to Europe, USA & Asia.

A prudent part of any company's export planning – whether involving products, services or know-how – is to ensure that potential intellectual property exposures have been properly assessed and the protection of IP rights considered. At this stage it is also essential to identify other parties' IP rights, thereby establishing the exporter's freedom to operate. A lack of due diligence in these areas can result in potentially expensive lawsuits, including injunctions from entering a marketplace, or the surrender of infringing goods and the payment of damages.

The insurance solution

Company D was presented with a range of coverage options. These had been tailored to meet its requirements and budget, and also its desire to retain a proportion of the risk.

Insurers were able to offer liability coverage options to protect Company D arising from its infringement of IP rights as a result of the sale and distribution of its products through other parties worldwide. Protection was also offered to Company D's sales and distribution partners in their export territories. In addition, a quote for optional cover was provided, to include pursuit costs incurred in enforcing the rights of Company D's own patents, design rights and trademarks. To reduce costs, Company D was happy to pay a fixed amount of any claim (GBP 50,000) and a proportion of any amounts claimed under the policy.

Company D's IP risk management procedures were key to obtaining viable and cost-effective insurance quotations.

The outcome

Insurance protection was successfully purchased, as outlined above. During the first annual period of insurance, the insurance contract was used, along with the professional advice of the insurance brokers, underwriters and their legal advisors to successfully rebuff spurious allegations of infringement.

CONCLUSION

With guidance and advice, companies can use insurance as a valuable tool to provide financial security and technical expertise to meet the needs of their business and for protection of their intellectual property. As companies focus on ways to minimise risks within their businesses and protect the value of company assets, the importance of using insurance as a cost effective measure to protect both tangible and intangible assets is becoming increasingly recognised.

Part Three

Aids to Innovation

3.1 INFORMATION SERVICES SUPPORTING INNOVATION AND IP PROTECTION

Steven Johnson and Vedran Biondic, J&B Partners Ltd. – Patent and Scientific Research

The importance of being fully informed before making decisions is not a new concept, and in the current age there is no shortage of information at our fingertips. The focus now is on identifying the most pertinent information to make sure that it is useful in helping businesses and individuals make their decisions.

This is of huge relevance to fuelling innovation, where a balance needs to be struck between having all the information on a technology and risk being swamped, and having just enough to be able to move forward with research and development without any surprises, and with the most useful practical knowledge.[1] [2]

Innovation feeds into research and development and hopefully will ultimately lead into the production of a successful product or process capable of commercialisation. Along this timeline the type and amount of information required changes, and so the types of searches required will also change. In the early stages of the process, landscape and state of the art searches can provide broad, high level insight into a particular technology field. When dealing with large numbers of references in the identified dataset, the initial value in the information lies in the dataset as a whole, and the trends apparent therein.

When areas of interest are more focussed, more precise searching is required which

---

1. Patent information to stimulate innovation in small and medium sized companies; Koch, A.; World Patent Information, Vol. 13, no 4, November 1991, pp. 201-205

2. Managing External Information in Manufacturing Firms: The Impact on Innovation Performance; Frishammar, J., et al.; The Journal of product innovation management, ISSN 0737-6782, E-ISSN 1540-5885, Vol. 22, no 3, May 2005, pp. 251-266

will highlight specific cases that are important to the technology.[1] These can help with the question of novelty and patentability, identifying disclosures that would potentially prevent the granting of a patent, or help with drafting to ensure that the new innovation does not overlap with the prior art.

The commercialisation of the assets gained from the processes of innovation, research and development, will bring with it questions of freedom to operate, and potential oppositions or questions of validity of protection. The importance of comprehensive coverage and wide ranging search scope becomes apparent in order to find all potentially problematic patent cases for the FTO search and any disclosure, even of the most obscure kind, which may affect the validity of an IPR that has been, or is about to be granted.[2]

Patents themselves hold a huge amount of information; aside from the obvious technological content, they must provide full disclosure of the invention. There is also the detail on the corporate sources, so it can be seen who else is innovating, in what technology areas, and in which places around the world.[3]

Here we look into the ways that patents and non-patent literature can be searched, categorised, and analysed to provide vital and hugely useful insights and guidance into the process of innovation and IP protection. We will look at the different stages, and the related ways in which searching can help with providing the right information in the right format.

GENERAL SEARCH TECHNIQUES

Using search strategies through appropriate databases, a patent dataset needs to be brought together that represents the technology field that is under investigation. There are a multitude of approaches that can be taken, but by combining different search strategies a sensible set of references can be brought together. Different approaches include using classification headings from the various patent publishing bodies, along with keyword searches, forward and backward citations searches, and investigations using the names of assignees, inventors, and authors. Specific classification systems include:

- International Patent Classification system (IPC)[4] from the World Intellectual Property Office (WIPO);

---

1. Sources of information as determinants of novelty of innovation in manufacturing firms: evidence from the 1999 statistics Canada innovation survey; Amara, N. and Landry, R.; Technovation, 2005, Vol. 25, no 3, pp. 245-259

2. Patent information survey: Information for innovation: Surveys of innovating and patenting small firms; MacDonald, S. et al.; Computer Law & Security Review, Vol. 13, no 5, September-October 1997, pp. 344-348

3. https://papers.ssrn.com/sol3/papers.cfm?abstract_id=1510560

4. http://web2.wipo.int/classifications/ipc/ipcpub/

- Cooperative Patent Classification system (CPC)[1] which is intended to supersede the previous systems used by the US (USPC) and the European Patent Offices (ECLA); and
- Japanese F-Terms[2].

Patent classifications are assigned to applications based on their technical content and are primarily for the use of examiners in the IPOs. They are constantly evolving systems and are adapted and updated to represent new and emerging technology fields.

There are specialist databases and tools available, each with their own strengths and data coverage. Some, which can be technology-specific, include searches using chemical structure, and protein or nucleic acid sequences.

Once arrived at, the dataset can then be manually inspected and categorised/ rejected, or automatically categorised according to the keywords and classification headings used. The aim of the search is to provide a dataset which is as comprehensive as possible, whilst reducing the amount of noise from unrelated references. Depending on the search type, the importance of comprehensive coverage will determine how focussed the search strategies need to be.

LANDSCAPE ANALYSIS

In working out the lay of the land it makes it easier to decide the best route to take in order to reach your destination. In relation to business innovation decisions this is likely to be the route that is the road less travelled. A landscape study can help to identify activity in a technology area, both in terms of specific technological innovations and what the major players in the field are doing.

Technology Review

A large dataset is identified, usually based on a broad technology area, and often relying on search strategies using broad classification headings. This can then form the basis of the landscape analysis. The records are investigated and categorised according to their main technological features and grouped accordingly. Manually inspected datasets can ensure that the focus of the invention is correctly identified and the reference is categorised appropriately. More automated characterisation techniques may be a quicker and more cost efficient approach; however, the value in the data can be compromised with a higher amount of noise that could potentially affect the final outlook.

From the categorised data a picture will emerge of areas of technical innovation, which will be well represented by multiple patents and patent applications relating to a particular feature and ancillary features. Conversely it is also possible to identify

---

1. https://worldwide.espacenet.com/classification
2. https://www5.j-platpat.inpit.go.jp/pms/tokujitsu/pmgs_en/PMGS_EN_GM101_Top.action

the areas of white space. These areas represent areas of potential innovation; they can be used as signposts directing R&D goals into less crowded areas, and may yield breakthroughs in the technology field.

The existing disclosures are also a valuable tool for R&D departments so that already investigated areas do not have to be covered again. The information and findings of previous work can be used as a platform for the technology to reach the next level.

Indicators such as citation counts on particular patents can indicate any references in the area that are important to the technology. The most cited may well be held as a standard in the field and could prove essential to either avoiding the specific technology or providing insight into finding potential alternatives.

Corporate Review

Similarly, using a large dataset representing a technology field, with further analysis a corporate review can provide valuable information on the activity of other businesses and institutions. By looking at the numbers of applications in the area, details of the major players may become apparent. Information on granted patents will provide similar insight into the major players and also their patenting strategy.[1]

Timelines may be important to keep abreast of who is currently active in the field, as opposed to others that may have a history in the development of the technology but now no longer pursue an aggressive patenting agenda.

Opportunities may become apparent for collaborations or partnerships, where it appears other players are working toward similar goals. An informed licensing strategy can help to neutralise any potential conflict where another assignee's patent protection could otherwise be a barrier to further development or commercialisation.[2]

STATE OF THE ART AND COLLECTION SEARCHES

As mentioned, the patent art constitutes a gold mine of technological information. The consequence of full disclosure of an invention in order to gain IP protection allows detailed research and development to become available for all to use to continue to advance the technology field. Whilst care must be taken not to infringe on the activities of the existing IPRs, the knowledge can still be of great importance.[3]

State of the art searches should constitute a complete picture of the specific

---

1. Patent landscaping for life sciences innovation: toward consistent and transparent practices; Bubela, T. et al.; Nature Biotechnology, Vol. 31, 2013, pp. 202-206

2. How to Use Patent Information to Search Potential Technology Partners in Open Innovation; J. Jeon et al.; Journal of Intellectual Property Rights, Vol. 16, Sep 2011, pp. 385-393

3. Business models for sustainable innovation: state-of-the-art and steps towards a research agenda; Boons, F. at al.; Journal of Cleaner Production, Vol. 45, April 2013, pp. 9-19

inventive features known in the field. While a large portion of this can be found in the patent literature, in some fields there is a need to look also at the scientific and industrial literature. Journal articles, conference proceedings and trade publications can provide valuable information on the state of the art, especially in areas where little patent art is available.

Collection searches should aim to provide a thoroughly comprehensive investigation of all patent references pertaining to a specific technology; they will provide the information required to show exactly what has been, what is, and provide insight into what soon may become, the state of the art.

PATENTABILITY

Where early searches can result in a large dataset, complex analysis and a broad range of information, they will hopefully lead the innovative ideas into a better-defined objective. That objective may well include seeking patent protection. In order to be in the best possible shape to have a patent granted, a patentability search can help to ensure that there are no surprises when filing and the search step is undertaken.[1]

A small-scale search, the patentability search aims to highlight disclosures that may affect what protection can be gained. It will look for references that already describe the invention, or that represent the closest prior art that may then be deemed to preclude the new invention as an obvious progression, destroying the inventive step.[2]

When taken into account, the results from patentability searches can be an essential tool for deciding whether to seek protection at all, but also to those who may be drafting the claims of a patent application. The closest related art will give an indication as to what the scope of the application can be, and what areas need to be avoided.

FREEDOM TO OPERATE

One of the many pitfalls of innovation, particularly in crowded technology areas, is that the interests of other parties may dictate or block your progress owing to pre-existing IPRs. It can therefore be useful, at as early a stage as possible, to identify any potential IPRs that will influence the freedom to operate in the technology space.

The freedom to operate search is a comprehensive search aiming to identify any patent or patent applications that may contain claims covering or overlapping with

---

1. Selective search, sectoral patterns, and the impact on product innovation performance; Köhler, CH. Et al.; Research Policy, Vol. 41, no 8, October 2012, pp. 1344-1356

2. Prior art: To search or not to search; Atal, V. et al.; International Journal of Industrial Organization, Vol. 28, No 5, September 2010, pp. 507-521

the products or processes that you are hoping to commercialise. Of most interest would be granted patents which are currently in force, but applications that have the potential to be granted can also not be ignored. Whether you are seeking to obtain patent protection or not, making sure that your activities do not infringe another's rights can help to avoid any costly confrontations further down the line.[1]

SUMMARY

In an increasingly competitive business world, technology and technological advances are key to gaining an advantage. We have shown that an important tool is to have the right information available to move the technology forward, and in turn move the business forward. Using all the different types of search, which draw on the many different strategies for identifying the most relevant data, it is possible to navigate the process from stimulating innovation, guiding R&D, and intelligently protecting the IP and business interests that come from it.

---

1. New Product Clearance: Freedom to Operate Search and Analysis; Sheridan, Jamie; Intellectual Property & Technology Law Journal, 2011 Vol. 23, no. 1, p 14

3.2 BUSINESS GROWTH THROUGH INDUSTRY-ACADEMIA INTERACTIONS

Dr. Brian More, Coventry University

INTRODUCTION

I have spent over 40 years working in first industry then academia on business collaborations and partnerships. I now relish the opportunity to dispel some long ingrained prejudices and look to evidence how both sectors are increasingly driven by economic, social and political pressures to engage more for the benefit of society at large. In the United Kingdom universities are seen as essential pillars in the communities in which they reside, offering services not witnessed before as they strive to provide a central focus for society.

Many are classified as large businesses with turnover exceeding £500 million, and provide far more services than just teaching and research to businesses, charities and Government organisations. Universities are seen not only as a source of young talent for business but a cost effective way of industry improving both products and services, discovering new technologies and building upon the skill base of employees. Government sees the universities as prime locations for funding to develop new products and deliver business services to industry. From a theoretical collaborative business model to delivery of tangible results the Triple Helix[1] of Government/ Academia/Industry interaction is starting to deliver impact for many countries, a reassuring fact as we enter the Brexit and Trump eras with more uncertainty and risk for international trade.

Industry-academia- interactions are naturally two way; companies of all sizes and legal structures can support the Government's research and education agenda

---

1. https://triplehelix.stanford.edu/3helix_concept

by providing more industry and societal challenges to drive relevant and focussed research. As the skills needs of new business sectors change, the academic base has to be responsive to provide these skills at the right level and right time for global growth in international markets.

Industry has to compete in the global marketplace as international political changes since 2016 have simultaneously opened up opportunities and closed doors to trade and commerce. As UK Government focus shifts towards scale-up business support to grow our economy, no matter what the size of the industry or the state and stage of their development, a collaborative approach to working with academia is recommended.

Internationally developed economies approach industry-academia interactions in essentially the same way, with the trade-off between freedom of publication and intellectual property lock-up the most cited area of conflict[1]. Out of Canada, Japan, the UK and USA only Japan permits companies to control exclusively most collaborative inventions and to censor academic publications. Even in this situation companies are reported as not developing university discoveries to their full potential.

This is a practical chapter aimed to articulate current industry-academia interactions, and offer some guidance as to benefits and challenges going forward.

INDUSTRY-ACADEMIA INTERACTIONS MAKE A DIFFERENCE

One of the latest and most influential reports on the evidence underpinning industry-academia research collaborations is the 2015 Dowling Report[2] issued by the UK Government. Both qualitative and quantitative evidence demonstrate why it is important for both sectors to collaborate to improve their respective businesses. Ideas and creativity from both industry and academia, and more importantly the multidisciplinary collaboration between both, create new products, processes, services and business models. Early pre-competitive research and an open innovation approach involving many companies and universities has proven to increase innovation through sharing of research results, for example the Structural Genomics Consortium[3].

In the Dowling Report the UK Government recognises the importance of their role in providing strategic leadership and financial support to collaborations in order to drive economic growth. For every pound spent by Innovate UK on collaborative research the Gross Value Added (GVA) was £9.67 where there were 2 or more academic partners, compared to £4.22 without academic partners. Businesses who invest more in R&D are on average 13% more productive than those with no R&D

1. Industry-University Collaborations in Canada, Japan, the UK and USA –With Emphasis on Publication Freedom and Managing the Intellectual Property Lock-up Problem

2. The Dowling Review of Business-University Business Collaborations, 2015, www.bis.gov.uk

3. The Structural genomics Consortium, http://www.thesgc.org/

spend; these innovative businesses also see additional benefits in that they are more likely to:

- Be active exporters and achieve better value added per employee;
- Exhibit faster growth – it has been estimated that 51% of labour productivity growth between 2000 and 2008 could be attributed to innovation; and
- As collaborators, produce higher quality research outputs than research conducted either within an individual firm, or on an academic basis alone.

Conversely, for academic researchers the benefits reported included the following:

- Gaining real industry problems to solve, automatic relevance of research;
- Benefiting from working with other disciplines on industry projects;
- Increasing the breadth and reach of funding opportunities;
- Making a positive difference to society, providing their work with meaning and purpose to make a positive difference;
- Accessing new networks;
- Witnessing laboratory research go to industrial scale;
- Seeing new technologies reach the marketplace; and
- Seeing societal impact from academic research– theory to practice.

WAYS OF INTERACTING WITH INDUSTRY

One of the major barriers reported by industry in engaging with universities was the lack of a clear entry point to start the dialogue, and no clarity of the potential benefits. These 2 issues have been overcome by most UK universities with dedicated business facing support teams, with an associated contact website. Figure 1. Shows Coventry University's contact details shown on social media.

Figure 1. Coventry University's Twitter Cover Image

Source: Coventry University, Enterprise & Innovation

Before industry collaborates with a university the following points, taken from the Dowling Report, are considered to be important in achieving success, for all parties concerned.

- Strong and trusting personal relationships;
- Shared vision, goals and objectives defined, setting in place clear expectations;
- Mutual understanding between partners;
- Ability of, and opportunities for, staff to work across institutional boundaries;
- Collaboration brings about mutual benefits;
- Available funding;
- Processes for agreeing contracts and IP are in place;
- Clear and effective communication between partners;
- Organisational support, including senior management buy-in and championing of projects; and
- Willingness from both parties to devote time and resources.

These points for success are mirrored in the USA[1] with additional emphasis placed upon:

- Identification of leaders who are capable of crossing boundaries between business and academia to foster strong ties; and
- Investment in long-term relationships. A long-term relationship allows parties to share risk and accountability without overburdening a single entity. Under a shared vision and a foundation of mutual trust, a long-term partnership can reap great results by building a body of work over time.

Most industry-academia engagements start with a single project whereby both parties gain trust. If this interaction meets both parties' expectations of outcomes then multiple projects lead to larger collaborative research, strategic partnerships and other large scale projects. For strategic partnerships, universities and industry partners will employ a dedicated client manager to deal with all interactions or touch points between partners.

For practical purposes interactions fall within 10 distinct but not mutually exclusive categories as below:

Collaborative projects and partnerships
In collaborative projects and partnerships, costs are usually shared between parties because each will benefit from the collaboration, e.g. developing a new product,

---

1. How Academic Institutions Partner with Private Industry, https://www.rdmag.com/article/2015/04/how-academic-institutions-partner-private-industry

process or service for the industrial partner based upon applied research. Once the intellectual property has been protected by the industry or academic partner, then publications disseminate the results as widely as possible. Often the industry costs are subsidised by Government grants and/or academic partner contributions. In addition to publications, depending upon the collaboration contract, the academic partner may receive an on-going royalty payment through a commercial licence for product sales.

Contract research

In cases where the industrial partner needs to own and control the use of intellectual property from the academic partner then contract research is used. Industry generally will be expected to pay the full economic costs for the research, and their expectation is that the contract will be professionally managed and delivered to industry standards of time and quality.

Continuing Professional Development (CPD)

Continuing Professional Development (CPD) of staff is a key differentiator for industry in growing and competing in the commercial world. Universities deliver accredited CPD courses in most industrially relevant subjects from law, engineering, sciences, leadership, languages and management. Courses are delivered in all the required media formats and locations to meet industry needs – at the university, at the industrial site, at residential locations and, more frequently, on-line. CPD courses and seminars are also delivered by industry, providing an opportunity for academic staff to maintain and build on their knowledge and skills. CPD courses are an excellent way of staff networking and for building lasting relationships on both sides. In addition to CPD, industry/academic staff secondments are a very popular way to build partnerships and expose staff to respective working environments, processes, procedures and priorities.

Expert Consultancy, practical problem solving

Expert consultancy is where industry wants to access the expertise of certain academics when they have an urgent problem which needs solving, in the short term rather than through long or medium term research. The consultancy contracts would be expected to be paid for in full by the industry requesting the service. Examples here might be engineering expertise when a process line fails, or for expert witnesses in court cases. Academic consultants are also used widely for business advice and in the medical sector.

Business space and conferencing facilities

Larger universities run incubator, accelerator and co-working spaces for businesses to locate, work and access academic expertise. These science or technology parks provide both laboratory and office space for spin-out and spin-in companies, often accompanied by large conference centres and meeting rooms. Science and technology parks are also run by industry and will have a specific sector focus, often dictated by the anchor industry, for example pharmaceutical companies (Cambridge BioPharma Cluster[1]), environmental (Hong Kong Science Park[2]) or digital industry (Stanford Research Park, California[3]). Clustering businesses in a sector on a science park, located at or near a university or universities, is a well-documented method of creating value in cities and regions. Running a shared science park with academia and industry co-located creates a hotbed of ideas from cross-disciplinary contacts.

Access to Funding

Hundreds of funding schemes are available for industrial-academic collaborations, particularly in the field of pre-competitive research, for example national (Innovate UK), regional (Northern Powerhouse, Midland Engine), sub-regional (Local Enterprise Partnerships), European (Horizon 2020, Europe Enterprise Network) and international (Research Councils UK, The Newton Fund, the Industry Engagement Fund). Businesses who collaborate with universities can often use university specialist teams of bid writers who can support them gain access to grants, debt and equity finance. The industry-academia landscape for interactions remains complex (as seen in figure 2 below), so care needs to be taken in using the right scheme for specific desired outcomes.

1. Bidwells Cambridge BioPharma Cluster, http://www.bidwells.co.uk/assets/Uploads/downloads/biopharma-clusters/research-biopharma-cluster-cambridge-report-rebrand.pdf
2. Hong Kong Science and Technology Park, https://www.hkstp.org/hkstp_web/en/what-we-do/innovation-for-a-brighter-future/clusters-in-focus/Green%20Technology
3. Stanford Research Park, www.stanfordresearchpark.com/

Figure ². Research and Innovation landscape Map (Taken from the Dowling Report²)

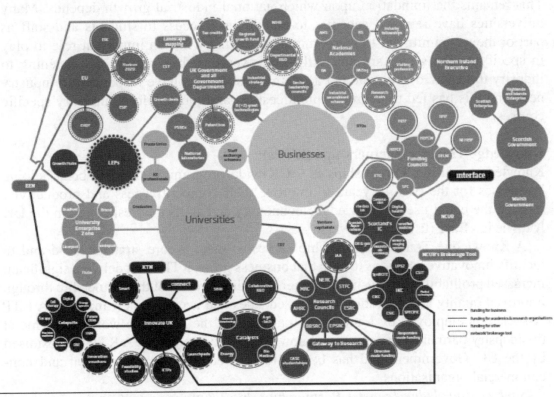

⁊ Figure 10 is an attempt to capture the major organisations and funding sources, relevant to business-university collaboration, in the UK's research and innovation landscape. Due to the complexity of the landscape there will inevitably be information missing.

Source: The Dowling Review of Business-University Business Collaborations, 2015, www.bis.gov.uk

Access to intellectual property

Despite opening up the opportunities for both parties for economic growth, IP ownership, use and commercial terms need to be well thought out for both industry and academia when collaborating on projects. This is still the most significant barrier to industry collaborating with academia, and the second most significant barrier for academia collaborating with industry. To help in reaching mutually acceptable terms for IP the Lambert Agreements[1] have been drafted by legal experts in consultation with industry and academia. These agreements have recently been updated and are a good starting point for negotiations, but will require amendments, additions and deletions for each specific contract.

1. University and Business Collaboration Agreements: The Lambert Toolkit, https://www.gov.uk/guidance/university-and-business-collaboration-agreements-lambert-toolkit

Access to talent, student placements, internships and recruitment

This remains the foundation upon which national industrial growth depends. Many universities have regional schemes to enable easy access to students and staff as part of their commitment to the community. Industry has an important role to play in specifying the sector specific skills and expertise they require. By listening to industry the UK Government and academic institutions have responded to industry need and this has led to degree apprenticeships and more tailored industry specific courses.

Knowledge Transfer partnerships (KTPs)[1]

Knowledge Transfer Partnerships is a UK-wide programme that has been helping businesses for the past 40 years to improve their competitiveness and productivity through the better use of knowledge, technology and skills that reside within the UK Knowledge Base (usually a university).

A Knowledge Transfer Partnership serves to meet a core strategic need and to identify innovative solutions to help that business grow. KTP often delivers significant increased profitability for business partners as a direct result of the partnership through improved quality and operations, increased sales and access to new markets. A KTP Associate is employed by a university partner, but the Associate works full time at the industry partner to transfer their knowledge to the company. A KTP is subsidised by the UK Government and has been widely used by both commercial and non-commercial organisations.

Source: Knowledge Transfer Partnerships, http://ktp.innovateuk.org/

Access to state of the art equipment

State of the art equipment is made available both in industry and academic institutions. Catapult Centres are a recent attempt to drive good research results through technology transfer to market; they were set up to support industry in the eight great technologies identified as important to the growth of the UK economy. Similar centres found in Germany are the Fraunhofer-Gesellschaft[2] Institutes.

CONCLUSIONS

Many examples and case studies exist to demonstrate the importance, significance and impact of industry-academia collaborations and partnerships. This includes, for example, the REF Impact Case Studies[3], a collection of 6,975 case studies submitted by

---

1. Knowledge Transfer Partnerships, http://ktp.innovateuk.org/
2. Fraunhofer Institutes and Research Establishments, https://www.fraunhofer.de/en/institutes.html
3. REF Impact Case Studies, 2014, http://www.hefce.ac.uk/rsrch/refimpact/

UK universities under the research excellence framework in 2014, and the University Industry Innovation Network good practice series 2016[1].

Good partnerships and collaborations can be long lasting and rewarding; many are characterised by committed individuals and champions on both sides. However, challenges tend to arise where the driving force behind the collaboration moves on, where university researchers fail to appreciate the commercial drivers for industrial work or where an industry strategy changes rapidly. Strategic differences for each sector remain; however, the interaction between both is improving as the academic sector employ teams who cross the boundary to specifically grow partnerships.

Today, more than ever, it's time industry started to work closer with the academic base, and universities listen harder to the real world needs of industry to ensure a prosperous and sustainable future.

1. University Industry Innovation Network, Good Practice Guide 2016 Series: Fostering University-Industry relationships, Entrepreneurial Universities and Collaborative Innovation. ISBN 978-94-91901-19-5

3.3 ONLINE PRESENCE: IGNITE THE DIGITAL SPARK

Yasmin El-Saie, UK2 Group

Statement:
In our technologically driven reality, can any business afford to forgo an online presence? asks Yasmin El-Saie, Content Manager at UK2 Group

TECHNOLOGY IS OUR FUTURE

"If you're not changing, you're dying[1]."

The internet has opened doors to endless possibilities, and has forever changed our perception of reality. Not only do we live in a physical three dimensional existence, we also are part of a virtual landscape that is constantly evolving. Websites, blogs, online shops and social media have become the dominant form of business presence, news channels and communication with customers. Our society's demand for instant gratification requires access to anything and everything, at any time, at our fingertips. Search engines are the portals into the internet's fabric, and the results they deliver carry powerful influence when it comes to decision making.

As a direct consequence of the internet, in conjunction with technological advances such as Artificial Intelligence and Blockchain, the way businesses are structured, marketed and how they interact with their consumers has changed forever. The doors have been opened to new and disruptive ideas, using digital innovation to drive growth and thinking outside of the box. Customers' demands and expectations are also

---

1. https://www.allbusiness.com/9-ways-to-inspire-innovation-and-transformation-in-your-business-104262-1.html

changing, and a successful business must strive to meet their new and evolving needs. A business which still relies solely on word of mouth and non-digital marketing must ask themselves one simple question: "**What are the consequences for my business without an online presence and the digital innovation it brings?**". If financial profit is the only consideration, then perhaps for some well-established niche businesses the need to conquer the internet and enter the world of digital marketing might not be a priority right now. However, it won't be long before such businesses are left behind. Without an online presence a business is limited – the innovation will always reside on the other side. To start the digital journey the first consideration is to find the right infrastructure to build on. Once this is in place, the innovation can begin.

WEB HOSTING SOLUTIONS

How Can a Website Enhance Your Business?
Online presence is synonymous with credibility in our digital age. Furthermore, it is almost impossible to digitally innovate without being digitally connected. The first step to take when investigating a future business partner, supplier or service provider is to "Google" them, and the decision on whether to hire or fire can be heavily based on what information about them you find online. The primary online presence is of course your website, followed by a company blog and active social media accounts. Even if your website has the sole function to dazzle and create awareness, the digital innovation that is possible through it is in itself essential.

How to Choose the Best Web Hosting Solution for Your Business

Current and Future Needs
There are two basic considerations when choosing the appropriate web hosting for your business: your current hosting needs, and future expansion. To small businesses starting out online this may seem a long way off. But growth can happen at unexpected exponential rates, and if your web hosting cannot keep up and your website crashes, the disruption in service can not only earn you a bad reputation, it can also lead to huge financial losses. To then change to a new hosting provider can cause even more disruption, and lead to high costs as well as unforeseen technical issues. To avoid such a situation, it is crucial to choose your infrastructure provider carefully.

Infrastructure Providers and Considerations
When choosing your web hosting package, there are some important factors – other than the type of hosting – to consider. For one, investigate the service provider before committing. Ideally you would choose a provider who has data centres around the world. This means that if you target different countries, you can have your website hosted in a data centre closest to your target market. This can reduce loading times

at peak traffic hours, providing a better service to your customers. The bandwidth a provider offers is also crucial as fundamentally it is the rate of data transmitted to and from your website. The greater the bandwidth on offer, the more complex processes your site can handle at a faster speed. Slow-loading websites are a recipe for failure, as even search engines penalise lack of speed. Looking slightly further ahead, once you have set up a network of virtual or bare metal servers (once your business is established), you can choose to have them positioned in various data centres in various locations to spread risk: if something goes wrong in one location, your servers in the rest of the data centres will still be up and running, serving your website.

Web Hosting Solutions: Shared Hosting, VPS and Dedicated Servers
There are three main types of web hosting:

1. Shared Hosting
Perfect for anyone starting out in the online world. This type of hosting is cost effective as multiple websites share the resources of one server (or computer). However, one repercussion is that the activity of any one website on the same server will affect all others. This means that if one particular website suddenly receives a massive influx in traffic, the bandwidth and loading speeds of all other sites could be severely slowed down.

2. VPS (Virtual Private Server)
A VPS solution is a halfway house between shared and dedicated server hosting. A VPS allows you to choose the specifications such as RAM, disk space and bandwidth, and is entirely flexible as to how you wish to set it up. You do not share the VPS with anyone else; it is like having your own environment, just virtual. And as it is virtual, you can scale up and down by adding more VPS servers to your network as and when required. This does not involve physically adding hardware, and is generally more cost effective than a dedicated server.

3. Dedicated Server
A dedicated server is the ideal solution when your website becomes well established and you start to receive high volumes of traffic on a regular basis. This type of hosting allows you to configure the actual hardware and software it runs according to your needs. A dedicated server hosting solution will require regular maintenance of the server, and to scale up will involve physically configuring the added servers. However, this will be the most cost effective, secure and reliable solution in the long term.

To get a tangible idea as to what kind of website requires what type of hosting, it all depends on how much of the available server resources you are using and the amount of daily visitors and simultaneous visitors your website receives. One of the biggest factors influencing how much traffic your shared hosting can cope with is the actual coding of the website itself. An optimally coded website will allow for a substantial number of simultaneous visitors. If you already have a VPS or dedicated server, the system load and memory usage figures will enable you to work out when you need to either grow the VPS and move to a dedicated server, or upgrade an existing dedicated server to a bigger one.

Once you've chosen the right type of hosting for your business, then comes the exciting task of building a state of the art website, with SEO, security and, of course, user experience in mind. A good web hosting provider will be able to provide you with all of the tools needed to get you started. If you are starting big, you will need to hire a reputable web development and design team to build a custom website for your business and its needs. This can be extremely interesting if you are adding special interactive features, a highly evolved ecommerce solution or a spectacular streaming/gaming platform.

DIGITAL INNOVATION SOLUTIONS

What Is Digital Innovation?

In a nutshell, digital innovation is the use of technology to improve what already exists as well as creating new concepts based purely on possibility.

The digital revolution is accelerating, and with it arise matters of privacy and security controversy. But looking at the phenomenon of advance in itself, there has never been a more exciting time to reinvent the wheel. Artificial intelligence is already transforming the internet, digital marketing and our homes. Whether it's Alexa at your service or a Facebook algorithm interpreting and commenting on posts, clever technology is everywhere.

The main reason why any business should seriously contend with going digital is to remain competitive and possibly to reinvent itself to accommodate new demands. Most customer journeys nowadays begin online, resulting in mountains of behavioural data which in turn can be used to define the future direction of a business.

Digital Innovation in Action

"Gartner, a leading technology research firm, has predicted that by 2025, all industries will have been transformed by the capabilities of digital technologies.[1]"

To illustrate the impact digital innovation has already had on businesses and entire industries, here are some examples:

---

1. http://www.pwc.com/gx/en/ceo-agenda/ceosurvey.html

The aviation industry uses the internet of things (IoT) at an industrial level to gather data via sensors on the aircraft, analyse it and deduce maintenance schedules and optimised landing flight paths to save fuel.[1] Tech industry giant Apple used digital innovation for over a decade to make technology sexy. Not only the hardware devices were revolutionary – the software platforms to harbour content, which then could be consumed by the devices, were also something brand new. The launch of iPod in 2001, with the associated iTunes in 2003, were both revolutionary concepts and have changed the way we listen to music forever.[2]

Sports legend Nike has embraced digital innovation by announcing its first "Digital Officer" in 2016.[3] Trying to reinvent itself as a service design company, Nike can target markets with consumers that effectively expect more.

Innovation Through Artificial Intelligence

AI is probably the hottest innovation around, and one of its many applications relevant to business is marketing. There are several forms of AI capabilities applied at different stages of the customer cycle. Some examples are ad targeting, propensity models and predictive analytics, dynamic pricing and web and app personalisation. Here we highlight some of the less well known AI technologies.[4]

AI content writing programs can create relevant articles by picking and choosing the right information from any given data. The result is a highly relevant "human sounding" post. These types of AI writers are extremely well suited to the financial services sector, where the content is based on data-focused events. For example, earnings reports, outcomes of sports matches and games and stock exchange data fit well with AI writing capabilities. To gain an impression of the popularity of AI writing, "WordSmith" produced 1.5 billion pieces of content in 2016 and they are offering a free beta version of their AI:

https://automatedinsights.com/

Content curation techniques, in which potential customers are shown content relevant to them, are also widely used, increasing engagement levels. For example, large ecommerce sites use this in the form of "customers who bought this also purchased that". Also, subscription-based services collect large amounts of data from their users, enabling them to better understand what they enjoy and are looking for. Netflix is a great example of being able to recommend to you what you would like to watch next, based on your general streaming habits.

Semantic SEO will be even more relevant due to an increase in voice search. Semantic

---

1. http://www.businessinsider.com/sc/farnborough-airshow-digital-aviation?IR=T

2. https://yourstory.com/2016/09/digital-hub-strategy-apple-innovation/

3. http://www.thedrum.com/news/2016/02/10/why-nike-has-finally-hired-chief-digital-officer

4. https://www.linkedin.com/pulse/15-applications-artificial-intelligence-marketing-robert-allen?trk=v-feed&trk=v-

SEO differs to regular SEO in that it not only relates a search to a given target phrase, it also needs to include all semantic phrases that could link to it. Basically, one target landing page (URL) needs to consider all possible ways of asking roughly the same question in different ways. This data needs to weave into a given URL to answer as many questions as possible connected to the overall topic a search phrase touches on.[1]

Disruption: Blockchain Decentralisation

There's digital innovation and then there is sheer disruption: getting rid of things as we know them and replacing them with brand new ones. One of the best examples of a disruptor is Blockchain technology, which is famously known as its cryptocurrency manifestation, Bitcoin. Blockchain basically is a mechanism of distributing digital information without duplication, and without a centralised entity regulating it.[2] The transparency and non-corruptibility of Blockchain makes it extremely appealing in our age of digital insecurity. In the world of finance, a growing market is international remittances, where Blockchain effectively cuts out the middleman. Data storage will also benefit from Blockchain, creating much needed security and protection from hackers.

Blockchain will create the startups and disruptors of the future. For example, Ethereum – an open source blockchain project – created smart contracts which will automatically pay the dividend of a financial investment once the conditions of the contract have been met. Another innovation is the concept of the sharing economy. Features such as ride-sharing, available through an intermediary like Uber, may eventually cut out the middleman through peer-to-peer payments via Blockchain. Imagine a general election made completely transparent through technology. Blockchain would revolutionise the way votes are counted. Now that could be the latest outrage! For many more interesting concepts have a read here: https://blockgeeks.com/guides/what-is-blockchain-technology/

Successful Ways to Digitally Innovate

Basically, if you can apply or create a technology to enhance your existing business or completely revolutionise it, you are digitally innovative.

> *"Gartner Survey of CEOs found that 47% of CEOs are being challenged by the board of directors to make progress in digital business. 20% of CEOs report they are now taking a "digital-first" approach to business change and 56% said that their digital improvements have already increased profits.[3]"*

---

1. http://www.smartinsights.com/search-engine-optimisation-seo/seo-strategy/semantic-seo-future-seo-strategies/
2. https://blockgeeks.com/guides/what-is-blockchain-technology/
3. http://www.gartner.com/newsroom/id/3689017

There are 3 main ways digital innovation can influence your business[1]:

1. Upgrade the traditional business model and how it executes tasks through new digital technologies:
- Collect data about your customer's behaviour.
- Invest in software/AI to evaluate the data and make predictions as to how to better satisfy your customers' demands, and identify and meet their new needs. It's all about mapping the physical into a digital counterpart.

2. Transform an existing business model into its digital technological counterpart:
- Take your offline business and go online. If you are a retailer, ecommerce with a sophisticated data analysis system is the way forward.
- Look outside the box: other industries can provide inspiration on how you can operate within in your niche area. For example, Saudi Telecom Company did exactly that: they hired a team of researchers to find out what their millennial customers were looking for. This lead to the creation of Jawwy App, which enables mobile planning, billing and charge overview.[2]

3. Disruption? Create a completely new type of business model based on new digital engagement:
This requires identifying a need that has arisen due to innovation, and fulfilling it by creating something new. For example, the need for security in a way has given rise to Blockchain technology, which in turn can revolutionise business models. Another example is Augmented Reality, which has already touched the retail experience through augmented mirrors, creating a projection of the customer (from all angles) virtually trying on clothes. The IoT is already a game changer to manufacturing, allowing the connectivity of devices to create a new playing field. Hybrid wireless technologies are hot on the list, basically enabling all types of input sources to communicate amongst each other. Hybrid software and interfaces translate the signals into a universal language. For example, a hybrid positioning system is able to use GPS, cell tower signals, wireless internet signals, Bluetooth sensors and IP addresses all together.[3]

SO WHAT'S THE ANSWER?

Whatever the question may be, it seems that technology has the answer. For existing businesses the idea is to change, evolve and adapt to new demands and needs as much

---

1. http://www.tivix.com/blog/what-is-digital-innovation/
2. https://www.visioncritical.com/digital-transformation-strategy-examples/
3. https://en.wikipedia.org/wiki/Hybrid_positioning_system

as possible. For startups, however, it is an exciting time to build a business using state-of-the-art ideas and technologies to truly revolutionise. In either scenario, it all begins by connecting to the internet and going digital. So to answer my initial question on what the consequences of your business would be without an online presence, you'd be mad not to!

3.4 THE USE OF PATENT INFORMATION FOR INNOVATION AND COMPETITIVE INTELLIGENCE

James Cooper and Rahman Hyatt, Minesoft Ltd

Although exploiting your own patent portfolio effectively can be an excellent basis upon which to build business decisions and strategy, it is not sufficient to only know and understand your own portfolio. In this increasingly competitive and global world, understanding your competitors' patent portfolios and how they compare to your own is critical for business survival. The rate at which new inventions are being patented is ever-increasing, therefore, the continuous monitoring of new patents is vital to ensure corporate success and financial stability when attempting to access new markets, exploit existing ones and scoping the profitability of emerging products.

To understand how patent data can be used both to drive innovation at a strategic level and to remain aware of the movements and intentions of the competition, we should first define some of the terms involved:

- A patent provides protection for a disclosed invention, with a government providing a temporary fixed-term monopoly on the monetisation of the invention in return for full disclosure on how the invention is created and used
- An invention simply refers to the creation of something new, while innovation is the implementation of an invention

MODELS FOR INNOVATION

According to Chesbrough (2005) (Open Innovation: The New Imperative for Creating and Profiting from Technology: Harvard Business Press), there are two models for how innovation takes place, Closed and Open innovation:

- Closed innovation is where the target market and end goals are pre-defined, the scope of the research limited and the boundaries within which the firm works impermeable. Research projects are guided down the funnel laid out by the existing markets whilst projects deviating too far from the desired criteria are abandoned or de-prioritised
- Open innovation, by contrast, removes the boundaries set down by existing target markets and looks outside of the project/company to locate both internal and external ideas. This allows new concepts to permeate into and out of the business to enhance the innovation process, create new markets and to identify collaboration opportunities

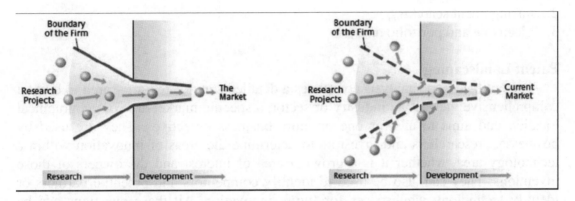

Patent data, publicly published and readily available, is an excellent source of external ideas and information that can be used in the open innovation model to identify opportunities and threats to a business and improve its survivability and profitability in the modern marketplace.

This information is also of vital importance to competitive intelligence, which makes use of public information to accrue data on competitors and the market environment to drive strategic decision making.

A general approach to gathering competitor intelligence is as follows:

1. Identify the information that a decision-maker needs
2. Collect publicly available raw data
3. Analyse the data and convert it into intelligence
4. Communicate the finished intelligence to the decision-maker(s)
5. Decision-maker(s) use the intelligence to inform business strategy

As patents are often the first and only source of disclosure for new inventions, a business that ignores patents as a potential source of information risks building an incomplete competitive intelligence picture and delaying or even preventing innovation.

Acting on an incomplete picture can be even more dangerous, with potential revenue loss through wasted research and development, loss of intellectual property rights or litigation costs following infringement of third party patents.

USING PATENT DATA FOR INNOVATION AND COMPETITIVE INTELLIGENCE

This article will briefly cover 3 different approaches to using patent data and the potential information each approach can generate to drive decision making:

1. Patent landscaping
2. Infringement searching
3. Licensing and portfolio analysis

Patent Landscaping

A patent landscape analysis comprises a detailed state-of-the-art search to build a comprehensive view of an industry or sector, a specific market area or geographical location and aims to answer one or more business objectives. They are used by businesses, researchers and investors to determine the areas of innovation within a technology area, whether it is a growing area of interest and the owners of those inventions. They can also be used to identify competitors and potential partners or identify technology whitespaces for future innovation. All these questions can be boiled down to a single query: where should we invest our time, effort and money to achieve the best return on investment?

Prior to any analysis or searching, the scope of the landscape study should be defined, based on the topic, time period and the reasons for the study.

Once the scope of the study has been agreed the analyst will begin by reviewing the main articles and literature on the topic, to gain an understanding and to pull out key terms that will be used to build the initial search strategy. In our example, the analyst is investigating the recent Ebola epidemic.

Background reading gives several variations and abbreviations for the virus, including the family (filoviridae) and its close relationship to the Marburg virus. Additional keywords identified at this stage include: Bundibunyo virus (BDBV/ BEBOV), Reston virus (RESTV or REBOV), Sudan virus (SUDV or SEBOV), Taï forest virus (TAFV or CIEBOV), Ebola virus (EBOV or ZEBOV). An additional virus that generates haemorrhagic fever is the Arenavirus, a member of a different viral family but related to the Ebola virus.

4. <u>Generation Of Virus Like Particles And Demonstration Of Lipid Rafts As Sites Of...</u>
In this application is described a method for the formation of filovirus like particles for both Ebola and...

5. <u>Trojan Inhibitors Method For The Production And Use Thereof</u>
...filo viruses and in the treatment and prevention of viral haemorrhagic fever activated by Ebola or Marburg viruses and in the therapy of tumoral diseases whereby the tumour cells are characterised by a specific...

6. <u>Compositions And Methods For Detecting Preventing And Treating African Hemorrhagic Fever</u>
There is a substantial degree of structural similarity although not sequence similarity between the carboxy...

7. <u>Identification Of Two Linear Epitopes On Ebola Or Marburg Virus Glycoproteins...</u>
The present invention relates to a linear domain encompassing F88 and a linear domain encompassing F159 or...

8. <u>Sulfonyl Semicarbazides Semicarbazides And Ureas Pharmaceutical Compositions...</u>
...but not limited to Arenaviridae Junin Machupo Guanavito Sabia and Lassa Filoviridae ebola and Marburg viruses Flaviviridae yellow fever omsk hemorrhagic fever and Kyasanur Forest disease viruses and...

9. <u>Recombinant Proteins From Filoviruses And Their Use</u>
...formulations The subunit proteins include GP95 GP FL VP40 VP24 and NP derived from Ebola Virus and Marburg Virus Adjuvants include saponins emulsions alum and dipeptidyl peptidase inhibitors The disclosed...

10. <u>Treatment Of Hemorrhagic Viral Infections Using A Tissue Factor Inhibitor</u>
...relates to novel methods for the treatment of hemorrhagic viral infections such as Ebola and Marburg virus by administering a tissue factor...

11. <u>Antiviral Drugs For Treatment Of Arenavirus Infection</u>
Compounds methods and pharmaceutical compositions for treating viral infections by administering certain novel compounds in therapeutically effective amounts are disclosed Methods for preparing the compounds and methods of using the compounds and pharmaceutical compositions thereof are also disclosed In particular the treatment and prophylaxis of viral infections such as caused by hemorrhagic fever viruses is disclosed i e including but not limited to Arenaviridae Junin Machupo Guanarito Sabia Lassa Tacaribe and Pichinde Filoviridae Ebola and Marburg viruses Flaviviridae yellow fever Omsk hemorrhagic fever and Kyasanur Forest disease viruses and Bunyaviridae Rift Valley fever

12. <u>Antiviral Drugs For Treatment Of Arenavirus Infection</u>
...Arenaviridae Junin Machupo Guanarito Sabia Lassa Tacaribe Pichinde and LCMV Filoviridae Ebola and Marburg viruses Flaviviridae yellow fever Omsk hemorrhagic fever and Kyasanur Forest disease viruses and...

13. <u>Monoclonal Antibodies For Ebola And Marburg Viruses</u>
Described herein are a number of Ebola and Marburg monoclonal...

14. <u>Methods Of Use Of Antiviral Compounds</u>
...of influenza viruses e g influenza A virus and other similar viroporins e g VP24 of Ebola and Marburg viruses and NS3 protein of Bluetongue The present invention further relates inter alia to compounds...

15. <u>Methods Of Use Of Antiviral Compounds</u>
...of influenza viruses e g influenza A virus and other similar viroporins e g VP24 of Ebola and Marburg viruses and NS3 protein of Bluetongue The present invention further relates inter alia to compounds...

16. <u>Inhibitors Of Filovirus Entry Into Host Cells</u>

Once the keywords have been defined, patent search tools can be used to cross reference them with existing patent classification codes to find the specific codes that relate to the area of study. These codes can be used to refine the search by technology area, increasing the accuracy and specificity of the final result set.

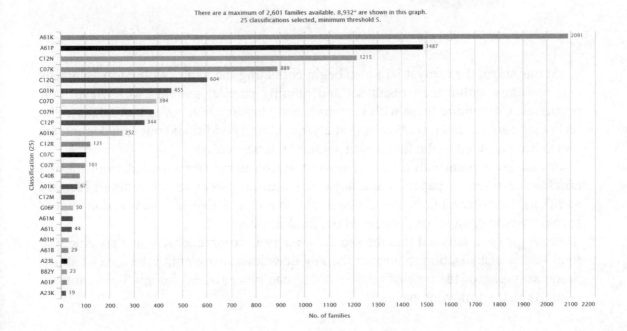

During this process, the relevant classifications for RNA viruses in general, the filoviridae family and the Ebola virus were identified. A keyword analysis was used to refine the result set, for example, the analyst identified that the families reporting both Ebola and HIV virus in their title, abstract and claims were not relevant to the overall study and so could be excluded from the final landscape. This process of cutting out irrelevant results is vital to ensure the final landscape is as focussed as possible.

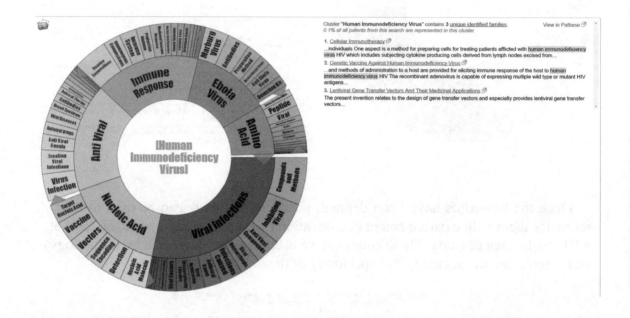

At this stage, the analyst will also begin collecting the names of the top assignees and inventors within their result set and running parallel searches to retrieve their portfolios. Combining them with keywords and classification codes that relate to the technology area of interest allows the analyst to identify additional relevant documents which can be added to the final result set that will be studied.

So, having begun with a basic keyword search using terms pulled from journal articles and research papers, the analyst has utilised patent search tools to identify additional keywords, international classification codes, active assignees and inventors to improve the comprehensiveness of the final result set.

Once they are satisfied that the search strategy is comprehensive and specific, the final step is visualisation to answer the key questions surrounding the area of study. Some examples of the type of questions that can be answered for any landscape are outlined on the following pages.

1. Is this a growing area of interest?

   Visualising the number of patent families, applications and grants published
   over time allows us to identify whether this is a growing area of interest.
   The significant increase in the number of granted patents over the past 10
   years is a good indication that the research and development in Ebola has
   grown. Furthermore, it can be seen that following the end of the outbreak this
   technology area has been shrinking as a field of study given the recent drop off
   in the number of patent applications and granted patents.

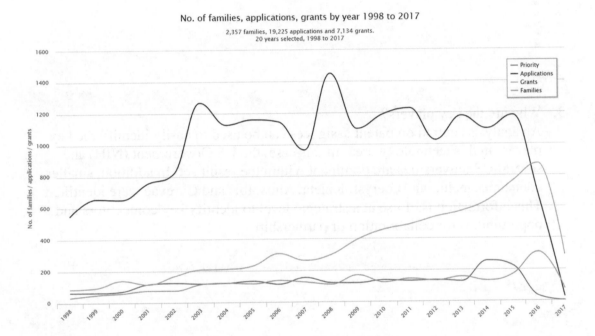

No. of families, applications, grants by year 1998 to 2017

2,357 families, 19,225 applications and 7,134 grants.
20 years selected, 1998 to 2017

2. What are the fields of interest?

   Analysing the results by classification code allows the identification of the top
   codes for the set and thus the fields of highest interest. In this example, the
   codes for anti-viral compounds (A61P31 and A61K31) and vaccines/antibodies
   (A61K39) are among the top IPC and CPC codes.

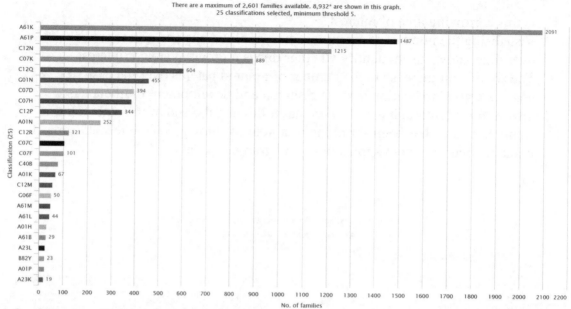

There are a maximum of 2,601 families available. 8,932* are shown in this graph.
25 classifications selected, minimum threshold 5.

3. Who are the key players?

An analysis centred on patent assignees can be used to easily identify the key players in this technology area. In this case, the US Government (NIH) and several US universities are dominant within the result set. In addition, smaller companies including Biocryst, Kineta, Alios, Ibis and Curevac were identified. This information is of use at a strategic level to identify key competitors and opportunities for collaboration or partnership.

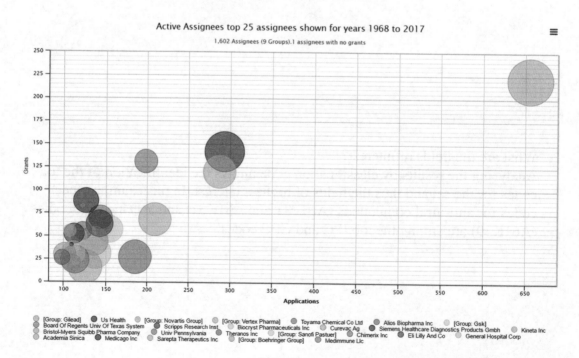

Active Assignees top 25 assignees shown for years 1968 to 2017

1,602 Assignees (9 Groups).1 assignees with no grants

4. Where are the key players filing their inventions?
    Drilling down into the data to determine where specific assignees (patent owners, usually the corporate affiliation) are filing their patents is useful to determine the markets that they are seeking or have obtained patent protection in. This is useful information to guide a filing strategy in this area and to determine the markets which your competitors deem most important.

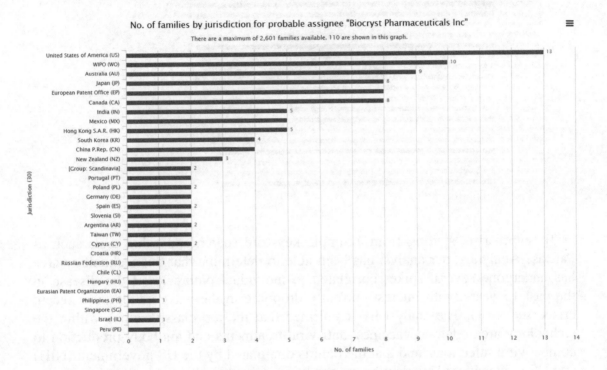

5. Who are the key thought leaders in the field?
    Finally, an analysis of the top inventors in this area can help to identify the key opinion leaders in the field. Sorting or grouping them by company/institution can also give some insights. For example, in this case the top inventors are from US universities who could be willing to collaborate or could be your potential next employee!

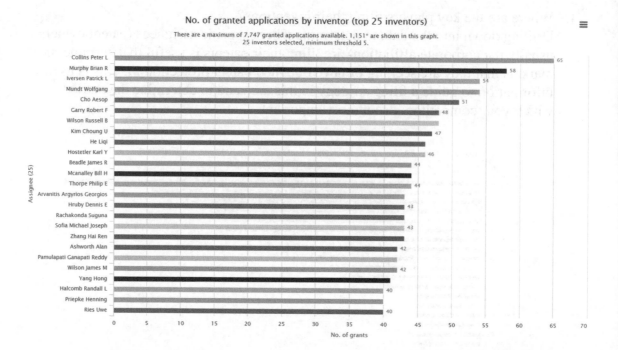

To summarise, starting from a simple keyword search and using tools such as PatBase Analytics, our analyst has been able to determine that this technology area has undergone several spikes correlated to individual outbreaks of the disease in the past 15 years, with interest currently dropping in the wake of the most recent crisis (see fig.1). The analyst has confirmed that the top classifications within the technology area relate to vaccines, anti-viral treatments and antibody production to combat viral infections, and that the field is dominated by the US government (NIH) and US universities. This dominance can be explained by this field of study rising to prominence through a world public health crisis rather than market forces, prompting universities and Western governments to become involved in its development. This is also supported by the jurisdiction analysis which found the US to be the most common filing country for families within the result set.

The assignee analysis also found several smaller companies that could be competitors or partners and are worthy of further investigation at a corporate level.

The analyst was also able to determine the top inventors within the field, which may be of interest for talent acquisition, knowledge sharing or intelligence gathering.

Used in this way, patent landscaping can give both broad and detailed insights into a technology field and the companies and individuals that lead it.

Infringement searching:

An infringement search (AKA: Freedom to Operate, FTO, Clearance) is a critical analysis for any company wanting to market a product or service anywhere in the world. The risks and consequences of patent infringement can be significant and could involve litigation or the withdrawal of your product or service. Simply put, an infringement search involves identifying any third-party patent which would be infringed by selling a product or service in a specific country or jurisdiction.

The search involves identifying any patent rights in that country/jurisdiction where the claims cover all or part of the product or service which you plan to market or sell.

In this example, a biotechnology R&D company has developed a therapy making use of the Sonic Hedgehog gene. Using genetic engineering they plan to increase the expression of Sonic Hedgehog in cardiac tissue following a heart attack to help increase blood vessel density and reduce tissue damage. They will be conducting an infringement search to determine whether any existing patents may prevent them from monetising their discovery.

To achieve a comprehensive and effective patent search, we have detailed 5 key steps to consider:

1. Spend time creating a comprehensive search strategy: As in our previous patent landscaping example, the process begins by identifying some initial search terms through research, background reading and ideation. Furthermore, using thesauri, like the PatBase Thesaurus, can help build a comprehensive set of relevant terms, synonyms, acronyms and foreign language translations which can be used to build a comprehensive search strategy.

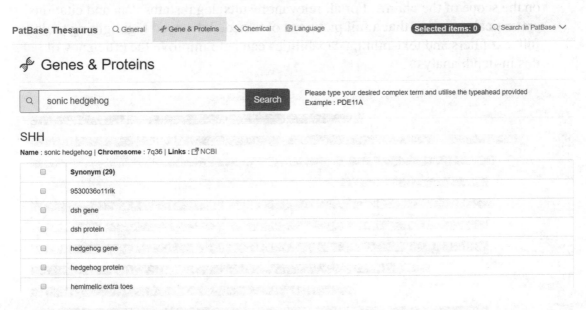

2. Run an initial search and use the results to refine your strategy: The initial terms are used to retrieve likely patents from your search tool. By analysing keywords

and classification codes, the analyst is able to identify additional search terms and relevant classification codes which they can use to refine their search strategy.

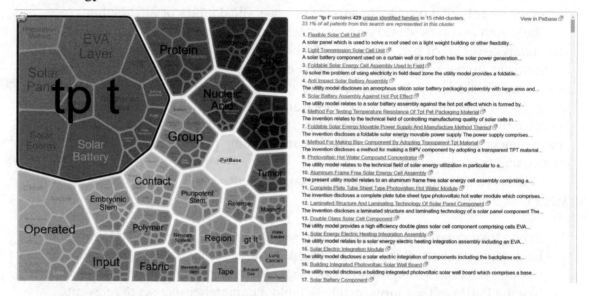

3. Run the refined search strategy and identify relevant results: The analyst will then take the time to review the retrieved results in depth, specifically focussing on the scope of the claims. For all relevant results, legal status data and citations are critical to ensure that a full picture is obtained. Advanced highlighting tools, full text filters and text-mining capabilities can help improve the efficiency of this in-depth analysis.

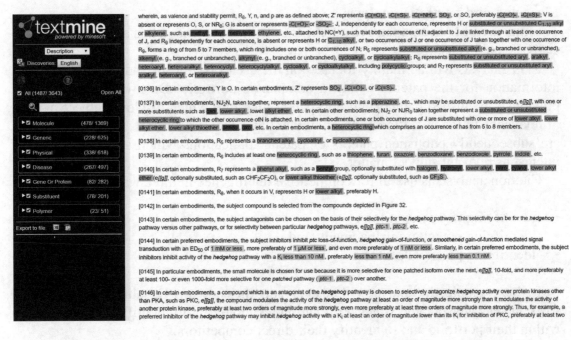

4. Store, share and report relevant results: having identified the relevant patents within a result set, the ability to store these results within folders is critical to allow the analyst to manage their workflow. Ranking the results within a folder and being able to add notes against each patent allows the analyst to prioritise their results and share or export this information with colleagues or customers.

5. Set up alerts for new patents and changes in the status of the patents deemed relevant: The final stage in the process is to create alerts to monitor new patents in the technology area of interest so that the analyst is aware of new innovations. Furthermore, for those patents deemed relevant, monitoring changes in legal status is critical as they may subsequently lapse, grant or a new equivalent covering a different jurisdiction may publish.

To summarise, infringement searching builds on the use of keyword and classification analysis which we described in our patent landscaping example. For an efficient, in-depth analysis of the relevancy of a patent to the subject matter of interest, legal status data and text analysis tools can help. These tools add vital detail by taking the results found from our search and allowing us to determine two key points:

1. Whether the claims cover part or all of the product or service in question; and
2. Whether the patent is still in force.

Licensing and portfolio analysis

The final use of IP in competitive intelligence to be discussed in this article is portfolio analysis and licensing.

This analysis will be mainly focused on the use of backward and forward citation information for the patents within a company's portfolio. Backward citations are previously published patents and non-patent literature which disclose subject matter of relevance to the invention claimed within the patent. In contrast, forward citations are subsequently published patents or patent applications which cite the patent of interest as relevant subject matter.

Citation analysis is useful for competitive intelligence in three ways:

- Identifying key competitors;
- Identifying potential infringement; and
- Identifying potential partners

In this example, the analyst will be analysing the company Desalitech, who mainly work in seawater-potable water purification technologies, to identify the valuable IP within their portfolio and to identify their direct competitors.

First some basic information on Desalitech's portfolio, which consists of 6 distinct patent families, 5 of which contain a grant.

Summary

pa=desalitech

- 31 Jurisdictions
- 24th February 2005 to 17th May 2017
- 12 years, 2 months, 23 days
- 1 assignees (1 with granted patents)

ⓘ	Families	Applications
Totals	6	76
Grants	5 (83.33%)	41 (53.95%)

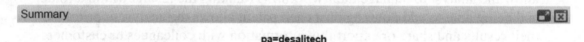

| Patents: 89.81% | Designs: 0% | Utilities: 0% | Other: 10.19% |

Large result sets can take a few moments to prepare, please be patient.

* Please note that non-unique items are marked with an asterisk. For example; families often contain patents from multiple jurisdictions meaning that in some instances families can be counted more than once (once for each jurisdiction).

The company's portfolio covers 28 jurisdictions, with the top 5 being US, CN, IN, PCT and EP.

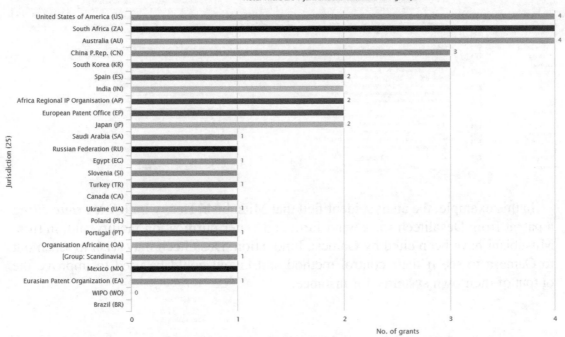

No. of granted applications by jurisdiction (top 25 jurisdictions)

There are a maximum of 41 grants available. 41 are shown in this graph.
25 jurisdictions selected, minimum threshold 0.
Note: There are 1 jurisdictions contained in 1 groups.

When viewing the citation information the analyst must first determine which families are currently the most cited within the company's portfolio. Citations are a good starting point to judge how valuable a patent is to the company and others. Each forward citation represents another invention or company that is building on the work detailed in your patent and developing further innovations from it.

It is important to note that there is a time lag for forward citations. Newer publications will initially have no forward citations against them, and it can take months for citations to be added. However, in this example, two of Desalitech's patent families which were filed in 2010 have minimal forward citations. This could indicate that these families are of lesser value for the company and could be candidates for pruning.

An analysis of the companies who are citing the Deslitech portfolio can provide useful competitive intelligence and indicate close competitors to Desalitech, potential partners or potential licensees. Tools like Citation Explorer provide the ability to review citations in detail and compare, side by side, the citation to the patent it cites.

In this example, the analyst identified that Mitsubishi Heavy Industries were citing a patent from Desalitech for a wind-farm and water purification facility and, in turn, Mitsubishi have been cited by Gamesa Innovation. Desalitech may wish to reach out to Gamesa to see if their control method and layout could be used to improve the output of their own systems, for instance.

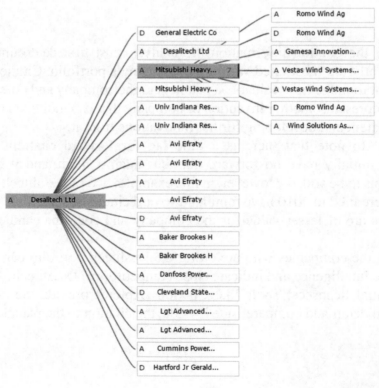

By assessing the forward citations for their entire portfolio, Desalitech could compile a list of known competitors in their technology field. This list of company/assignee names can be monitored for new publications using automated alerting features, such as PatBase alerts.

To summarise, citation information is particularly useful to identify close competitors, collaborators and even potential infringers. Furthermore, citation information can be an integral part of the package of information when deciding which of your IP portfolio to maintain or abandon. Highly cited patents represent valuable IP which should be maintained in as many jurisdictions as financially viable and which provide a market for the invention being protected. In contrast, patents with few or no citations may be of lesser value and could be cut back to only cover key markets (e.g. EP, US, CN, JP and KR) or abandoned altogether.

In conclusion, patent information contains valuable insights and information that can assist companies in identifying new/emerging markets, give insights in to the actions of competitors and partners and inform the company which parts of their portfolio are most valuable.

Using tracking and alerting products, a company can be alerted as soon as a change is detected in their own portfolio or in a competitor's portfolio, allowing swifter responses to the decisions and actions of competitors and State Patent Offices worldwide.

The examples covered in this article touch upon just some of the ways in which patent information can be used by companies to protect and enrich themselves in the global marketplace of ideas and innovations. For more information about how IP data can help your business, visit www.minesoft.com and download our whitepapers for free.

3.5 PROTECTING INNOVATION WITHOUT PATENTS

Aaron Wood, Wood IP

Patents provide a substantial protection for innovation: they provide a monopoly against third party use, and can provide the basis for additional benefits such as preferential tax treatment in certain circumstances. Patents are not always available or appropriate, however, and an innovative business should consider other forms of protection – particularly where patent protection is set to come to an end, where a company is keen to avoid disclosing its processes as part of a patent application or where protection cannot be obtained at all because the innovation lies outside the protectable subject matter of a patent. This chapter introduces the other forms of intellectual property that are available and typical issues which businesses need to consider.

TRADEMARKS – PROTECTION FOR BUSINESS INDICATORS

A trademark is a registered right which gives a monopoly in the mark protected for the goods or services for which protection is obtained. Whilst words and logos are what people traditionally think of as trademarks, it is in fact possible to register other kinds of material as trademarks, such as shapes, colours and colour combinations.

Once registered, a trademark lasts for an extended period (in the UK and many other countries this is 10 years) and can be renewed for further periods so long as the owner has an interest in it.

In the context of innovations, patent owners may seek to promote their innovation under a particular name or broader brand to create awareness and loyalty so that when protection with a limited life-cycle (notably patents and designs) comes to an end, consumers continue to buy their products. A major sector which adopts that strategy is the pharmaceutical sector, where brands and product design are used to take over from patents at the end of their lifecycle, when the value of the business is typically at its highest.

A trademark depicting the product (or part of it) may sometimes be the focus of protection, since a registration for the shape of the product or its packaging may often provide effective protection for the product. There are, however, some inherent difficulties which need to be considered when taking this approach:

1. Trademarks protect signs which "distinguish the origin" of the goods or services. Trademarks must be distinctive – either inherently or because of the use made of them in the trade – and the various registries take the view that consumers do not typically see shapes as indicating the origin of the product or service. This can be overcome with evidence, but there can sometimes be a tension in the evidence where the product was previously covered by a patent: if only one company has produced an item in that field (because there was a patent), does the consumer recognise it because there was no competition, and would they rely upon that shape to identify the source of the product if there were others in the market?

2. In making the application, the applicant must show or describe the mark ("graphically represent" it). In the case of a product which is likely to be copied to some extent by others, the temptation is to try to draft a description or "claim" to catch all manner of other copies within the description. Doing so can, however, lead to the conclusion that what is being sought is not so much a "sign" as a plurality of signs or a property. This is the outcome in a number of cases, including:
    a. Dyson's application to register a transparent bin for vacuum cleaners (to defend against competitors that sold, or threatened to sell, vacuum cleaners with transparent containers);
    b. JW Spear's attempt to register a tile shape which featured a roman letter and a number on the top surface (i.e. the concept of the SCRABBLE tile); and
    c. Cadbury's attempt to register the colour purple, as applied "to the whole or the predominant surface area of the goods."

3. Certain types of marks have specific exclusions which prevent their registration if they consist exclusively of matter which:
    a. Results from the nature of the goods themselves;
    b. Is necessary to obtain a technical effect; or
    c. Adds substantial value to the goods or services.

These "shape" exclusions led to the cancellation of the shape of Philips' three-header shaver (the shape of which was deemed to consist exclusively of a shape which was necessary to obtain a technical effect i.e. improved shaving performance) and the shape of a particular speaker sold by electronics company Bang & Olufsen (on the basis that the speaker would be purchased for aesthetics and so the shape added substantial value). The test is whether the mark consists *exclusively* of such material, so important elements ("essential features" to adopt the legal wording) which do not have these issues should mean that registration will be possible even if some features have a technical effect.

DESIGNS – PROTECTION FOR PRODUCT APPEARANCE

Designs (called design patents in some countries) protect the appearance of products. Designs are protected by a mixture of registered rights (which require using an application procedure) and unregistered rights (which arise automatically). The protection for designs varies in terms of length and what it covers and so can be complicated, but design rights form an important part of the patchwork of rights available to creators.

In terms of the protection available, protection can be had for the appearance of the whole or a part of a product, and protect against the use of another design which gives the same overall impression. Where you are relying on a registered design as the basis for any claim against a third party a Court will look at the registration document itself, so if the *entire product* is registered under a single design registration then the fact that one feature or part of the design can be seen in another product may not be sufficient for the alleged infringer to be found to have infringed the registration.

In selecting what to register it is therefore very important to consider what is to be protected. Whilst there are often very good reasons to want to protect the entire product under a design registration, it is also worth considering whether further registrations are needed for part of a product (or even part of a part!).

Equally, the way in which the item is shown can have an impact on the rights obtained. Typical ways of showing an item in a design application in the UK or EU are line drawings, 3D computer models or photographs of the item on a neutral background. The danger of 3D models or photographs are that these can show up contrasting colours or textures which are not intended to be part of the design protected. This is a problem which befell the maker of the TRUNKI children's suitcase, in their case intending to stop the sales of a suitcase which was a copy (we can say this safely, as the defendant admitted that they copied it!). Reproduced below are the TRUNKI as sold, the copy and the way in which the design was shown in the design registration. Ultimately, the UK Supreme Court held that the design registration had a lack of surface decoration as part of the registration, and the addition of the surface decoration (along with other changes) meant that the defendant's case gave a different overall impression.

There are certain types of designs which are excluded from protection – most importantly these stop the valid registration of designs which are dictated *exclusively* by function (i.e. there is no aesthetic aspect to the product or the part) and designs where the features must be in specific dimensions and placement to fit around other items. Typically even those features of a product which have a functional element to them will also have been given some further aesthetic element during the design process, and so a valid registration is often achievable even where the design has some functional aspect.

In order to be valid a design must also be novel (i.e. the same design must not already be on the market) and the design must have individual character (i.e. there must not be a design already disclosed which, whilst not identical, is sufficiently close to this later design as to not give a different overall impression).

The length of protection of a design registration in the UK and EU is 5 years, extendable to 25 years through 5-yearly renewals. In some countries (although not all) it may be possible to obtain a valid registration even though the product has been launched on the market – the European Community Design, for example, has a period of one year during which a product may be marketed before the registration would be invalid because of the prior marketing and sale of the product. This means that a company that finds that a product has been very popular can still obtain registration if it does so within this period. It is important to note, however, that if a competitor were to launch a very similar product during that one-year period this copy may be a cause for any subsequent application by the first company to register the design to be invalid – as a result it is not always safe to rely upon this one year period as it only protects against invalidity based upon your earlier disclosure of the product.

Alongside registered designs there is also unregistered design protection. This protects against the use of the design in broadly similar situations as those for registered designs, with two important distinctions:

a. In the UK there is no unregistered design protection for "surface decoration" – i.e. patterns which are on the surface of objects, which includes logos; and
b. The term of protection is much shorter than registered design protection (15 years from creation of the design or 10 years from first marketing (whichever comes first) for UK unregistered designs; 3 years for European Community unregistered designs).

CONFIDENTIAL INFORMATION – KEEP IT SECRET AND KEEP IT FOREVER

The potential for never-ending protection for your product is an appealing one, and it may be the correct approach for some products. Whilst patent protection is the state monopoly for disclosing new inventions to the public by way of the patent application, the law around confidential information or "trade secrets" (also known as the law of confidence) protects against unauthorised disclosure of information to the general public by third parties. It does not, however, protect against third party discovery and so is not a monopoly on the invention itself. Used correctly it can be part of the mix of protection.

The information can take many forms, such as food recipes, production methods and source code or algorithms not otherwise disclosed to users. Very well known examples of confidential information include the recipe to the coating for KENTUCKY FRIED CHICKEN (which is professed to be a secret blend of herbs and spices) and the recipe for the syrup which is used to flavour the COCA-COLA soft drink.

In order to benefit from protection, the company disclosing the information must show that the information over which it is claiming protection is not already in the public domain and that it was disclosed to the company misusing it in circumstances where an obligation of confidence existed. Generally a company will demonstrate this last point by showing that the other company signed a non-disclosure agreement which identified that the material disclosed to them was done on a confidential basis, was not to be used other than for a defined purpose and was not to be shared, copied or otherwise used other than in accordance with that purpose.

Where a company is unsure about whether to seek patent protection (or simply is not ready to file their patent) then it is advisable to use non-disclosure agreements to preserve the confidentiality of any information that they may disclose to third parties they interact with, or at least to document that the party receiving the information understands it should be kept confidential.

3.6 RESERVING PATENT RIGHTS FOR YOUR SECRET PROCESSES

John Moetteli, Da Vinci Partners LLC

Abstract

Provided innovators do not file any non-US patent applications and request non-publication of the U.S. patent application at the time of the U.S. regular (i.e. non-provisional) filing, their U.S. application is kept secret and is not published by the U.S. Patent Office until it is granted. Therefore, innovators who practise a secret process need not relinquish trade secret protection until they're willing to trade in this protection for a granted US patent.

INTRO

Most business people, and many IP attorneys unfamiliar with US practice, believe that trade secrets and patent rights are mutually exclusive. It is commonly believed that if you choose to keep innovations a secret, then you cannot attempt to patent them. If you attempt to patent them, you obviously cannot keep them secret, because they will be published about 18 months after the earliest claimed priority date. In addition, many non-US based companies believe that a prior user right will enable them to claim a defense if threatened with a law suit from a US patent holder. To most persons reading this article, it will come as a surprise that the above assumptions are simply not true, at least in one very significant situation.

NOT MUTUALLY EXCLUSIVE

The fact that trade secret rights and patent rights are mutually exclusive is indeed the case in Europe (including Switzerland), China, Japan, South Korea, India, Russia, and essentially every industrialized country in the world. This means that if you choose to protect your invention with a patent application, you subject yourself to publication of that patent application at 18 months after the earliest claimed priority date or the date of filing of the application, whichever date is earlier. Publication destroys trade secret rights in the published information.

Yet according to the Uniform Trade Secrets Act (UTSA) and most countries' laws, you can enjoy limited trade secret protection to the extent that you've taken "efforts that are reasonable under the circumstances" to ensure information about your invention has been kept secret.[1]

Regarding reasonable efforts to maintain secrecy, the UTSA maintained that actions such as restricting access to a "need-to-know basis" and informing employees that the information is secret met the criteria for reasonable efforts. The UTSA stated that the courts do not require procedures to protect against "flagrant industrial espionage" as these were not necessary.

However, almost without exception, the filing of a patent application is an authorisation of publication of the application's contents, which takes place at 18 months. Once the previously secret information is published, one can no longer rely on trade secret protection. Consequently, it is clear to essentially all IP professionals that the choice to file a patent application comes with an obligation to give up any trade secret rights in the content of this patent application at least after a period of time when it is too late to prevent publication at 18 months.

There are, however, two significant exceptions.

Firstly, the filing of a US provisional application does not constitute acceptance of publication at 18 months because US provisional applications are never published until they are claimed in a regular patent application[2].

Therefore, if you file and pay the fees for a US provisional application, and do nothing further, the US provisional application will *not* publish and so, unless you or someone else publishes previously secret information about your invention or unless you fail to make a reasonable effort to keep it secret, your invention will indeed remain secret and so you may preserve your trade secret rights in this information.

Secondly, if a regular US application is filed together with a non-publication request, then, provided that *the invention disclosed in an application has not been and will*

---

1. UTSA § 1.4

"Trade secret" means information, including a formula, pattern, compilation, program, device, method, technique, or process, that:

(i) derives independent economic value, actual or potential, from not being generally known to, and not being readily ascertainable by proper means by, other persons who can obtain economic value from its disclosure or use, and

(ii) is the subject of efforts that are reasonable under the circumstances to maintain its secrecy.

2. See 35 USC 122(b)(2)

not be the subject of an application filed in another country, or under a multilateral international agreement, that requires publication of applications eighteen months after filing, the application will not be published, assuming further formalities are met. Such formalities include the requirements that:

1. A request (nonpublication request) is submitted with the application upon filing;
2. The request states in a conspicuous manner that the application is not to be published[1]; and
3. The request contains a certification that the invention disclosed in the application has not been and will not be the subject of an application filed in another country, or under a multilateral international agreement, that requires publication at eighteen months after filing.

THE CERTIFICATION MUST BE PROPER

Before making the latter certification, the person who signs the certification must make an actual inquiry to determine whether the certification can be appropriately made, to determine that:

a. The application has not been the subject of a foreign or international application filed in another country, or under a multilateral international agreement, that requires publication of applications at eighteen months after filing (e.g. a counterpart PCT application); and
b. The applicant's intent at the time the nonpublication request is being filed is that the application will not be the subject of a foreign or international application filed in another country, or under a multilateral international agreement, that requires publication of applications at eighteen months after filing.[2]

Only when both conditions are satisfied, can applicants file a nonpublication request[3]. A nonpublication request is not appropriate if applicants have already filed a counterpart foreign or international application in another country, or under a multilateral international agreement, that requires publication of applications at eighteen months after filing. A nonpublication request is not proper even if the foreign or international application is abandoned before it is published. Therefore, the mere filing of the PCT application precludes the proper use of a nonpublication request, since the invention disclosed in the U.S. application was the subject of an application that was filed under an international agreement requiring publication at

---

1. under 35 U.S.C. 122(b)
2. under 35 U.S.C. 111(a)
3. under 37 CFR 1.213(a)

18 months (the PCT application). If applicants filed a nonpublication request in a U.S. application that claims the benefit to an earlier foreign or international application, the Office will not accept the nonpublication request and will assign a projected publication date. The applicant will be notified that the certification is inconsistent with the priority claim. The notice will provide a non-extendable time period of 30 days from the mail date of the notice for the applicant to provide a satisfactory explanation as to how the certification submitted is valid in light of the priority claim. If applicants fail to provide a satisfactory explanation, the Office will publish the U.S. application. One potentially acceptable argument, however, is that the content of the US application includes significant new matter not present in the earlier filed application. If a petition is filed requesting non-publication with a showing that such application is indeed different than the one filed earlier outside the US, then publication may be avoided.

A nonpublication request is also not appropriate if the applicant has not yet made a decision whether to file a counterpart application in a foreign country, or under a multilateral international agreement, that requires publication of applications at eighteen months after filing. A certification cannot be made based on lack of knowledge of the applicant's plans concerning the filing of any counterpart application that would be subject to eighteen-month publication or the applicant's past practices or tendencies with respect to the filing of foreign counterpart applications[1]. The fact that a particular applicant has a tendency to file counterpart applications for fewer than fifty percent of its U.S. applications is not alone an adequate basis for filing all or any of the U.S. applications with a nonpublication request. The applicant must have an affirmative intent not to file a counterpart application, and not just the absence of any intent or plan concerning the filing of any counterpart application that would be subject to eighteen-month publication. A nonpublication request is only appropriate if the applicant's intent at the time the nonpublication request is being filed is not to file a counterpart foreign or international application that would be subject to eighteen-month publication.

GRANT OF A US PATENT APPLICATION CAN BE POSTPONED FOR LEGITIMATE REASONS

Thanks to the highly flexible legal regime protecting patent rights in the US, the grant (and therefore publication) of the contents of a regular application can be legitimately postponed through the filing of requests for continued examination, continuing applications such as divisionals, continuations and continuations-in-part. It may make sense to file such continuing applications in order to ensure that you obtain the maximum scope of patent protection to which you are entitled. As mentioned, no such

---

1. under 37 CFR 1.213(a)(3)

request need be filed with the US provisional application because the US provisional never publishes in and of itself. Typically, for legitimate reasons, non-publication can be ensured for many years after the filing of the US regular application.

NOT WITHOUT ITS RISKS

Deliberate attempts to delay prosecution of your US patent application can be grounds a competitor might use to invalidate any patent which might be granted on your application.

If you filed a nonpublication request and later decide to file a counterpart foreign or international application in another country, or under a multilateral agreement, that requires eighteen-month publication, you must either: (1) rescind the nonpublication request before filing such foreign or international application; or (2) notify the Office of such filing no later than 45 days after the filing date of the counterpart foreign or international application. Failure to file the proper notice can place your US patent rights in jeopardy by automatic abandonment. Consequently, care must be taken to timely notice the USPTO of any publication-initiating filings.

In fact, other related patent applications may go abandoned because a notice of foreign or international filing was not filed for applications simply having related subject matter.

NO PRIOR USER DEFENSE

The Leahy-Smith America Invents Act of 2011 (AIA) provides a "prior use defense" to patent infringement. Specifically, a party may defend a patent infringement suit by establishing with clear and convincing evidence, that the patented subject matter was "commercially used" in the U.S. at least one year before the effective filing date of the claimed invention[1].

The new prior use defense provision applies to any patent issued after September 16, 2011. This defence is similar to what one finds in countries like Germany and Switzerland, in that the prior use had to take place a certain amount of time before the filing of the third party rights asserted against the defendant, and such rights are based on use in their country, not elsewhere. This means that all those practising secret processes outside of the US simply have no prior user defence. Therefore, failure to have timely reserved your patent rights in the US may leave you with no means to preserve the US market for your product, should a competitor assert patent rights against you there.

---

1. 35 U.S.C. § 273(a)(2)

CONCLUSION

To preserve your trade secret rights using methods difficult or impossible to reverse engineer from study of the final product and reserve significant patent rights at the same time, file a US patent application first (a provisional or non-provisional, the non-provisional being filed with a non-publication request), and make a reasonable effort to protect the content of the patent application and of your trade secret process. Given that the valid filing of a non-publication request is not possible once a foreign-to-the-US application has been filed, this requires that the priority applications for such technologies be filed in the US first. Doing so preserves all your options, maximises your US rights, and can offer significant strategic advantages should you receive a cease and desist letter from the owner of a US patent covering your secret process.

Unfortunately, preserving trade secret rights and patent rights in this manner is simply not possible once a European, Swiss, Japanese, Chinese or Korean patent application is filed. However, it may indeed be possible to file a PCT application on these secret processes on the very day that the US patent grants, making sure that the US patent has indeed published as granted before filing the foreign-to-the-US application (the US application is no longer a "patent application" under US law but a granted patent), in order to ensure that the US patent application is not constructively abandoned due to the filing of the PCT. Such a decision to file the PCT should be made after the filing of the original secret US application to ensure that there was no intent at the time of that filing to file "in another country, or under a multilateral international agreement, that requires publication of applications eighteen months after filing".

If you currently use IP counsel that has no US patent attorney on staff, we'd be happy to help train someone in your patent department to file US provisional applications directly, and so do away with the need of a US patent attorney for this first step. Such training would require only a few hours of their time yet give your company the ability to take the initial step in preserving your valuable rights, thereby helping you stay on equal footing with your US competition. If you do have important secret processes, then this tact should be given serious consideration. Feel free to contact us to discuss this option further.

John Moetteli is an International patent attorney (US and Swiss) and managing attorney of Da Vinci Partners LLC (www.DaVinciPartners.com), an IP firm based in Switzerland specialising in preparing and filing US and European patent applications for globally-minded clients. Besides his almost 28 years' total IP experience, John has more than 20 years' experience filing US patent applications directly from Europe.

He may be contacted via email at moetteli@davincipartners.com.

Although this chapter is subject to copyright © 2017, the author does not object to its reproduction and redistribution provided it is copied and distributed in its entirety including endnotes.

3.7 GRANTS AND INCENTIVES WITHIN THE UK

Olaf Swanzy, PNO Group

INTRODUCTION

Despite current political uncertainty surrounding the UK, numerous grant funding measures are available to strengthen UK industry by stimulating growth, employment and the development of state of the art technology, allowing the UK to compete effectively in the global market. There is a regular supply of varied UK grant funding programmes which are beneficial over loan or equity investment as they are non-repayable and do not require the dilution of shareholdings.

Thousands of different grant schemes, worth well over £5 billion each year, are available for UK companies to encourage, amongst other things, innovation and economic development.

In general, there are four types of public funding incentives available in the UK:

* Grants – where funding is secured ahead of the launch of a project;
* Soft loans – where loans are secured for projects that fall outside the parameters of normal business banking;
* Tax incentives – recognising advanced financial incentives for those with leading edge Research and Development (R&D) or capital programmes that are aligned with government strategy; and
* Awards – that retrospectively recognise industry excellence in many functional areas of business – usually a financial prize, which has the advantage of significant PR.

Outside of obvious fiscal benefits, for successful applicants the receipt of public funding can help achieve the following:

- Increase project leverage and project development;
- Improve company image – a successful grant application equates to being awarded a quality stamp from a grantor body;
- Gain a competitive advantage over others in your sector;
- Help raising additional 'harder finance' – comparable investment criteria; and
- Establish collaborative relationships – these are an ideal opportunity to work with academia, or other industrial organisations, including potential customers.

Funding is always used by governmental bodies or policy makers to address key policy issues and to stimulate first movers by reducing financial risk in that area. Such incentives are therefore always in line with Government policies and key drivers. It is essential that potential applicants consider this throughout their applications.

Although other forms of public funding are available, this article will focus predominantly on grants, as they represent the largest sums of money available for UK organisations.

MAIN GRANTS AND INCENTIVES IN THE UK

A key funding body that supports UK businesses is Innovate UK (formerly the Technology Strategy Board), a fully public funded executive body established in July 2007. Innovate UK is our national innovation agency, dedicated to driving innovation for wealth creation in the UK, so that technology-enabled businesses sustain or attain global significance. It gives extra support for Research and Development (R&D) to build partnerships between business, research and the Government to address major societal challenges and to run a wide range of knowledge exchange programmes to help innovation flourish. Funding is available for business and sometimes the academic base. Innovate UK aims to make the UK a global leader in innovation and a magnet for innovative businesses, where technology is applied rapidly, effectively and sustainably to create wealth and enhance quality of life. Further information can be found at https://www.gov.uk/government/organisations/innovate-uk.

Other sources of guidance and support for UK investment include: www.ukti.gov.uk, www.scottish-enterprise.com, www.wales.gov.uk and www.investni.com.

Generally, the range of funding programmes available for UK businesses is in one of three principal areas:

1. Research and Development;
2. Training and Education;
3. Capital Investment.

howman
solicitors

Build branding success

Legal advice on:

Branding

Business structures

Specialising in:

Fashion and media

Technology

Technology and office solutions

Asset finance

Contact
Gary McGonagle 07887 774656
gmg@howmansolicitors.co.uk
www.howmansolicitors.co.uk

17 Bolton Street,
Mayfair, London W1J 8BH
Tel: 020 7629 1801

mmercial Litigation - Corporate & Commercial - Commercial Property - Debt Recovery - Intellectual Property & Branding - Restructuring & Insolvency

INTEGRATED RESOURCES

We solve people problems

We help to grow your business

HR consultants working to release potential, improve performance and inspire growth.

Design HR Strategy
Our experts provide a complete spectrum of tools to guide your business towards success.

Boost Potential
We work with clients across a wide range of sectors to implement quantifiable change.

Consult In Partnership
Our team of consultants have a proven track record helping businesses manage people.

A one-stop shop across the entire HR lifecycle

Well established for over a decade, our team of top-quality consultants and interims can eliminate your HR headaches and help you to grow your business in the direction you want.

Compliance	Search	Performance
Reward	Coaching	Psychometrics

"Indispensable now to our business for recruitment."

Tim Clark
MD, iE Music

"The benefits of having an independent third party are enormous."

Richard Palmer
Head, St Christopher's School

"We can turn the HR tap on and off depending on our business needs."

Lindsay Melvin
CEO, CIPP

"I find their services very helpful in reducing my HR headaches."

Steve Barry
MD, Munro Group

Call us on
01223 640 605

Email us at
director@integratedresources.co.uk

Visit us at
integratedresources.co.uk

Inspire Improve Impact

Are you looking for R&D grant funding opportunities?

PNO Consultants

PNO Group is Europe's largest independent public funding advisory, employing more than 230 staff across 12 European countries. Supporting small businesses, large enterprise and universities across all research disciplines and sectors, PNO has extensive experience of all principal national and European funding programmes with a service model that covers the entire grant acquisition process. This includes the identification of grant funding opportunities to support project ideas and company activities, a comprehensive but flexible writing service that includes full writing support through to peer review guidance and support in the post award reporting process to ensure that the full draw down of a grant is achieved once an individual project is underway. PNO also offers an extensive range of project services including project management, technology intelligence, development of exploitation strategies and dissemination. With a client base of more than 15,000 organisations throughout Europe, PNO can also help with finding suitable project partners as well as identifying potential projects for our clients to join.

Our Services:

1. Initiate
   - Assessment of projects for grant potential
   - Linking with potential partners/ projects
   - Grant education and training
2. Apply
   - Bid writing support: Full support, co-writing and peer review
   - Development of project budget
   - Contract negotiation with Grantor Body
3. Comply
   - Advice on administrative requirements
   - Project management assistance
   - Support to ensure full draw down of grant
   - Managing project spend against project deliverables

Grant Schemes

There are a range of funding programmes available for UK businesses that aim to help take projects from research to as close to commercial viability as possible to support the development of new products, processes or services. Key national funding programmes include:

- **SMART -** a single applicant scheme open to all R&D performing UK SME's from any sector
- **Collaborative R&D** – supports industrial and research collaborations in strategically important areas of science, engineering and technology
- **Catalyst Programmes -** a form of research and development funding which focuses on a specific priority area. Current areas include Industrial Biotechnology, Energy, Agri-Tech and Biomedical
- **Small Business Research Initiative (SBRI) -** supports the engagement of the public sector with industry during the early stages of development across a range of industry sectors.

Key European R&D funding programmes include **H2020** and **Eureka Eurostars.**

Contact Us:
Olaf Swanzy, Director
Telephone: 07810 837479 **/** 0161 488 3488
Email: olaf.swanzy@pnoconsultants.com
Web: www.pnoconsultants.com

INNOVATION PLACE
Projects, networks and funding
Sign up to our free online innovation portal
www.innovationplace.eu

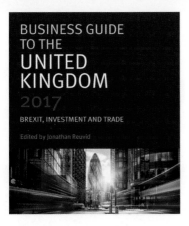

Published: 30 September 2017
ISBN (Paperback): 9781785079139
ISBN (Ebook): 9781785079122
Rights: World

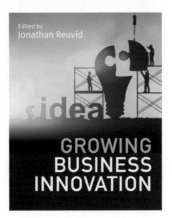

Published: 31st October 2017
ISBN (Paperback):
9781787198937 ISBN (Ebook):
9781787198920
Rights: World

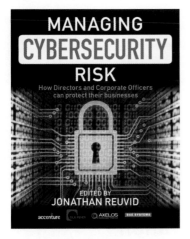

Published: 30 November 2016
ISBN (Paperback): 9781785079153
ISBN (Ebook): 9781785079146
Rights: World

Published: 30 November 2017
ISBN (Paperback): 9781787198913
ISBN (Ebook): 9781787198906
Rights: World

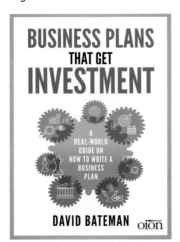

Published: 30 April 2016
ISBN (Paperback): 9781785079320
ISBN (Ebook): 9781785079337
Rights: World

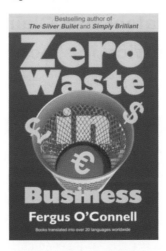

Published: 28 May 2011
ISBN (Paperback): 9781907756382
ISBN (Ebook): 9781908248169
Rights: World

1. RESEARCH & DEVELOPMENT

Innovation remains the key focus for most UK funding bodies. Many schemes are available for businesses irrespective of sector, company size and Technology Readiness Level (TRL). The core national funding programmes (summarised below), designed to support businesses in their R&D activities, offer up to 70% grant funding for projects up to £1million in cost.

For technical feasibility studies and industrial research, funding rates are:

- 70% for small businesses;
- 60% for medium-sized businesses; and
- 50% for large businesses.

For experimental development projects, funding rates are:

- 45% for small businesses;
- 35% for medium-sized businesses; and
- 25% for large businesses.

The Open Programme (Innovate UK)

The Open Programme supports UK-based enterprises with projects aiming to develop highly innovative processes, products or services that can potentially deliver significant business growth. Run biannually, the competition is open to all sectors and supports projects at different maturity levels (from initial ideas through to advanced prototype development). Suitable proposals must show:

- cutting-edge, disruptive or game-changing innovation leading to novel, new products, processes or services; and
- clear and anticipated growth impact leading to significant returns on investment.

Manufacturing and Materials (Innovate UK)

This competition, again deployed biannually, aims to stimulate and broaden innovation in advanced manufacturing and materials, to increase productivity, competitiveness and growth for UK businesses, especially SMEs. Suitable projects cover at least one of two areas:

- innovation in a manufacturing system, technology, process or business model; e.g. more flexible/efficient processes and those that allow greater customisation of products;
- innovation in materials development, properties, integration or reuse; e.g. materials for ease of manufacture or for targeted performance.

The project challenge should be in the manufacturing process or materials development rather than product innovation.

All projects must enable a step change in productivity and competitiveness for at least one UK SME. Applications are particularly welcome where the innovation can impact multiple sectors.

Emerging & Enabling Technologies (Innovate UK)

Another biannual competition that aims to identify and invest in new technologies coming from the research base that allow things to be done that were not previously possible (emerging) and the underpinning capabilities that improve existing industries (enabling). Proposals must show innovation in one of the key priority areas (see below), have outputs applicable to multiple markets or sectors, and improve business growth, productivity or export opportunities. Key priority areas include:

- Emerging technologies, e.g. novel single-layer (2D) materials, cutting-edge imaging technologies, etc;
- Digital, showing significant development in one or more of: machine learning and artificial intelligence (AI), cyber security, data analytics or 'big data', distributed ledger technology (e.g. blockchain), Internet of Things (IoT), immersive technology (e.g. virtual/augmented reality) and innovative services/ applications employing new forms of connectivity, including 5G;
- Enabling capabilities, such as electronics, sensors and photonics (ESP), robotics and autonomous systems, and creative industry technologies;
- Space applications with innovation in at least one of the following: satellite communications, satellite navigation, or earth observation and environmental monitoring services.

Health and Life Sciences (Innovate UK)

Aims to stimulate innovation in health and life sciences that significantly increases competitiveness and productivity with a focus on SMEs. This competition runs twice a year with key priority areas including:

- Agricultural productivity;
- Food quality and sustainability;
- Precision medicine;
- Advanced therapies;
- Medicines discovery and preclinical technologies;
- Biosciences.

Infrastructure Systems (Innovate UK)

Also biannual, this competition aims to stimulate innovation in infrastructure systems that provide critical services to our economy, environment and society, across multiple sectors, including energy, transport and city/urban systems. Solutions can include technologies such as communications, digital, electronics, novel materials and sensors. Projects must meet one of the specific competition themes:

- 'Smart' infrastructure: solutions bringing the digital and physical worlds together to improve whole-life cost and/or performance, resilience, security and/or sustainability.
- Energy systems: with the ability to flexibly match changing energy supply and demand;
- Nuclear fission;
- Offshore wind;
- Connected transport: innovations that encourage more efficient transport of people and goods across more than one mode of transport, addressing at least one of capacity, accessibility or sustainability.
- Urban living.

The Catalyst Programmes (Innovate UK)

Catalysts are run by Innovate UK in conjunction with Research Councils. A Catalyst is a form of R&D funding which focuses on a specific priority area, aiming to help take projects from research to as near to commercial viability as possible.

The Catalyst model supports projects in priority areas where UK research bases have a leading position and where there is clear commercial potential. Three levels of funding are usually available, varying according to how close a project is to commercialisation, with applicants able to join at any phase. Current Catalyst programmes include:

1. Biomedical Catalyst: open to both SMEs and academics looking to develop innovative solutions to healthcare challenges, either individually or together. Support will be available for projects arising from any sector or discipline that is aimed at addressing healthcare challenges. Depending on the maturity of the research, applications can be made to feasibility, primer, early or late stage awards (all with varying levels of funding available). Applications are accepted on a rolling basis with batch assessment dates typically every four to six months;
2. Agri-Tech Catalyst: supports businesses and academia in developing innovative solutions to challenges in the agri-tech sector. The Agri-Tech Catalyst will fund proposals relating to: primary crop and livestock/aquaculture production, non-food uses of arable crops, food security and nutrition challenges in international development or challenges in downstream food processing, provided the solution lies in primary production;

3. The Energy Catalyst supports businesses and research organisations, including academia, to respond to challenges across the energy sector. It will fund projects delivering innovative solutions that address all elements of the energy trilemma. The Energy Catalyst can fund projects from early concept stage through to precommercial technology validation.

Digital Health Technology Catalyst

This new competition launched recently to support UK organisations with innovative solutions to healthcare challenges that have digital technology at the core of development and delivery. These solutions must meet one or more of three key criteria: (i) improving patient outcomes, (ii) transforming healthcare delivery, and (iii) enabling more efficient delivery of healthcare. Collaboration is compulsory to access the higher funding levels of up to £1m available, with NHS collaboration particularly encourage. This competition covers a number of areas including informatics, data analytics, machine learning, artificial intelligence, Internet of Things (IoT), clinical decision-making support and digitally-enabled medical technologies.

Small Business Research Initiative (SBRI) (Innovate UK)

Supports the engagement of the public sector with industry during the early stages of development, supporting projects across a range of industry sectors through stages of feasibility and prototyping stages. Targeted towards SMEs and early stage businesses, it provides them with funding for the critical stages of product development, and gives them a fast-track and simplified process for working with the public sector. Typically, funding available is £100,000 for a feasibility stage project and £1 million for a development stage project.

Full information regarding all Innovate UK managed funding programmes can be found at https://www.gov.uk/apply-funding-innovation.

EUREKA Eurostars (joint programme between over 30 EUREKA member countries and the European Union)

Supports research-performing SMEs to develop market-orientated innovative products, processes and services in a transnational context, i.e. involving at least one other partner from another Eurostars country. The main programme criteria are:

- Consortium leader is an R&D performing SME from a Eurostars country which includes the UK;
- Eurostars R&D performing SMEs contribution is 50% or more of the total project cost;
- The consortium is well balanced (no single participant or country is responsible for >75%);
- Project duration is up to three years;

- Market introduction is within two years of the project's completion;
- Any topics considered (except military projects).

In the UK, only research-performing SMEs qualify for funding under Eurostars. UK academics/universities and large companies are welcome to participate in a Eurostars project, but will not be funded by Eurostars. The same rules do not apply for other member states so for any potential collaboration please check the country specific terms. Up to 60% of eligible costs will be supported to a maximum grant level of €360,000 per UK partner in a Eurostars project. Further information can be found at https://www.eurostars-eureka.eu/.

Horizon 2020 (H2020, European Commission) – European Funding
H2020 is the largest European funding programme for research and innovation, with nearly €80 billion of funding available between 2014 and 2020. Horizon 2020 is the financial instrument implementing the Innovation Union and a Europe 2020 flagship initiative aimed at securing Europe's global competitiveness. With emphasis on excellent science, industrial leadership and tackling societal challenges, Horizon 2020's goal is to ensure Europe produces world class science, removes barriers to innovation and makes it easier for the public and private sectors to work together in delivering innovation. H2020 is open to everyone and has a simpler structure than previous programmes – reducing red tape and time enabling participants to focus on what is important. This approach helps new projects to get off the ground quickly and achieve results faster. Full details can be found at http://ec.europa.eu/programmes/horizon2020/.

Please note that UK organisations can still participate in all H2020 programmes until the point that the UK leaves the EU. The potential to access support after this point will depend on the negotiation process.

2. TRAINING

Training or retraining of employees is of eminent importance to keep the workforce up to speed in rapidly changing environments. In some areas within the UK, these types of training courses may be eligible for public funding. The focus is on training for personnel below NVQ level 2 or minority groups such as asylum seekers.

3. CAPITAL INVESTMENT

Few CAPEX support programmes remain in the UK, with a greater number of smaller schemes available at a regional/local level, depending on location. For larger scale investments, the main national funding programme is the Regional Growth Fund (RGF). RGF is a £3.2 billion fund, helping companies throughout England to create jobs between now and the mid-2020s. The payment of RGF money is spread between

2011 and 2017. RGF supports projects and programmes that are using private sector investment to create economic growth and sustainable employment. The bid threshold (a minimum amount of funding that can be applied for) is £1million. Any support will be phased in line with expenditure and/or job creation/safeguarding. If considering an investment that will lead to job creation, it is worth speaking initially to your Local Enterprise Partnership about the availability of funding: https://www.gov.uk/government/policies/local-enterprise-partnerships-leps-and-enterprise-zones.

THE GRANT APPLICATION PROCESS

Thorough preparation is key to success for grant applications. Having a credible business plan, a clear commercial/marketing strategy alongside a quality management team, before an application is submitted is an essential part of the application process. Application processing timescales differ significantly between schemes, ranging from four weeks to nine months. For any potential applicants, it is important that project costs are not incurred before the grant application process is completed and grant agreements signed with the appropriate funding body.

Careful preparation of applications will increase the chances of success. However, there are no guarantees of an application succeeding, regardless of its merits, as most UK grants are discretionary, meaning that they are awarded on a case-by-case basis and, more commonly, on a competitive basis. It is therefore vitally important to ensure that the application is of the highest quality to raise it above the competition. It is also prudent to maximise the chances of success by developing a total grants strategy, rather than pinning everything on a single application.

SUPPORT IN THE GRANT ACQUISITION PROCESS

Finding the most appropriate grant and applying for funds can be prohibitive. Successful grant procurement requires dedicated time and resources that many companies do not possess internally. Therefore, some businesses choose to maximise funding opportunities by appointing external expertise. Support advice and providers can be found through bodies such as the UK Government Business Link network and the Enterprise Europe Network as well as specialist funding consultants. One such public funding advisory is the PNO Group – Europe's leading innovation funding advisors. Employing over 270 staff across the EU, PNO's core business is advising organisations across all industrial sectors, in the context of the UK and EU grant funding landscape, helping them to identify and secure funds through available schemes.

Their client base includes an extensive range of SMEs, universities and multinationals including companies such as HP, Microsoft, Philips, P&G and Solvay (www.pnoconsultants.com). You can contact PNO's UK office to discuss the eligibility of any project ideas for funding potential on 0161 488 3488.

CONCLUSION

Public funding can provide a valuable means of supporting companies to achieve their strategic goals. For R&D activities especially there are a range of schemes available to support projects across all stages of development from initial conception through to large scale demonstration.

With many businesses struggling to raise private and bank finance to advance their activities, it has never been more important to review all forms of funding available, including public funds. If you are serious about being a market leader in your field, grant funding is the ideal mechanism to help you to achieve your goal.

Part Four

Extended Thinking

4.1 DEVELOPING A PATENT PORTFOLIO STRATEGY FOR TECHNOLOGY START-UPS

Dr Mark Graves and Julia May, May Figures Ltd

When discussing the benefits of patents, most people immediately think of the potential for securing monopoly rights to commercialise their invention by obtaining a granted patent.

Whilst this is certainly the primary raison d'etre for the existence of patents, they also confer benefits in terms of licensing revenue and taxation saving (through the Patent Box tax relief scheme).

However, the main benefit in developing a patent portfolio for technology companies (at least in the initial stages of their development), is the use of the portfolio to increase the likelihood of attracting Venture Capital (VC) funding and to increase the valuation of the company's business used to determine the investment per equity share.

Surprisingly, despite this widely acknowledged benefit of patent portfolios enabling start-ups to acquire VC funding on favourable terms, the research in this field is limited, and that which does exist is not typically studied by professional advisers. Consequently, many early stage technology companies are receiving limited or perception-based advice on how to optimise their patent portfolio strategy specifically for VC fundraising.

INCREASING COMPETITION AMONGST EARLY STAGE TECHNOLOGY START-UPS SEEKING VC FUNDING

Whilst developing strategies to fully advise our clients, we have analysed data pertaining to technology start-up companies and VC funding across 195 different technology sectors with a more detailed analysis in 45 specific technology sectors. Table 1 shows a summary of the number of early stage technology start-up companies seeking VC investment and the number that have been successful in securing at least one round of VC funding for some of the technology sectors analysed.

Technology	Founded	Funded	% Funded
Medical Devices	6868	3748	55
Smart Grid	533	288	54
Energy Efficiency	1929	801	42
Wearable Technology	1677	606	36
Industrial Robotics	851	266	31
Blockchain Technology	730	225	31
Virtual Reality	1661	373	22
3D Printing	2000	343	17
Drones	1614	270	17

Table 1 Showing the number of technology start-ups in different technology sectors with the number and % that received at least one round of VC fundraising.

The validity of the statistics is affected by two key factors: (1) A number of founded companies would not have sought VC funding, having access to alternative sources of finance; (2) The number of founded companies will be underestimated, as many are very small or in stealth mode. Our experience leads us to conclude that the percentage chance of an early stage technology company obtaining VC funding will be materially less than that listed in Table 1.

Across the 45 technology sectors analysed in detail, the smallest number of start-ups in any one field was 308 for the field Robo-Advisors in Fintech. Given that this is a rapidly growing field (up from only 140 start-ups in February 2016), this is likely to increase rapidly in coming months and is predicted to reach the 500+ benchmark by close of 2017.

In conclusion, even with the limitations of the dataset, our own experience is that VCs are overwhelmed with a huge number of companies seeking investment in almost every emerging area of technology.

To deliver their ambitious growth plans VCs do not typically invest in niche sectors but generally prefer to invest in fields and markets where there is the potential for huge growth.

Given that in a typical technology sector of interest to a VC there are likely to be at least 500 other companies also seeking investment, how can a start-up increase their chances of being heard amongst the noise of companies seeking investment?

WHAT CAN A COMPANY DO TO INCREASE ITS CHANCES OF VC FUNDING?

A company seeking VC funding can be considered to be operating in a market categorised by asymmetric information – i.e. one side of the market (the company) has much better information than that on the other side (the investor).

The theory of asymmetric information in markets has attracted considerable economic interest since Akerlof, Spence and Stiglitz shared the 2001 Noble Prize for their work in this field.

We are not going to delve into the economic theory but rather look at practical steps a company can take to increase its chances, level and valuation in an investment round.

Previous research has analysed VC funding rounds and compared them against factors such as: education of the founders, prior career backgrounds of the founders, affiliations associated with the company, number and quality of patent pending applications, number and quality of granted patents etc. Essentially the work has focussed on what information can be passed from or inferred about the company to the investors in order to re-balance the information asymmetry and de-risk the investment from the investor's perspective.

Braum & Silverman at the University of Toronto analysed 204 VC investments in the Canadian biotech sector over a ten-year period, concluding that patents were the second highest factor in determining whether a company would get funding, after the status of the founding president. They determined that every standard deviation above the mean for patent applications resulted in an increase of C$753,361 of investment.

Hsu & Ziedonis at the Universities of Michigan & Pennsylvania analysed 370 US semiconductor start-ups through over 800 rounds of investment over a 25-year period. They concluded a doubling of patent application stock increased valuations at fundraising by 24%, beyond what would otherwise have been expected. They determined that the role of start-up affiliations with prominent partners had little impact on fundraising once patenting activities had been taken into account. They also determined that the signalling value of patents (i.e. acting as proxy indicators for the strength of technology and the management) was far greater in earlier financing rounds.

A more recent study led by Hoenen et al at Wageningen University also identified the role that patent applications have in increasing the level of funding at the first round of fundraising. However, they determined that patent applications and granted applications have no effect on the growth of venture capital funds raised during the second round of financing, in line with a reduction in information asymmetries once the initial investment has materialised. This is in line with the earlier work by Braum & Silverman who determined that companies with a standard deviation above the mean for granted patents only increased the funding value by C$118,625, a dramatic reduction compared with the increase of funding of C$753,361 for a standard deviation beyond the mean for patent applications.

In our opinion, for relevance in advising clients on patenting strategies for securing VC funding, the most interesting academic work in the field is the work of Haeussler et al at the University of Munich. They concluded (unsurprisingly in view of earlier research findings) that having at least one patent application reduces the time to first VC investment by 76%. However, more interestingly, they also determined that the final grant decision shows no additional effect on time to VC funding.

Indeed, opposition events (competitors opposing the application of a patent) were actually considered a positive signal by VCs; the conclusion being that VCs prefer to finance endeavours with high commercial potential where oppositions are more likely to occur and, potentially, that VCs are capable of determining high-quality patent applications long before the assessment is confirmed by citation or examination outcomes.

PRACTICAL IMPLICATIONS OF THE ACADEMIC RESEARCH

Given that company founders cannot practically change their educational or career backgrounds, one area over which they do have control, to improve their chances of securing VC investment, is in developing a high-quality patent portfolio.

The key take-away from the academic research is that in order to maximise the opportunities and valuation of VC funding, it is necessary to have as large and high-quality a patent application portfolio as possible **before the first round** of VC funding and that if resources are limited they should be focussed on widening the application portfolio even at the expense of delaying the time to grant for other pending applications.

Companies should also push for early searching of the results and not be overly concerned if the search news reveals lots of prior art in the field – indeed, they should see this as an opportunity to explain to an investor how their IP differs from the prior art.

Securing a large and high-quality patent portfolio is an expensive process. In many cases a technology start-up is faced with the agonising decision as to whether to divert funds from early prototype development / proof of concept trialling to developing their patent portfolio.

In many cases the company makes what seems a pragmatic decision to just file a single patent application and spend whatever funds are available on product development, with a view to securing first-round funding and then using the financial resources available after the first round of financing to fund the development of their patent portfolio.

Whilst understandable, the effect of such a strategy is that the resulting weak patent portfolio increases the time to fundraising and lowers the initial valuation so that founders end up giving away more equity than they could achieve with an alternative approach.

FUNDING OF PATENTS FOR EARLY STAGE TECHNOLOGY COMPANIES

Aware of the dilemma faced by early stage companies, a number of patent investment firms (not VC investors investing in equity) have devised schemes whereby they will help finance the initial patenting but in return they will hold the patents and license them back to the company for an on-going license fee.

One disadvantage with securing third party investment (and devolving ownership of the patents) is that this acts as a huge disincentive to future VC equity investors. Whilst all equity investors are hopeful that the company will grow and become a great success, a key part of their investment strategy is to minimise their losses and seek to salvage what they can from an investment which is unsuccessful.

Often when an early stage company fails the only assets of value are the patents and if these are owned by a third-party and licensed back to the company, then the investor does not have any scope for liquidating these in the event of company failure.

A POSSIBLE WAY OF FINANCING THE PATENT FUNDING GAP?

Whilst companies are developing their proof of concept prototypes, they are spending valuable resources (often initial seed funding from family and friends). In many cases, at the end of their financial year (assuming their cash position is not so perilous as to be unable to meet the going-concern requirement) they will be able to make an R&D Tax credit claim, recovering cash as a proportion of their historic R&D expenditure.

We ensure early stage companies recover their R&D Tax credit cash refund as soon as possible by finalising their accounts and filing a claim within days of their year-end.

It has been frustrating to observe a number of technology start-ups limit the development of their patent portfolio (and thus lose valuable traction to securing funding) due to limited financial resources, despite being aware that a recovery of cash from the R&D Tax credit scheme would arrive just a few months later.

EARLY STAGE PATENT SEED LOAN FUND

We have therefore launched our Early Stage Patent Seed Loan Fund. This provides an interest-free loan to companies to fund the development of their patent portfolio, with the loan being repaid through the subsequent R&D Tax credit claim. This avoids the need for companies to divert funds from the development of their early prototypes whilst being able to fund a high-quality patent portfolio, without conceding equity nor having to assign and re-license back the use of their patents.

We hope this exciting new offering will enable technology start-ups and their founders to secure a solid patent portfolio, succeed in raising funds at a higher valuation, retain a higher equity stake and ultimately benefit more from the risk and hard work required to build an early stage technology venture.

REFERENCES

Baum, J.C. and Silverman, B.S. Picking winners or building them? Alliance, intellectual and human capital as selection criteria in venture financing and performance of biotechnology startups. Journal of Business Venturing 19 (2004), 411-436.

Haeussler, C., Harhoff. D. and Muller, E. To be financed or not ... The role of patents for Venture Capital financing. Discussion Paper 2009-02 Munich School of Management, University of Munich.

Hoenen, S., Kolympiris, C., Schoenmakers, W. and Kalaitzandonakes, N. (2014), The diminishing signalling value of patents between early rounds of venture capital financing. Research Policy 43 (2014) 956-989.

Hsu, D. and Ziedonis, R. Patents as Quality Signals for Entrepreneurial Ventures. DRUID Summer Conference on Appropriability, Proximity, Routines and Innovation, Copenhagen, Denmark, June 18-20, 2007.

4.2 INNOVATION IN HR PRACTICE

Claire Vane, Integrated Resources Limited

Before talking about innovation in the workplace, from the aspect of human resources and the people that run, lead and operate in businesses, it is important to think about what innovation really is and a dictionary definition is not very helpful, i.e. "The action or process of innovating". It is about looking at new methods, new ideas and new products. Where the product is intangible, this still applies. Most learned articles explain that innovation is crucial to the success of any organisation and it implies making changes in something which is already established.

Those of us who are old enough, remember Tom Lehrer, a mathematics professor at Harvard, who used to make fun of anything that was too serious. He wrote a song called "Plagiarism" and it is extraordinary to think that we can always be original, by challenging the status quo and what has been established as a norm.

INNOVATION IN THE WORKPLACE

In business, adding value through innovation has to be looked at from the customer/client perspective. It is a combination of coming up with ideas but also the effect of implementing them. It is no good coming up with great ideas if they are not practical. There are internal customers for the HR function as well as external ones in the field of recruitment.

In order to innovate in HR, it is important to listen to the internal customer/client and properly utilise the existing resources that we have, including the ideas that all teams generate.

Innovation and challenging the status quo depend on certain factors. One is that individuals have to feel safe enough to come up with ideas, safe enough to cope with them being shot down and confident enough to make mistakes. It isn't enough to ask for ideas; we have to make it safe for the ideas to be suggested and then think about how we treat people who come up with these ideas.

HR is well known for its language of jargon and hyperbole. "World class" comes to mind; it was coined by ICI when it launched its (then) new logo in the 1980s. But sometimes hyperbole is appropriate. One of the things that matters in innovation is thinking big and not settling for mediocrity, whereas many HR departments have a reputation for maintaining the status quo and settling for the midpoint – abnormal is considered bad, i.e. it is away from the norm. Remuneration undoubtedly drives behaviour also and it is important to provide reward for ideas where these are worthy of application in practice.

So we need an environment that gives enough safety and security to innovate, that allows ideas to be generated and then to be applied, with an environment that rewards that innovation.

EFFECTIVE HR

I'm very keen on Stephen Covey's 'Seven Habits of Highly Effective People', but the one, to me, that stands out above all others is 'knowing what your outcome is'. If individuals don't understand what it is to innovate and have great ideas, they will not be able to deliver the outcome. They need to have an understanding of the outcome, the freedom to think creatively, the time to do so and the support to apply those ideas in practice. The outcome is critical and if there isn't a problem to solve or a challenge that requires change then innovation isn't worth the creative effort. The word 'innovation' itself is even seen in many organisations as slightly negative because it is not 'the usual way', so it is seen as risky.

Often, the HR function is seen as limiting and risk averse, particularly in the application of employment law, but good HR can foster an environment that thinks big and believes and rewards innovation. Without the HR function supporting innovation, then I don't believe that anything useful can be achieved. Pay and rations; hire, fire and inspire; match, hatch and dispatch, whatever the definitions you have of HR, it is now a function that requires rapid change and rapid response to changes within a business. Demand and technology have increased the desire for a response to that demand. HR must move with the pace of change and must be open to fostering risk.

If inequality exists and there is a lack of reward that would improve the welfare of staff, then the HR function is failing in its duty. However, for innovation to take place, we must go a step further, as a function through strategic planning, grooming of potential leaders, career development and maximising the impact of each individual in an organisation, not least of all through recruitment and then the maximisation of organisational capability.

Many organisations do not allow HR on the top table and, where the function is struggling for a seat on this table, then there is unlikely to be the kind of environment where HR can sit as a backcloth and encourage innovation.

STIMUATING INNOVATION

HR needs to be open-minded, accepting of risk and able to open up a variety of experience and opportunity to different kinds of people to make the perfect team out of imperfect individuals.

For innovation, we need leaders who are creative, adaptable and flexible. We have seen only too clearly on the social, political and economic stage, where there is an insufficient amount of these three ingredients, how an organisation or a country then finds itself in trouble.

Innovation is bound to be linked to engagement and if employees are not engaged, then there is no desire to innovate and without it there will be no catalyst for growth. We can innovate in relation to processes, products, labour costs, recruitment, leadership development and career and rewards. This is core to the HR function. We need to invite innovation and reward it, to utilise full capability and maximum collaboration.

The first part of any innovation programme is to ensure that the recruitment process is spot on and, secondly, that the environment fosters risk-taking, innovation and acceptance of failure, which is one of the steps towards innovation, and the differences of motivation between different generations and the positive effect of unconscious bias. These generational differences and any unconscious bias needs to be fully understood as the motivation and engagement of each generation is affected by many different and varying factors.

So if the HR function is to do its job properly when things are changing so fast in every aspect, there is a contradiction between ensuring stability for the hope of stable careers, with cooperation and collaboration and a certain amount of competition, and the need to take risks. We are thus faced with contradictions and, if HR is going to foster innovation, it needs to look at its recruitment processes, the creation of the right environment to allow for innovation and the compensation systems to reward it. Innovation needs to be at the centre of competency architecture.

Most HR problems centre around the inability to bring in the right people at the right time and to know for sure that they are the right people. Having made a mistake the error is often compounded by a failure to manage the mistake, to manage expectation and to articulate the truth. It is very important, therefore, that we invest the time and energy into establishing the right mechanisms for recruitment in the first place and by so doing we will avoid the basic issues in the workplace, such as mental and physical violence, aggression, anxiety attacks, performance issues, long term sickness, short term repeated patterns of absence, drug addiction and alcoholism. We will also positively seek out innovation.

DEFINING COMPETIVENESS

Competency architecture is the key to all good recruitment and retention. So, let us examine what we mean by this. Both in recruitment and retention, employers tend to talk in platitudes and generalisations about behaviour and refer to attitude and fit: "They're just not up to it…", "….their face doesn't fit…" and the employer automatically blames the employee. Whose responsibility is it for this misfit? It is usually the employer's.

What are competencies? They are skills, knowledge and attributes, and they divide into two groups – technical/hard/quantifiable competencies and non-technical/soft/behavioural competencies. With hard competencies it's quite easy to articulate what is required, e.g. contribution to the bottom line, the target revenue the individual is required to deliver, the labour turnover the leader is supposed to foster, the promotion policies that are to be managed with X number of successes, the reduction of absenteeism or the number of people made redundant and the consequent cost. These are all quantifiable/ hard competencies. They have numbers attached to them and many leaders think that these criteria are all that matters. So, what to do?

It is surprising how often not even these numerical measures are sufficiently articulated, especially at the recruitment stage. It is even less likely that the soft competencies have been clearly articulated; what behaviours do we actually want to see demonstrated in a role? So often these are not articulated, usually because the employers do not have the language to articulate what they mean. You can't describe an attitude, any more than you can seek a state of mind, e.g. happiness, but you can articulate the behaviours you want, even if it is by knowing what behaviours you don't want. Articulating soft or behavioural competencies is, in my view, the only way forward. And if we want innovation, it needs to be defined, articulated, sought and rewarded.

This is a cost effective way of avoiding unnecessary labour turnover, not to mention the subsequent cost of recruitment advertising, potential agency/consultancy fees, management time spent interviewing, lost opportunity cost for the time of the manager, induction, internal or external HR time and the cost of removing people through contractual and statutory payments, not to mention the lengthy procedures that are inherent in any statutory process that will stand up to legal scrutiny and avoid costly claims for unfair dismissal, discrimination and the like.

So, if we are going to retain the right people, then we must have a clear set of behavioural competencies that are promulgated company wide. These behavioural statements allow the interviewer to describe the behaviour required in post, and defining these is therefore the first building block to predicting whether a candidate can produce that behaviour in the future; if the individual has done it before then he/she will be likely to do it again. If we want innovation, we must articulate this and interview for it.

If you have a set of behavioural competencies then you are able to frame your interview questions around clear behaviours. Interviews often fail because there was insufficient preparation, insufficient articulation of competencies and therefore a consequent inability of interviewers to ask questions that provide the evidence for behaviours required in the role. Will the interviewers do this for innovation?

THE CANDIDATE'S VIEWPOINT

Flipping this approach on its head, let us examine the area of interviewing from the candidate's point of view. Candidates, especially good ones, become frustrated when they aren't given the opportunity to describe their successes and their successful behaviours, and it is not 'cheating' to encourage a candidate to articulate interview answers in a certain way. In our organisation, we use the acronym 'CEO' – Context, Event, Outcome and explain to the candidate that we are conducting competency-based/behavioural interviewing. The interviewer should be looking for examples of behaviour from the past that are required to be replicated in the future. So, we should be encouraging the candidate to give specific examples, not generalisations. It is easy to coach someone to make generalised intelligent comments and statements but when the candidate is vague, rather than write them off because the candidate is unable to demonstrate particular competencies, we coach the candidate to deliver specific examples within the framework of Context, Event, Outcome – "Give me an example of when you have........please frame your answers by giving us the Context, i.e. tell us a little bit about the background, explain your intervention, i.e. the Event, and tell us the Outcome", i.e. give the interviewee the chance to explain their success. If we seek innovation, then it is important to break innovation down into behaviours and seek evidence of those behaviours, i.e. give the interviewee the chance to explain their success.

When you recruit to a company you are making one of the most expensive decisions you will ever make, not to mention the additional costs if anything goes wrong. There are not only the direct annual salary and benefits costs, but also the overheads, the support functions that enabled the employment to take place, office accommodation, desk space/heat/light etc.

From the candidate's point of view too, it is important to know what behaviours you are looking for in an interview. If you, as the employer, don't know what those behaviours are, then there isn't a hope of assessing them through the interview process, nor a hope of the candidate providing competency-based examples to do him or herself justice. Once competencies are articulated, including those that are necessary for innovation, you can prepare your interview questions, both quantifiable and qualifiable, and encourage and prompt the candidate to deliver examples from their past where they have demonstrated the very behaviour you are looking for. Then you make good decisions based on data, the recruitment becomes successful and you also have a language at your disposal which you can then use for feedback in post and ultimately for rewarding the behaviours that you want – including innovation.

INTRODUCING INNOVATION INTO THE JOB SPECIFICATION

It is very rare that we see innovation described sufficiently in a job specification and this needs to be highlighted for innovation to be part of the defined competency architecture around which we are recruiting. This means we need to recruit risk takers, as well as those who don't take risk. This is very hard to assess unless one starts introducing psychometric profiling.

Having recruited the 'right' people, then it is necessary to make sure that the environment that has been managed and created in theory through recruitment, is actually delivered in practice. The buzz words need to be curious, open-minded, creative, ideas-driven, supportive and customer-focussed, because innovation is a driver of growth and any lack of leadership support, whether time or money, is going to contradict the statement that innovation is the name of the game in a particular organisation.

Not all employees should be engaged in innovation as some will be and should be risk averse. We don't want financial controllers who are risk-takers; we want them to produce accurate information. Innovation is not for everyone but certainly needs to be embedded in an organisation if it is going to happen. Constant examination and regurgitation of detail, which is appropriate in some roles, will stifle innovation in others. Again, there is a tension between the risk-takers and the non risk-takers and there is a place for both. We must also run psychometric profiles as a check to ensure that we are recruiting enough innovators and risk-takers and this requires the right kind of psychometric innovation.

THE DEMANDS OF INNOVATION

Innovation requires time as well as aggressive but constructive argument. Time has to be laid aside to solve problems when the pace of life is fast, but more time needs to be diarised for creativity and innovation. Innovation will have to be raised as a challenge by the HR function and fostered company-wide to allow that time to be laid aside. We all know the difficulty of constantly dealing with shrapnel which has to be done because it is urgent and is an important cog in the wheel, but it does not drive the business forward. HR departments can foster the driving of 'innovation' by having a working party with the purpose of running the business through innovation and training those who are prone to take risk to be secure in their risk taking.

So HR is vital to innovation through recruitment, the fostering of a risk-taking environment, a reward policy that encourages innovation and a competency architecture that defines it, in addition to the various tools of psychometrics to look for this quality.

4.3 ADAPTING DEFENCE TECHNOLOGY TO BUSINESS ENTERPRISE

Paddy Bradley, Swindon and Wiltshire Local Enterprise Partnership

On the 23 January 2017, the Government released for consultation its Green Paper, "Building our Industrial Strategy". The consultation sought responses on a range of issues including views on industrial sectors and the structures and processes necessary to enable the UK to be a competitive and successful global innovator and trader. In addition, areas of the country were asked to identify what made them special and distinctive and which would warrant investment to produce world class products and process performance. The 38 local enterprise partnerships in England singularly, and in some cases collaboratively, responded with enthusiasm to describe their versions of potential local industrial strategies.

In its response, the Swindon and Wiltshire Local Enterprise Partnership (LEP) identified the outstanding features of the area's economy and focussed on those future-oriented opportunities with excellent scope for expansion. Amongst those economically powerful combinations was the location of major defence technology expertise and the increasingly productive routes to commercially successful enterprises.

The Swindon and Wiltshire LEP is at the heart of a thriving defence science and security technology cluster in central southern England and is home to a range of leading companies including QinetiQ, Porton Biopharma, and Chemring Countermeasures, and also major research led organisations such as Defence Science and Technology Laboratory (DSTL) and Public Health England (PHE). Wiltshire is home to a quarter of the British Army and has major assets in defence and security technologies, including the Chemical Biological and Radiological research and development capability at Porton and through DSTL and the Ministry of Defence (MoD) site at Lyneham, which hosts the Defence College of Technical Training (DCTT), which includes the Defence

School of Electronic and Mechanical Engineering. The MoD site at Boscombe Down is an established centre of excellence for aerospace defence and security technology, hosting 2000+ staff.

DSTL manages £380 million per annum of UK Government funding on science and technology projects. The new Porton Science Park, forming part of a wider campus, is a unique opportunity offering a state of the art 10 hectare defence and security research and development facility. Porton carries out research to ensure that the UK's military and wider public benefit from the latest technical and scientific developments. The UK Government is investing £115 million in developing new facilities at Porton, which will bring 650 new jobs to the area. Porton has close links to PHE, world leaders in high quality microbiological research and testing, and DSTL, specialising in development of effective countermeasures against chemical and biological events, and Porton Biopharma Limited, established in 2015 to commercialise research outputs into pharmaceutical development and manufacturing. Recently, Boeing Defence UK (BDUK) selected Boscombe Down as its preferred choice for its new UK headquarters, delivering 1,500 jobs and a multi-million pound investment. It will work with QinetiQ on defence-related aerospace activity. The LEP sees this as the first step in the development of a commercial defence technology site in the south of Wiltshire.

Swindon and Wiltshire is already home to a wide range of world class advanced engineering companies, including Honda, which has recently invested £250m in its plant at Swindon and has employment levels back above pre-crash numbers. Dyson, one of the UK's leading high technology engineering companies and the country's largest investor in robotics, is creating a new campus at the Hullavington Airfield, near Malmesbury, increasing its footprint in the UK by ten-fold. This is in addition to its £560m commitment to its existing campus at Malmesbury and is a significant vote of confidence in the Swindon and Wiltshire area and the UK. Dyson already employs 3,500 people in the UK, half of whom are scientists and engineers.

Swindon and Wiltshire has a range of education and skills facilities to support the expansion of the advanced engineering sector, including: the Defence School of Electronic and Mechanical Engineering at Lyneham; QinetiQ Apprentice Training School at Boscombe Down; the Empire Test Pilots School also at Boscombe Down and apprenticeship opportunities at DSTL at Porton.

The combination of these assets and their supply chains lays a firm foundation for additional skills development in defence engineering and aerospace across central southern England. This will require teaching and research work across a range of colleges and universities and will support other private sector businesses operating in the advanced manufacturing and aerospace sectors. In the future, these assets will be enhanced by the co-location of defence and public-private defence-related activity as an unique feature of Swindon and Wiltshire, which has the potential to transform not only the local economy but that of neighbouring areas, linking activity in Swindon and Wiltshire with Bristol and Bournemouth and beyond. However, the advanced engineering workforce at higher levels is mobile. This means that the challenge to any area with this type of sector clustering is to cultivate home grown talent to deliver the technical and higher level skills needed to support accelerated developments in this field.

AUTONOMOUS UNMANNED VEHICLES

The development of autonomous vehicles technologies has the potential to revolutionise logistics and distribution, from the use of drones through to innovation in agri-tech and energy applications. Defence industry-related activity in this area will be the catalyst for growth and new technology development in this field in Swindon and Wiltshire and relates well to the foci of the Industrial Strategy Challenge Fund. The opportunity is there to transform the technology of military drones into commercial and public sector applications.

Defence Technology
The defence industry has led much of the development of unmanned autonomous vehicles on land, sea and in the air. Growth of technological developments and applications are continuing to expand at a rapid rate. IHS Markit, a business providing critical information, analytics and solutions for the major industries and markets that drive economies worldwide, commented in January 2017 that over the next 10 years sales of unmanned military aerial vehicles would exceed $82 billion globally, involving 63,000 new vehicles. Many of the unmanned ground vehicles, such as those used in combatting the threat of improvised explosive devices, were delivered more than a decade ago. The IHS forecast is for sales of circa 30,000 vehicles up to 2025, largely to replace existing stock with technologically more advanced applications. Between 2016 and 2025, approximately $4.9 billion will be spent on unmanned ground vehicles globally. Unmanned sea vehicles have been used for decades for mine hunting and exploration, but are still at a relatively early stage of development. The growth in sales for unmanned sea vehicles will be $900m by 2025, compared to the growth of $800m for unmanned ground vehicles. Globally, sales of unmanned sea vehicles will reach $6.5 billion by 2025. The overall market for military unmanned vehicles is huge and growing, accounting for sales close to $100 billion over the next decade.

Figure 1 Military Drone

Commercial development

Albeit at a much earlier stage of development and with a smaller market, we are beginning to see applications of drone technology within the private and public sector. Dorset Police recently announced the creation of a high-tech drone unit and in so doing are amongst the first police forces to deploy such technology through a dedicated unit. Through collaborative research, the forces across Dorset, Devon and Cornwall began exploring drone use in November 2015. The drones will be used in missing person searches and crime scene photography as well as major traffic collisions. They will also track along the 600 miles of the Dorset coastline to help combat wildlife crime. They will provide operational support across Dorset, Devon and Cornwall. Drones can reach sites of emergencies quicker than road vehicles and are already operating to send aerial video to emergency planning teams. Delivery of first aid equipment and drugs by drones will also enhance survival chances of victims of emergencies.

Private use of drones has caused a lot of concern due to irresponsible and highly dangerous flying of drones near airports and in planes' flight paths. The government's intention to introduce licensing of drone flying is welcomed. Thankfully, there are already businesses that have taken a responsible route to exploitation of drone technology and are registered with the Civil Aviation Authority. Commercial aerial photography is an obvious development, from initial military use to spy on forces and activity from a safe height and in a largely undetectable unmanned vehicle. It provides a cheaper alternative to photography from fixed-wing aircraft or helicopters, whose technology also emerged from military use. For example, in the earlier example of Dorset police's use of drones, they are deploying unmanned vehicles costing in the region of £1,300 to £2,000. Thermal cameras for drone application cost £6,000 and a zoom camera £800. Helicopters cost the Police about £800 per hour. The numbers do add up for drone use and the equipment costs will only reduce as deployment increases.

Drones enable a range of applications as the size and manoeuvrability of the vehicle enable it to get close in and take detailed pictures of small features. This capability lends itself well to inspections of buildings and surveying of sites. It is also a boon to people looking for dramatic views to market products, ideas or to see the impact of a large infrastructure improvement such as a major road or rail-bridge or the regeneration of a city centre site.

Drone technology is also helping to open up the world of planning and development of new and heritage buildings. Using the ability of cameras on drones and application software to render levels of accuracy to millimetres, potential clients and members of the public can see what a building looks like now in its current setting, what the views are like from the building and how light and shadow play out during a day. The new design can be incorporated into the aerial photography to show the proposed updated arrangement and what will change and what will remain the same. Most people find it difficult to translate a two dimensional drawing into a three-dimensional view in their mind. We can already translate a drawing into a three dimensional image on a computer screen and with high-resolution, it is already a much improved product. The merging with actual aerial photography takes the proposition further. It has the great potential to make better informed decisions about building design and planning decisions and can really make public consultation worthwhile and widely accessible.

Figure 2 Commercial Drone

Use in Agriculture

There is exciting research being carried out by Harpur Adams University, in collaboration with Precision Decision Ltd, into an alternative approach to robot farming. They have called the project the "*Hands Free Hectare*"[1]. The aim is to carry out a full farming cycle from preparation of the land, planting, maintenance and harvesting without any human setting foot on the field. The site will be developed by unmanned ground vehicles and overflying drones controlled by humans using application software. It is the case that a modern farm tractor can already use GPS to decide where, for example, to deposit pesticides and fertilisers and how much in each case. Making the tractors fully autonomous is the next logical step. However, the Harpur Adams study is looking at this issue from a different viewpoint. Existing tractors are heavy, which means they can crush and compact the soil, which reduces yield and their size limits their accuracy when spraying the expensive chemicals. The Harpur Adams team is using prototypes of smaller, lighter and cheaper vehicles which will leave the soil in good condition and can deploy chemicals with pinpoint accuracy. The debate is yet to be decided as to whether farming in the future will be dominated by a few large, self-driving tractors or a fleet of smaller robot machines. It is likely the decision will be different on the plains of the USA and East Anglia in this country compared with more compact farms elsewhere in the UK.

Elsewhere in the world, developments march on – with minimum human intervention. Wine makers, despite their industry's reputation for tradition, have been using drones for years to inspect crops and assess the health of the soil. Now, as is often the case, the existence of a problem has created a novel solution. In Burgundy, the shortage of labour to work the vines led to the invention by Christophe Millot of a four wheel vine trimming robot, which learns as it goes and powered by solar panels can operate for between 10 and 12 hours without a charge. In Japan, by 2018, there will be a farm producing 30,000 lettuces a day, which after seeding, have been entirely tended by robots. The impact on workforces is profound. The International Labour Organization estimates that between 1950 and 2010, the proportion of agricultural labourers as a percentage of the workforce declined from 35% to 4.2%. The application of unmanned vehicles will speed up this reduction, with the sector requiring fewer, but more highly skilled, operators.

The commercial reason for this interest in the market for unmanned agricultural vehicles is one of the most developed outside the military. One report, by US firm WinterGreen Research, forecasts that the market will grow from $817m in 2013 to $16.3bn by 2020. But investment bank Goldman Sachs is far more bullish, predicting a $240bn market over the next five years. Manufacturers including John Deere, CNH Industrial and AGCO are all fighting to corner the market in driverless tractors. This places the budget in the agricultural sector on unmanned autonomous vehicles at more than twice the level of the military.

---

1. BBC News Report 13 December 2016

Ploughshare

The story of transforming defence technology into commercial business enterprises would not be complete without a mention of Ploughshare. This business was established in 2005 as DSTL's Technology Transfer Office to actively pursue the commercialisation of publicly funded research for the benefit of all, whilst supporting DSTL's obligations to the MOD. It does this through a mixture of licence agreements and the establishment of spin-out companies. The process of releasing the economic potential of public sector research establishments is often complex and lengthy with a high degree of uncertainty. The research at places like DSTL may be at quite a fundamental level and many steps away from commercial exploitation. Despite these difficulties, since its inception, Ploughshare has commercialised more than 120 technologies and launched twelve spin-out companies, principally for civilian applications. It anticipates that by 2018, its licence agreements will have created more than 500 high-value jobs, generated exports to the value of £223m and attracted £130m of external investment.

We are now seeing the civilian benefits of years of military research and development. Markets are now well established and surpassing known military spend and economics drives further innovation. We are witnessing cross-over and integration of systems as different sector specialists share ideas and learn from each other. The UK is in a position to consign to the dustbin the oft-used adage that we are not good at converting research into commercial applications. From defence technologies, business enterprises are thriving.

4.4 EMBRACING TECH TRANSFORMS A BUSINESS PRACTICE

Sumit Agarwal, DNS Accountants

A PERSONAL JOURNEY

I started my own practice, DNS Accountants, from my bedroom in 2005. It started off as something more traditional than it is now, but I always wanted to grow it into a small firm to be proud of. Within two years, I had an office and two staff; a huge milestone for me. But my practice didn't really take off until I started thinking about technology.

Rather than using an existing software package to modernise my practice, I decided to create my own. I wanted us to spend less time on bookkeeping and compliance, and more on adding value and setting ourselves up to grow. The results were beyond expectations.

We started using our own cloud software in 2010. By 2013, our productivity significantly increased, client retention and referrals went up, and year-on-year profits started soaring. My staff were happier too, having ditched their more tedious tasks in favour of more engaging advisory work. We had also expanded our business through acquisitions in 2012, which brought in a whole new client base.

At the end of that three-year period, DNS Accountants won Online Accountant of the Year at the British Accountancy Awards. It was an extremely proud moment, and we couldn't have done it without technology.

Any business meets with conflict when trying to manage all the tasks involved in running a profitable company efficiently and with integrity. If you ask most business owners what their number one priority is, it would probably be: provide the best possible service. In reality, it's not always that simple.

Company law, the market, the competition, compliance, shareholders; all of these things take time away from improving your service and growing your client base.

What technology provides is a cost-effective way to basically outsource these basic business functions, freeing you up to plan ahead, upskill your staff and provide better advice to your clients.

It also speeds up these processes, allowing you and your practice to be more agile and able to react quickly if your client has a problem. This is incredibly valuable to our clients. Suddenly your services are a lot more valuable.

For me, it's very important that the tech I use delivers everything I need from a practice management perspective. You don't want to be worrying about data security, for example, or having experienced, qualified accountants wasting time on admin. Make a list of all the tasks you want to get off your plate, and source software and technology that both takes away the tedious tasks and gives you the tools and information to build on your client services.

Cloud software is allowing accounting practices to do more and more for their clients without costing them the earth. It may sound like strong words, but it is genuinely revolutionary. Embracing technology in my practice changed my life. It could change yours, too.

HOW FIRMS CAN MAKE A CHANGE

Let's look at the typical challenges for accountancy practices at the moment. We surveyed firms about the biggest issues they currently face. Three major hurdles emerged as common problems for firms. Attracting and retaining clients is far and away the biggest, with 70 per cent of respondents listing it as a major problem. Controlling costs is the next highest at 37 per cent. Third is the pressure to ensure the firm makes efficient use of technology (33 per cent).

Although it comes third on the list for most firms, getting the technology right is critical in order to tackle the first two issues. To be competitive in today's world, a firm needs to be a digital practice.

Marketing

Take marketing. Most firms now have a website, but most of them would also agree that their website is not a great sales tool. Better lead generation means getting the digital marketing strategy right through (to name only a few channels) better search engine optimisation (SEO), blogs, Twitter and other social media. Most firms don't do any of this. Most don't even measure the success of what they are doing; only 38 per cent of respondents did any kind of measurement of their marketing activities.

IT, in the form of customer relationship management (CRM) software, can also handle lead management and monitor the success of your marketing effort, so you can see what worked and what did not.

Increasing revenue helps to make your practice profitable, but reducing costs and increasing productivity will have an even more direct impact on your bottom line.

Outsourcing

One important approach to consider is outsourcing. That doesn't have to mean outsourcing to (say) India; it could mean outsourcing accounts work to your local bookkeeper. The point is that you can concentrate on where you can best add value – advising the client – rather than be tied up with bookkeeping or completing tax returns.

Outsourcing also means that your practice can grow without adding significantly to costs such as office space or human resources.

Meanwhile, with the right IT, the firm can reduce manual processes, automate repetitive tasks, cut down on duplication and reduce the risk (and cost) of errors. Better IT also means you can have access to critical information in real time. The keywords are "efficiency" and "integration". If you get this right, you can increase your efficiency and productivity by at least 20 per cent. That's a potential to raise an additional 20 per cent of revenue without increasing costs in any significant way. It could make a real difference to your bottom line.

Exploiting the Cloud

Cloud-based solutions are increasingly central to this digital strategy. There's an analogy with the mobile phone sector – mobiles initially had a limited capacity, and could only be used for making calls or sending text messages. Today, of course, they do so much more.

Similarly, the cloud was originally, from the accountant's point of view, useful for online bookkeeping. Cloud-based software can do much more than that now, and an online bookkeeping service is the bare minimum you can offer your clients. Our aim, with Nomisma Solution, is to deliver an end-to-end package for accountancy practices. With current modules including Bookkeeping, Payroll, Accounts Production, Corporation Tax and Self-Assessment, our software is already well on its way to being the premier software to meet all of your compliance needs. Later in 2017 our practice CRM and Company Secretarial modules are set to be released.

Small business CRM systems

The introduction of small business CRM systems allows organisations to start integrating disconnected processes while managing the complete business cycle. Small businesses are looking for enhanced flexibility and top-notch productivity from CRM software that is easy to operate, yet providing comprehensive information. CRM software assists small businesses to achieve their goals by improving operational agility through automation, management of business processes and efficient and effective workflow management.

CRM systems help to reorganise current working styles. Tools are able to set a baseline of how things should be. You can then analyse the data to show how the business process should be restructured.

USING TECH TO BETTER UNDERSTAND YOUR CLIENTS

The Nomisma approach is: "One practice, one software". This way, integration is easier and you can save time and money. Updating information is more seamless and it will be easier to get a real-time view of the whole practice.

Business mobility is not a different business process. Rather, it is an addition to the modern working environment. As for any business process, a bit of focus and structure can take the business a long way.

Internal and external business processes can become complex, because they are beyond the scope of some CRM systems present in the market. These processes are not very difficult to manage; they just require the correct CRM system that best integrates all the business processes.

The last point, and possibly the most important, is that nothing can work without the right people in place. If your team isn't on the same wavelength it will be tough – many people are inclined to resist change. You need people around you who are happy to embrace it.

The profession is changing – and accountants are becoming more business-savvy. Young accountants are especially open to new ways of marketing, for example.

It is high time that firms revolutionise their working style and take a step towards a new and more productive way of working, based on clever use of technology, analysis and application of data, and the right people, with the right mix of skills. There are noteworthy strategic advantages and insights available thanks to today's technology, but it all boils down to choosing the right system around which to build the firm.

If firms can see the benefits of the technology available and implement and integrate it in the right way, I can see good days ahead for accountancy.

4.5 SCOTLAND'S INNOVATION JOURNEY

Jim Watson, Senior Director of Innovation and Enterprise at Scottish Enterprise

Over the last three years Scotland has seen significant growth in its innovation activity. More companies are innovating, new investments have been made, new jobs have been created and Scotland is now the most popular location for research and development (R&D) foreign direct investment. That's because in 2014 we launched our Refreshed Innovation Strategy.

Whilst Scotland is recognised globally for it strengths in invention – penicillin, telephone, television, vacuum flask and Dolly the Sheep – its business innovation performance remains stubbornly weak. Too few companies innovate and those that do don't create sufficient turnover and export growth to shift Scotland's globally competitive position. As the latest Scottish business expenditure in R&D (BERD) figures highlight, the country has historically underperformed compared to the rest of the UK and EU and remains around half of the UK figure (1.09% of GDP) and a third of the EU 28 average (1.22% of GDP).

SCOTLAND'S AMBITION

As Scotland's main economic development agency, addressing this imbalance has been a priority for us. We want to transform Scotland's innovation performance to equal the best performing nations by 2023, which in turn will lay the foundations for significant growth in Scotland's export and productivity performance.

Evidence shows it's those countries topping the OECD competitiveness rankings (Finland, Israel and Sweden) which have high levels of innovative business and are more likely to export successfully and generate growth, when compared to non-innovating countries.

To support innovation, however, we need to help companies understand what it means for them. For example, it is no longer just a few high tech manufacturing companies which are investing in R&D, technology and product development. Innovation is now ubiquitous, happening in every country and in all sectors.

OUR VISION

That's what our refreshed strategy set out to achieve – to grow a vibrant, innovative country driven by a company base which is using technology and know-how to innovate and create new products and services that are tailored for changing international markets. By 2023, we want to see:

- a better performing company base that is investing more in innovation and reaping the benefits in enhanced international sales;
- Scotland's standing increased as an innovation destination, resulting in the attraction and retention of more talent and foreign direct investment;
- more economic impact generated from the exploitation of academic research by Scottish companies; and
- growth in BERD and innovation activity to the OECD top performers.

The vision is for Scotland to be in the OECD's top quartile for innovation performance by 2023. To do this we will need 5,000 more companies to become innovators and Scotland's business expenditure on R&D to increase by £650 million, nearly double the 2014 figure.

Our vision is ambitious and involves a 'step change' in our innovation performance as well as a transformational shift in the ambitions of Scottish companies and sectors, but the rewards will be invaluable, some of which are already being realised.

DOING THINGS DIFFERENTLY

The opportunity to innovate exists in all companies and across all sectors. It is about trying new things, doing things differently and better. It's about exploring new services, processes, designs, business models, products, technologies and changing how resources are used.

We already work with many innovative companies and sectors and the impacts of our activities on performance and competitiveness are good at those individual levels, but to fully achieve our innovation ambition, we need to do so much more. Our refreshed approach refocused our innovation support, addressing the fundamentals which were holding back Scotland's innovation performance. Our approach now:

- emphasises the need for innovation in all companies and sectors;
- simplifies our innovation offer to companies and sectors;
- adopts a more targeted approach focused on innovation driven growth and international sales;
- introduces open, market pull approaches;
- places greater emphasis on the role of people and workplace participation in innovation success;
- recognises the need for greater collaboration and partnership across private, public and academic organisations.

Market demand driven innovation

Encouraging companies and public organisations to look outside their own organisation for solutions to their innovation challenges helps to overcome two fundamental issues holding back innovation – the lack of demand for new and different products and services and that all important first customer.

Our Open Innovation approach involves us working closely with businesses and the public sector to help identify innovation challenges which small to medium sized enterprises (SMEs) can respond to with new and innovative ideas.

This approach means companies and the public sector are no longer constrained to the limits of internal resources or knowledge to address the challenges they face. Instead, they are open to solutions from outwith their organisation, an approach which helps share the risk and more importantly the rewards as well as encouraging stronger collaboration between supply chain companies and larger multi-national organisations.

In June 2014, we saw the signing of our first strategic agreement with Norwegian headquartered oil and gas company, Statoil ASA, to deliver this new innovative approach. By March 2015, the first project was announced by Raptor Oil Ltd to deliver a £1.5 million R&D project to help boost performance in the oil and gas sector.

Since then, we're now actively working with 13 businesses and public sector organisations to bring a series of open innovation challenges to Scotland's SME community. Small businesses will be given the opportunity to do business with large corporations – from NHS Scotland, Doosan Babcock, Stena Line to Scottish Power Networks – helping them to tackle issues facing their businesses.

We will also launch our "Can Do Innovation Challenge Fund" in November, which will further enhance our market driven offering by focussing on public sector demands where Scottish company and sector capabilities have strength, depth and ability to compete globally.

Scotland is fast becoming a hub for market driven open innovation organisations looking for new solutions from a wide SME base and Scottish Enterprise's Open Innovation Challenge Portal is becoming the "go to" brokerage site for innovative SMEs looking to provide solutions and global corporates and public organisations that need new service and solution providers. It already has considerable traffic, with

34,000 twitter followers, 24,000 LinkedIn members, 28,000 newsletter subscribers and 5000 monthly visits to the webpage.

DELIVERING MORE INTEGRATED SUPPORT TO EXISTING INNOVATORS

As we work towards meeting our ambitious targets, collaborating with companies already investing in innovation will be important.

We want to help these companies to increase their national and international sales and generate even stronger growth by improving their capacity to create globally competitive products and services.

Through our account management system, which involves us working intensively with ambitious Scottish companies to maximise their growth potential, we are uniquely positioned to provide this service. Our in-house expertise to help companies establish the right mix of international, investment and company growth support at an early stage is also advantageous.

Take Alexander Dennis Ltd (ADL), for example. Our R&D and innovation support to ADL to help redesign its bus platform has helped to make it one of only 13 Scottish companies with more than £1 billion in revenues and one of only five manufacturers (data from February 2017 Insider rankings). This illustrates the economic power of innovation investment.

SUPPORTING SCOTLAND'S SECTOR CAPABILITIES

Our focus on sector capability aims to build on our competitive strengths using innovation to stay ahead of the game. It's about looking forward to the markets of tomorrow and aligning our talent and capability to be leaders in new markets. The approach requires industry, public agencies and academia to work together to identify the challenges, design the solutions and to co-own the response.

Take oil and gas for example. Over many years technologies developed in Scotland have revolutionised the worldwide oil and gas industry. But as the sector responds to the effects of the downturn, it must continue to invest in innovation to capitalise on these skills and maximise opportunities both at home and overseas.

In June 2017 Scottish Enterprise indicated it had provided £15.9m to oil and gas innovation projects valued at £43 million to develop and maintain companies' global competitiveness. Companies are using the funds for a range of innovation projects, including the development of new technology to improve efficiency and to contribute to a new subsea Centre of Excellence.

Scotland's global reputation as a hub for oil and gas skills can catalyse international investments. That is why Scottish Enterprise and The Nippon Foundation signed a Memorandum of Understanding (MOU), which will see both organisations work together to invest in R&D projects around subsea technology challenges.

Scotland currently accounts for around 14 per cent of the £50 billion global subsea market, comprising approximately 370 companies generating an estimated turnover of £7.5 billion annually. It has the largest concentration of subsea engineering in the world.

With the right investment and support the sector is perfectly placed to capture an even bigger slice of this market. Earlier this year (2017) we launched a Subsea Engineering Action Plan, in partnership with Scottish Development International, the Scottish Government's international arm, and supported by key partners and stakeholders such as Subsea UK, to help maximise the opportunities for Scotland.

Increasing business innovation, research and testing infrastructure will be a key factor of the action plan's success to support high levels of subsea related investment in the future. Momentum is gathering with a £4.9 million grant incentivising East Kilbride based NEL and Munich-based parent company, TÜV SÜD Limited, to invest £16 million to develop a new centre of excellence for subsea development.[1]

DEVELOPING A CULTURE OF WORKPLACE INNOVATION

Underpinning our vision for 2023 is the need to engage more of the workforce in the innovation journey. Workplace innovation is about introducing new ways of working that can help your business become agile, resilient and efficient, whilst creating a culture where employees' ideas are valued and they feel supported to reach their potential. There are three areas where workplace innovation can make a real difference: your people, your business practices and your workspace.

Since the launch of our Workplace Innovation Service in 2016 we have engaged with over 200 companies to raise awareness and provide tools and techniques. For instance, supported by their Workplace Innovation Specialist, Resources Director John Bain at Berwickshire Housing Association identified a need for fundamental change:

"*After working tirelessly on team development for three years, we realised that what we really wanted and needed was an innovative culture,*" says John. "*We now have people at all levels who feel more empowered, and around half of our team is involved in an innovation project.*" John elaborates: "*Although it's still in its early stages, we're already seeing real benefits from our workplace innovation projects. This builds on our breakthrough ideas, including installing solar panels on 750 homes during 2015 and 2016. That scheme not only brought down energy costs for our tenants, it also helped us to meet our environmental and commercial targets.*"

Other businesses, such as copywriters and investment specialist Copylab, are leading the way in workplace innovation. Founder and CEO, Ross Hunter explains: "*In some ways, Copylab has a very traditional business model but an innovative approach*

1. https://www.tuv-sud.co.uk/nel/tuev-sued-nel-news/unique-gbp16m-centre-of-excellence-to-cement-scotland-as-subsea-global-leader

to managing the business is contributing to our global successes." As well as being committed to ongoing training and development, Copylab operate a flexible working policy and hold a quarterly staff meet-up in Glasgow, an important opportunity for employees to share ideas and have face-to-face interaction.

Our Workplace Innovation service includes a number of change management programmes such as developing 'High Performing Participative Teams' and thought leadership master classes. In conjunction with partners such as the Business Gateway we have also piloted local workshops and funding for bespoke workplace innovation projects.

Scotland is increasingly being seen as a champion for Fair Work and Inclusive Growth and we will continue to work closely with partners such as Strathclyde University's Scottish Centre for Employment Research, Skills Development Scotland and the Fair Work Commission to share knowledge and experience in order to evolve our Workplace Innovation service.

RESEARCH AND DEVELOPMENT

Since the launch of our Refreshed Innovation Strategy in 2014, how and who we support with R&D activity has changed and this new approach has led to a significant increase in company activity, BERD Investment and Scotland's innovation performance. The following provides a flavour of our new approach:

- Manufacturing sector: we have targeted our manufacturing companies (which account for nearly 70 per cent of our R&D projects) and worked alongside them to bring larger projects to market sooner and hence increase overall productivity as well as augmenting expenditure in the Scottish supply chain.
- Increased focus on foreign direct investment: there was a tactical move to use R&D funding opportunities to attract new inward investors and establish Scotland as the place to locate. The success of this initiative is demonstrated by the recent EY report that cites Scotland as the number one location for R&D.
- Enhanced intervention rates: we reviewed our grant intervention rates against similar grant schemes in the EU and with a marginal increase, have increased demand significantly.
- Sectoral targeting: for example, we have supported oil and gas companies to innovate their way out of the downturn by offering an enhanced intervention rate for undertaking R&D.

DELIVERING RESULTS

Simplifying our offering to customers and focussing on a more market led strategy has made a big difference in the number of companies undertaking innovation activities.

Similarly, our sector focus has also seen us working with more companies to provide support helping them deliver projects more quickly and which are bigger and more impactful.

We're already seeing real progress towards our 2023 targets and vision for a more innovative Scotland:

- 3,000 more companies are innovating for the first time from a wide variety of sectors and stages of development.
- R&D investment has more than doubled from £11 million to £25 million in the last three years, with £250 million under management, close to a third of Scottish BERD.
- Every £1 invested on innovation generates a further £15 for the Scottish economy.
- Companies we have supported have delivered an additional £1.2 billion of turnover in the last two years as a result of their innovation activity.
- 50 per cent of the £1.2 billion of additional turnover came from sales outside of Scotland and we know that innovative companies are three times more likely to export successfully.
- 51 per cent of Scottish companies with more than 10 employees are innovating, up by 7 per cent since the 2013 Community Innovation Survey.

These results are down to a combination of a refocused approach within Scottish Enterprise and a bigger partnership approach across a number of public agencies. For example, we couldn't have increased the number of new innovative companies by 3,000 without working closely with over 20 local authorities.

Government support has also been a key factor and in Scotland we have this in spades. Just this month (September 2017) Scotland's First Minister said in a recent Programme for Government speech that she wanted Scotland to be the inventor and the producer of the innovations that will shape the future – not just the consumer of those innovations. She concluded by announcing an increase in our innovation support over the next three years by almost 70 per cent, from £22 million a year to £37 million.

By growing our innovation support and partnership approach with the public, private and academic sectors, together we will be able to drive forward Scotland's innovation performance and position us firmly on the worldwide stage.

4.6 INNOVATION, CREATIVITY AND CONSCIOUSNESS

Karren Brooks, Whitespace

Every company struggles to embrace three important concepts and indeed, the primary requirements which contribute to their short and long-term success:

* to inspire innovation;
* to encourage creativity; and
* to increase their employees' consciousness.

In our corporate consultancy practice, Whitespace defines **innovation** not only, as the Oxford Dictionary suggests, *"To introduce something **new**, especially a product"* but more broadly as,

"To make changes in something established, especially by introducing new methods, ideas, or products." The most prolific inventors would be stymied if they were bound by a strict definition of innovation, such as producing something **completely new**. In fact they understand, and never shy away from, the counter-intuitive process of "re-inventing the wheel" which leads to the biggest productivity gains.

Imagine the thousands of inventive engineers throughout the history of wheel development, who made incremental innovations, taking the roughhewn round rock wheels, popularised in the Flintstones cartoons and found lighter, stronger, rounder, and more durable materials and processes to evolve and adapt this basic transportation component. Modern F1 cars' wheels can be changed in less than 15 seconds and endure speeds in excess of 200 miles per hour with loads exceeding five tons. These racing wheels are constantly being 're-invented' in order to maximise performance and it is this innovation, inspired by F1 competition, which trickles down to make our road cars safer, smoother and more economical. The best engineers employed by these F1 racing teams are incremental innovators, constantly tweaking materials and processes while spending millions on research and testing in order to discover the minute changes, which may give them a competitive advantage.

Professor John Bessant teaches a course at the University of Exeter called 'Innovation and Entrepreneurship'. He further expands the definition of innovation for his students to include the concept of "creating value from ideas." The ultimate test for any business is the conversion of ideas into a viable commercial proposition and Professor Bessant emphasises the long and arduous road of this process of innovation.

When asked, "What are the key ingredients for business innovation?" Professor Besant responded with the following paraphrased bullet points:

- An organisational strategy or roadmap identifying the value and purpose of innovation;
- An atmosphere which promotes idea creation and collaboration between the innovators;
- A safe environment which permits failure and encourages experimentation;
- A managed portfolio of innovation which mixes long term and short term as well as high risk and low risk innovations; and
- Time and patience, which allow the corporate strategy and the innovators to adapt to the market requirements.

An important consideration for organisations wishing to create valuable ideas is the communication of the firm intention to foment innovation. All too often in our experience, corporations isolate both the innovators and the innovation strategy from their non-technical departments, clients and, indeed, competitors. Most corporate directors profess to communicate strategy and promote innovation but miss out on the preliminary step; the emotional commitment to have the decisive intention to inspire innovation. It is a corporate mindset which radiates creativity that attracts innovators and promotes inspiration.

One of the world's most successful creative companies is undebatably Google, which has its own Creative Lab. In its unique application for 5 paid positions, they announced they were looking for candidates who would work *"with talented folks who make things that matter,"*; again we see the link between innovation, teamwork and the concept of value. Google is proud of its reputation for creativity and from top to bottom the corporate mindset is proudly innovative. Steve Vranakis, Google Creative Lab Executive Creative Director speaks to that corporate mindset, *"When we talk about magic, we talk about the emotional connection you are going to make to something and the benefit and value it's going to bring you. From a brand perspective, our whole thing is about being the stage and our users being the stars."*

Creative 'types' conjure up images of thick spectacles, staring at multiple computer screens, and being 'nerds' or socially awkward. The reality is the best innovators enjoy the collaboration and ideas interchange with their colleagues, clients and, indeed, competitors. Whitespace works on the emotional requirements of creativity and builds confidence. Creativity requires a mental resilience towards failure and a dogged determination to develop one's own story. The 13th Century Persian Poet, Rumi, said it well: *"Don't be satisfied with stories, how things have gone with others. Unfold your own myth."* The following anecdote illustrates how to create your own story.

Whitespace Business Dynamics was recently contracted by a South London based SME to help raise the consciousness of one of their "fast-tracked" female directors, Martha. The Chairman and CEO of this SME requested that we help Martha break out of the boardroom paradigms and inspire her creativity. Martha related that all too often, when she had a good idea, the 'suits' would dismiss her suggestions as too emotional or not economically feasible. Whitespace counsellors analysed a typical boardroom problem and helped Martha discover a creative and innovative solution.

Martha's company was located in a 20 storey home office building with several floors sublet to other renters, which provided flexibility and important revenue to the SME. The problem presented to the Monday morning directors' meeting was described as a "continual and increasing complaint that the 8 lifts which serviced the building were too slow and causing waiting times of 4 to 6 minutes during peak usage." The tenants were threatening to break their rental contracts and even legal remediation. The two most popular solutions to the problem, proposed by senior male directors, included a new control program and lift segregation to dedicated floors, which promised to reduce waiting times by 20% and cost one million pounds. The second proposed solution would build two additional lifts and incur over two million pounds of capital expenditure while lowering waiting times by an estimated 40%. The two solutions were adamantly supported in a testosterone fuelled head-butting debate by their respective directors. The CEO asked Martha and the others to come up with some ideas for the next Monday meeting when a decision would be made.

Whitespace challenged Martha to view the problem from three different perspectives:

- A remote, helicopter view, as if Martha was watching the crowded lift lobby from above;
- A focused internal view; how Martha personally felt while standing waiting for the lift at a peak time; and
- An imaginative and empathetic exploration of the feelings of the frustrated tenants.

In the first, remote viewing perspective, Martha related that she could see the lift lobby filling up and the waiting crowd exchanging pleasantries in small groups, which soon disintegrated into a vocal and angry gang of frustrated tenants. Martha noticed how the men would fidget with their ties and phones and frequently check their watches. The women also would check their phones but often times fuss with their hair or make-up. In Martha's mind's eye, they appeared bored.

When Martha reviewed her personal feelings, she discovered that she had made it a habit to arrive early and leave late in order to avoid the 9am and 5pm rush periods. The recognition by Martha that she hadn't really experienced the problem to the same degree as the tenants, helped her realise why she hadn't been able to create a solution. She needed to be *present* to fuel her creativity.

In the third perspective, Martha was asked to empathise with the tenants and feel their frustration. This collaborative exercise is analogous to the prerequisite for successful innovation, which is to listen and understand what the client wants.

Martha developed three solutions which she confidently proposed at the next Monday meeting:

- Re-decorate the lift lobby with mirrors, so the waiting workers could check their 'look.';
- Install 4 television monitors showing headline news, giving information and further distraction; and
- Institute an alternative workday schedule for the home office employees, changing 9 to 5 to an easy to remember 8:30am to 4:30pm on even numbered calendar days and 9:30am to 5:30pm on odd numbered calendar days, therefore reducing rush hour concentration significantly.

Total cost for Martha's innovative solutions was less than one hundred thousand pounds. The CEO was impressed with the creativity she had brought to the solution and the proposal was adopted unanimously. Complaints about waiting times disappeared.

The popular admonition, "Think outside of the box," is further evidence of what is required to inspire creativity and foment innovation. Whitespace Business Dynamics is often asked to change mindsets – those preconceived notions which become a corporate paradigm. A simple exercise illustrates how we are constricted by our perspectives and suffer from the psychological affliction of **habituation**.

Habituation is defined by our friends at the Oxford Dictionary as, "*The diminishing of an innate response to a frequently repeated stimulus.*" In our world of standardisation we fail to notice things that may have once been fascinating during our childhood. To demonstrate the mind's propensity to *habituate,* Whitespace will ask a group of our executive clients, "*How many corners are there in this room?*" Overwhelmingly our habituated participants respond, "FOUR." Possibly having to sit in a *corner* for misbehaviour during our youth, combined with the ubiquitous GPS warnings to turn right or left at the next corner, contributes to the habituation of our two dimensional perspective. When Whitespace counsellors point out that there are eight corners, our habituation is removed to reveal a three dimensional space. We perceive the majority of our information from screens and printed words and maps and diagrams...all in two dimensions. Our mind has the ability to standardise and simplify our perception by eliminating the less used third dimension.

To "think outside of the box," one must first perceive the box and expand the perspective. Creativity and innovation are inextricably linked to the magic one experiences as a child. Picasso said, "Every child is an artist, the problem is to remain an artist once we grow up." Our mind has had years of working to simplify our existence by habituating our perceptions. The importance of pushing out our view to all corners of the room, both literally and figuratively, is basic to creativity.

The human ego and habituated mind tends to see all problems from the logical and simplified perspective of, *"What's in front of me and what's behind me?"* The realisation of our ego centred view allows our expanded consciousness to include the perceptions of, *"What's above me and what's below me?"* It takes further self-awareness to realise the importance of, *"What's inside me and how does that make me feel?"* And with truly expanded consciousness we can evolve our perception to understand the importance of, *"How does this make others feel?"* The late and great Steve Jobs encouraged his engineers to perceive how the clients would feel when using the Apple products. Watching his young daughter point to images on her computer would inspire Jobs to create the technology of touch screens, which have become a global phenomenon.

Whitespace is passionate about innovation, creativity and consciousness. We are constantly reminded of the inextricable links between these concepts and the urgency for all of us to experience the fulfilment and satisfaction of an expanded self-awareness. The beauty in repetition of conventional wisdom is that it is easy to remember even when turned on its head. The artful aspect of expanded consciousness is to constantly strive to "re-invent the wheel," and "to think outside of the box."

Whitespace works with leaders, not only of companies, but sports teams and indeed, families and each of these leaders become more effective and influential when they make the connection and embrace the challenges to inspire innovation, encourage creativity and expand their own and their followers' consciousness.

4.7 MONETISING INNOVATION

Jonathan Reuvid, Legend Business Books

Inevitably, money is a key element in every innovation. Funding is needed for research and new business start-ups, followed by intermediate finance for successive stages of technical development and developing channels to market. Up to the point where revenue from commercialisation of innovation supports cash flow, grants, debt and equity finance are required. Strong, sustainable revenue and positive cash flow will help growing businesses to fund further innovation, pay down debt finance, maintain necessary bank overdrafts and, hopefully, provide returns to equity stakeholders. Finally, the successful innovator will be able to evaluate and select available exit routes. This chapter offers an overview of each of these stages.

DEFINITION

Before discussing the successive stages which are integral to monetisation, it is helpful to define what we mean by "innovation". As Karren Brooks identifies in the previous chapter, innovation is not confined to just "introducing something new, especially a product", implying wholly new inventions, but embraces incremental improvements and by-products of the original invention. It also refers to the creative thought process that generates the introduction of new systems and practices within an organisation which are innovative because they generate enhanced performance, streamline administration or stimulate motivation. Unless a by-product of such activity is unique software or systems which can be packaged and licensed to companies in other industries or applied to other activities, this is activity which normally remains in-house.

The funding requirements for each of these types of innovation are very different from the research and development activities which result in wholly new inventions. In the case of incremental product innovation, the activity is most often part of an ongoing programme within a successful manufacturing company which has established a permanent research and development (R & D) resource as an overhead expense.

R & D activity within university departments certainly requires support funding, usually over a considerable period before generating income, particularly in the application of scientific research before a marketable product emerges. As Professor Graham Richards indicates in his preface to this book, financial support in generating patentable IP from scientific and, more broadly, technical R&D is needed by way of government grants.

The high tech innovation of Silicon Valley and similar IT hubs are an altogether different form of entrepreneurial activity. Mark Zuckerberg and Jack Ma are members of a rare breed. They are the twenty-first century successors to the mediaeval alchemist who have actually transformed base metal into gold.

EARLY STAGE FINANCE

Grant funding

For the entrepreneur or established SME the first ports of call for financing innovation projects externally are the grant funding sources identified by Olaf Swanzy in Chapter 3.6. The Innovate UK programmes, funded wholly by the British Government, are particularly attractive to small and medium sized companies. Phase 1 feasibility studies to be carried out within a period of 6 months can be funded up to 70% of cost for micro-businesses, 60% for medium-sized and 50% for larger businesses within a current limit of £25,000. Phase 2 experimental development programmes are funded up to lesser proportions of 45%, 35% or 25% of more substantial cost over 2 year periods.

There is parallel European grant funding for innovation under the Eurostar Eureka and H2020 programmes. There are 30 countries including EU members within the Eurostar group. Funding proportions of development cost according to business size under the H2020 programme are the same as for Innovate UK grants within limits of €50,000 for feasibility studies and €500,000 to €2.5 million for experimental development. Hopefully, Britain will retain Eurostar membership after Brexit.

Funding the balance

In all cases, the balance of funding for grant-supported projects must be provided by the applicant or third party support. Cost incurred before the start of a grant programme does not qualify for application of any grant calculation.

The balance of the funding required for a feasibility study, whether 30% for micro businesses or more for larger companies, may be sustainable from the innovator's own resources or existing bank overdraft or loan facilities. New bank borrowing for feasibility studies is likely to be difficult, if not impossible, for British companies under present conditions and, if available, will probably involve the provision of personal guarantees by the directors of smaller businesses. Loans or investment from family and friends are preferable for the owners of the smallest businesses.

Equity and/or debt funding from business angels or venture capitalists is unlikely before proof of concept can be demonstrated following completion of the feasibility study.

START-UP AND EARLY STAGE FINANCE

From the outset, it will have been apparent that permanent external funding will be required if ownership of an innovation is to be retained beyond the initial R&D stages. This should be no surprise to the entrepreneur innovator and it is never too early to engage in the self-questioning and detailed planning process described by Allison Sparron-Edwards in Chapter 1.2. The fruits of that exercise should be harvested now as the entrepreneur prepares to enter the professional investment arena.

Alternative investment sources

Venture Capital and Private Equity
The usual sources of investment partners are private equity or venture capital funds and business angels. The former invest on a professional basis, sometimes in millions and seldom, if ever, less than £250,000. They follow their own strict rules on investment rates of return (IRR) and look for recovery of their investment outlay within 3 to 5 years maximum. Most UK based venture capital funds and some business angel networks are members of the British Private equity and Venture Capital Association (BVCA). They are readily identifiable from the BVCA website.

There is a blurred distinction between venture capital and private equity funds. Venture capitalists characterise themselves as risk takers investing in early stage and start-up companies without a financial track record and expecting that no more than 30% of their ventures will be successful. Private equity funds are defined as longer term investors in more mature businesses, often in support of management buy-outs and buy-ins, and with the expectation of a close relationship with the proven management. However, venture capitalists and private equity fund managers each adopt the other's characteristics on occasion. When things go awry, equity fund managers are likely to behave the same as venture capitalists in looking to discard their investment in short order.

Angel Investors
Angel investors are a distinct category of wealthy private investor with a keen interest in taking a stake in early stage companies whose business is based on ground-breaking innovation, not necessarily hi-tech but with a clear prospect of rapid and substantial growth in defined markets. They will often have derived their wealth from businesses

that they have started themselves, grown successfully and sold on or brought to market. They have the same aim as other private equity investors of recovering a multiple of their original investment and exiting later. The expertise of angels acquired from experience makes them a particularly valuable asset to the original shareholders and managers of the companies in which they invest. They are likely to be sympathetic to the growing pains and problems of early stage businesses, having been there themselves, and often play an active role as non-executive directors.

Individual angel investments will typically be between £10,000 and £150,000 and angels often invest collectively as a consortium within the angel network of which they are members. One of the UK's first and leading business angel networks is the Oxford Investment Opportunity Network (OION) formed in 1994. OION is focused on technology companies with high potential seeking investment from £200,000 to £1.5 million. It has spawned two further successful networks: Thames Valley Investment Network (TVIN), which is focused on media, FMCG and green technology, and Oxford Early Investments (OEI), which is suitable for entrepreneurs seeking £75,000 to £250,000. The way in which OION operates is to form a fund at the beginning of each tax year in which investors will qualify for tax relief on disposal under the UK Government's current Seed Enterprise Investment Scheme (SEIS). Innovation projects submitted to OION are scrutinised by its network investment manager, who assists candidates to prepare a "pitch deck" conforming to OION guidelines, which they may be invited to present to a selection panel. The next step is an invitation to attend one of OION's monthly meetings where five or six businesses present to more than fifty angel investors at one sitting. Presentations are limited to less than 10 minutes each which is a daunting task for entrepreneurs who have spent weeks preparing their detailed business plans. Angels who wish have the opportunity to interrogate the business owners individually after the presentations to decide whether they have more than a passing interest.

Crowdfunding
A relatively recent phenomenon in fund sourcing, crowdfunding operates in the internet through its websites with pitches for investment direct to the general public. A Google search will reveal the special focus of each Crowdfunder from start-up finance to second stage debt and equity funding. Market leaders in this field include Crowdcube, Kickstarter, Indiegogo and Seedrs. The crowdfunders' rules and requirements for admission are strict, because their profitability and growth depend upon the subscription in full for each investment offering. There is an understandable preference in favour of share offerings for businesses which offer B2C products and services of high direct interest to members of the public who visit each crowdfunding website with a view to subscribing personally. B2B businesses may have difficulty in attracting the support of any crowdfunder.

Business plans and pitch decks

The rigorous business planning process set out in Alison Sparron-Edwards' chapter is an important self-discipline for business owners in ordering and articulating their thoughts and charting their plans for further growth. It is, of course, a reiterative process. This detailed business plan together with audited accounts and management accounts will provide the basis for the Information Memorandum which investors with a serious interest will require before arriving at a decision to make their offers. However, it is not an effective tool to engage preliminary interest from investors with whom there has been no prior contact.

There is an old central European saying that, "If you want to cook a good Hungarian rabbit stew, the first task is to catch the rabbit". And so it is with the investment community. Fund managers and angels are inundated with unsolicited funding proposals daily. One angel explained that he receives 50 to 70 proposals every week and simply does not have the time to read every multi-paged and closely written business plan. The practice he follows is to discard any proposal received of more than 10 or 12 pages displaying essential information, preferably in bullet point form.

This issue is addressed fully by David Bateman in his short book *Business Plans That Get Investment* published by Legend Business. His methodology and the templates developed in the book are endorsed by OION who recommend it as a model for investment applicants preparing their pitch decks for presentation. The website *www.businessplansthatgetinvestment* offers access to the templates and investor lists.

Forms of Investment

Some individual angels may offer finance by equity investment alone but angel investment funds, venture capital and private equity funds are more likely to offer a modicum of direct equity investment into the business plus debt finance in the form of interest-bearing secured or unsecured convertible loan stock. The conversion and repayment terms of the loan stock vary widely. In this way the investor limits the extent of his risk. More rarely the investment is offered in the form of cumulative convertible preference shares, giving the investor greater risk exposure but with the advantage that the business's balance sheet remains unencumbered.

In either case business owners will be subject to similar constraints and must expect to surrender between 25% and 35% of their equity interest over time.

PAYBACK TIME

The ultimate goal for the entrepreneur/innovator is the release of cash in the form of a capital gain for the original investors. This will be achieved by a trade sale, a private placement of shares or an independent public offering (IPO), typically on the AIM market of the London stock exchange. The outcome is predicated on building a profitable expanding business with the prospect of continuing strong growth. Along the way, there are opportunities for leveraging additional income and shareholder dividends by exploiting the fruits of innovation beyond the in-house activities of the business.

Exploiting IP

In order to generate additional revenue IP needs to be packaged so that it is transformed into an asset that is not vulnerable to industrial theft or direct copy by competitors. Parts Two and Three of this book provide extensive guidance to the management of IP and its defence in the forms of patents and registered designs, trademarks and copyright. Copyright is an intrinsic right, cheap to register but sometimes costly to defend against infringement. The other forms of IP are expensive both to register and maintain and also to defend. However, the costs are recoverable from licensing and sale of the IP rights created.

Copyright

Copyright is acquired naturally by authors and publishers of literary or science and technology works, music composers and originators of other creative works for the media and performing arts. Income for written works is derived from the licensing of their copyright for foreign language editions or adaptation into screenplays, television and theatre scripts. Licences may be sold for lump sums, royalties or a combination of the two. Ongoing royalties of major works provide the literary estates of deceased authors with substantial income many years after their death. Much of this traffic is managed by literary agents or the foreign rights specialists in publishing houses.

Trademarks

Well-known trademarks and the brands that they denote are a lucrative source of licensing income. Licensing of business names for use in defined territories only by other companies in the same industry manufacturing similar or different products is one way to go for those who do not plan to develop international distribution for their products or services. The disadvantage is that in this age of ecommerce, international borders are porous and it may not be possible to contain licensees within their own borders.

A more satisfactory route is to license the use of a brand in another defined application. The opportunities for famous brands to license their trademarks in this way are limitless and are exploited most commonly by personalities in the fields of sports and entertainment (think of Roger Federer and watches), cartoon characters, toys, clothing and consumer durables. For example, in the past few weeks ahead of the 2017 Brand Licensing Europe exhibition at Olympia London, deals have been announced between Paddington Bear and UNICEF, the Roald Dahl Literary Estate with LEGO and the launch of a footwear collection by Piaggio carrying the Vespa brand. Major brand licensors such as Disney or Premier League football clubs have their own in-house management, but the bulk of the brand and trademark licensing trade is carried out by merchandisers, some of them multinational companies in their own right. A subscription to the trade journal License Global will give access to international licensing news.

Patents and registered designs

The sale and licensing of patents and registered designs is big business. Million dollar transactions are commonplace. Patent infringement disputes and the defence of patents are also a major source of income for patent lawyers and brokers. In some industries the cross-licensing of new technology and componentry between competitors is endemic. Automotive industry constructors commonly license powertrain components, such as gearboxes, fuel injection or electronic management systems to each other. Similar licensing of componentry takes place between manufacturers of computer and telephony hardware with occasional well-publicised disputes between major global competitors such as Apple and Samsung. Patents require rigorous validation and due diligence before a transaction can be completed. The terms of transaction may be negotiated by a patent broker or on occasion by an auction process where demand is sufficiently high. Often the actual deal is struck post-auction by those who have declared an interest.

Major manufacturers with permanent R&D divisions and a continuing flow of patentable inventions accumulate portfolios of licenses over time. Occasionally, such licence portfolios come to market commanding a high value when their combined licensing income is determined actuarially on a discounted cash flow basis and offered for sale.

The final curtain

An outright trade sale is the cleanest and most certain way for the innovator/entrepreneur to realise the value of his investment and the accumulated IP in the balance sheet and ongoing royalty income may play a significant role in maximising the price. Nor should the retirement of venture capital funds with a substantial return on equity be contentious.

Stock market flotation or private placement may yield a higher share price than a trade sale, but it is unlikely that original owners and managers of the business will be able to sell more than a part of their shareholdings in the short term. If they have confidence in the future of the company, staying in with a continuing income may be attractive, but for those wanting to retire from the business, there will be a preference for "exit means exit" – to paraphrase a slogan in current use.

CONTRIBUTORS' CONTACTS

Bosideon Consulting Ltd
Charlie Wilson
Tel. +44 (0) 7880 654113
Email: cwilson@bosideon.co.uk

Cambridge Innovation Consulting Ltd
Dirk Mersch
Tel. +44 (0) 7572 460735
Email: d.mersch@camin.com

Consultrix Ltd
Allison McSparron-Edwards
Tel. +44 (0) 1793 726128
Email: allison@consultrix.co.uk

Coventry University
Dr. Brian More
Tel. +44 (0) 7974 984928
Email: BMore@cad.coventry.ac.uk

Da Vinci Partners LLC
John Moetteli
Tel. +41(0)7123 01000
Email: moetteli@davincipartners.com

DNS Accountants
Sumit Agarwal
Tel. +44 (0) 3300 88 66 86
Email: sumit@dnsassociates.co.uk

May Figures Ltd
Dr. Mark Graves
Tel. +44 (0) 1727 751 080
Email: mark@mayfigures.co.uk
Julia May
Tel. +44 (0) 1727 751 080
Email: juli@mayfigures.co.uk

Fieldridge Ltd
Andy Hill
Tel. +44 (0) 7540 746784
Email: andy.hill@fieldridge.org

GovGrant Ltd
Jeremy Tear
Tel. +44 (0)7789 557135
Email: jeremy@3dsolutions.tv

Howman Solicitors
Gary McGonagle
Tel. +44 (0) 7887 774656
Email: gmg@howmansolicitors.co.uk

Hunters
Gregor Kleinknecht
Tel. +44 (0) 207 4125122
Email: gjk@hunters-solicitors.co.uk

Integrated Resources Ltd
Claire Vane
Tel. +44 (0) 7801 982334
Email: claire@integratedresources.co.uk

Intellectual Property Office
Nic Fearon-Low
Tel. +44 (0) 207 0342841
Email: nic.fearon-low@ipo.gov.uk

J & B Partners Ltd
Steven Johnson
Tel. +44 (0) 7789 908470
Email: sjohnson@jandbpartners.com

Legend Business Books Ltd
Jonathan Reuvid
Tel. +44 (0) 1295 738070
Email: jreuvidembrooks@aol.com

Manchester University – The School of Chemistry and The School of Materials
Paul O'Brien
Tel. +44 (0) 161 2754652
Email: paul.o'brien@manchester.ac.uk

Mathys & Squire LLP
Ilya Kazi
Tel. +44 (0) 207 8300000
Email: ikazi@mathys-squire.com

Miller Insurance Services LLP
Keeley Patten
Tel. +44 (0) 207 0312725
Email: keeley.patten@miller-insurance.com

Minesoft Ltd
Caitlin Kavanagh
Tel: +44 (0) 203 4326176
Email: caitlin@minesoft.com

Oxford Drug Design Ltd
Graham Richards
Tel: +44 (0) 1865 261468
Email: graham.richards@chem.ox.ac.uk

Patentgate GmbH
Margit Hoehne
Tel: +49 (0) 3672 2059962
Email: mh@patentgate.de

PNO Group
Olaf Swanzy
Tel. +44 (0) 161 488 3488
Email: olaf.swanzy@pnoconsultants.com

Scottish Enterprise
Aileen Hotchkiss
Tel. +44 (0) 141 2282848
Email: Aileen.Hotchkiss@scotent.co.uk

STEMM Commercial Ltd
Sarah McCloughry
Tel. +44 (0) 1865 910289
Email: sarah@stemmcommercial.com

Stratagem IPM Limited
Nicholas Acham
Tel. +44 (0) 1223 550740
Email: Nicholas.Acham@strategemipm.co.uk

Swindon & Wiltshire LEP
Paddy Bradley
Tel. +44 (0) 1225 713205
Email: Paddy.Bradley@swlep.co.uk

UK2 Group
Yasmin El-Saie
Tel. +44 7833 142386
Email: yasmin.elsaie@uk2group.com

Whitespace
Karren Brooks
Tel. +44 (0) 557135
Email: karren@bewhitespace.com

Wood IP
Aaron Wood
Tel. +44 (0) 1327 315157
Mail: aaron@wood-ip.com

Other Legend Business Publications include:

Business Guide to the United Kingdom
Investors' Guide to the United Kingdom
Managing Cybersecurity Risk
Business Plans that Get Investment by David Bateman
Morocco: Emerging Economy of the Mediterranean
Chinese Court Judgements by Fei Ming
A Business Guide for Beginners by Des O'Keeffe
How to Sell and Market Your Book by Darin Jewell
Winning Ways to Work by Rupert Eales-White

Smart Skills Series:
Smart Skills: Meetings by Patrick Forsyth
Smart Skills: Negotiation byAnthony Jacks
Smart Skills: Persuasion by Patrick Forsyth
Smart Skills: Mastering the Numbers by Anne Hawkins
Smart Skills: Working with Others by Frances Kay
Smart Skills: Presentations by Frances Kay

www.legendtimesgroup.co.uk/legend-business